Contents

Table of cases

Free online study and revision support

Visit the online resource centre at:

www.oup.com/lawrevision/

Take your learning further:

➤ Multiple-choice questions

➤ An interactive glossary

➤ Outline exam answers

➤ Flashcards of key cases

➤ Download our free ebook, *Study and Exam Success for Law Students,* which includes:

• Guidance on how to approach revision and prepare for exams

• Guidance on how to use a statute book

'I always buy a Concentrate revision guide for each module and use the online resources. The **outline answers are particularly helpful** and I often use **the multiple-choice questions to test my basic understanding** of a topic'

Alice Reilly, Cardiff University

The Online Resource Centre has been **exceptionally useful**. In my first year, I used the resources to **quiz myself**, to test **my knowledge and understanding of cases**, and **to pick up extra pointers that could give me a few extra marks**'

Kelly Newman, University of Exeter

...edge ➤ focus revision ➤ maximise potential

To Lucy and Will.

New to this edition

Extended coverage of:

- The gig economy
- Zero hours contracts
- Brexit
- Gender pay gap reporting
- Restraint of trade

New cases include:

- *R (Unison) v Lord Chancellor* (2017)
- *Uber v Aslam* (2017)
- *Pimlico Plumbers v Smith* (2017)
- *IWGB Union v RooFoods* (2017)
- *Tillman v Egon Zehnder* (2017)
- *Chesterton Global v Nurmohamed* (2017)
- *Ruiz Conejero v Ferroser Servicios Auxiliares SA* (2018)
- *Naeem v Secretary of State for Justice; Essop v Home Office* (2017)
- *King v Sash Windows Workshop* (2017)

New statutes include:

- Trade Union Act 2016

Employment Law
Concentrate

6th edition

Michael Jefferson

Senior Lecturer in Law
University of Sheffield

OXFORD
UNIVERSITY PRESS

OXFORD
UNIVERSITY PRESS

Great Clarendon Street, Oxford, OX2 6DP,
United Kingdom

Oxford University Press is a department of the University of Oxford.
It furthers the University's objective of excellence in research, scholarship,
and education by publishing worldwide. Oxford is a registered trade mark of
Oxford University Press in the UK and in certain other countries

Third edition 2013
Fourth edition 2014
Fifth edition 2016

Impression: 1

Published in the United States of America by Oxford University Press
198 Madison Avenue, New York, NY 10016, United States of America

British Library Cataloguing in Publication Data

Data available

Library of Congress Control Number: 2018946363

ISBN 978–0–19–881516–7

Printed in Great Britain by
Ashford Colour Press Ltd, Gosport, Hampshire

Table of cases

✳✳✳✳✳✳✳✳✳✳

Table of cases

****

Table of primary legislation

Table of primary legislation

✳✳✳✳✳✳✳✳✳✳✳✳

Table of primary legislation

****

Table of secondary legislation

Table of secondary legislation

✳✳✳✳✳✳✳✳✳✳

Table of European legislation

#1
Employment status

Key facts

- The main legal distinction is between workers who have contracts of service (ie employees) and those who have contracts for services (ie independent contractors). Sometimes, however, Parliament protects not just employees but also 'workers' as defined in the relevant legislation such as the Equality Act 2010 in relation to discrimination (see chapters 4 and 5).

- The intention of the parties is not the sole determinant of employment status. The parties' views as to their relationship can be important but tribunals and courts will be wary of 'sham' arrangements.

- The fact that people have accepted self-employed status for some years does not prevent them arguing that they are, in reality, employees.

- Among the most important factors that tribunals and courts have used to decide whether or not a contract of employment exists are mutuality of obligation and personal performance.

- When an issue is raised about employment status, an employment tribunal must consider whether there is an implied contract between parties who have no express contract with one another.

- Employee shareholders can relinquish certain statutory rights in exchange for fully paid up shares with a minimum value of £2,000.

Reasons for distinguishing employees from other types of worker

Workers may be hired under a contract of service (ie employees) or a contract for services (ie independent contractors). Legislation may also protect some workers who are not employees, and the scope of that protection depends on the wording of the statute.

Revision tip

Be careful with the terminology here. It is important that you do not confuse a contract *of service* with one *for services*. The former is a contract of employment, the latter is not.

Although some legislation applies to both of these categories, such as the Health and Safety at Work etc Act 1974 and the Working Time Regulations 1998, other statutes do not. Employees alone get the benefit of a number of statutory employment rights, such as the right not be unfairly dismissed, the right to a redundancy payment, the right to maternity and **parental leave**. They are also covered by the unwritten general obligations implied into all contracts of employment (see chapter 2). In addition, when employees rather than self-employed persons are engaged, employers are required by statute to deduct tax under the Income Tax (Earnings and Pensions) Act 2003 (this is 'Pay As You Earn', PAYE) as well as social security contributions. Self-employed people are taxed differently and can set off business expenses against income for these purposes.

At common law perhaps the most significant difference is that the doctrine of **vicarious liability** applies to employees but not to the self-employed. According to this doctrine, employers are liable to third parties for the torts committed by employees in the course of their employment. Employees act 'in the course of employment' where they carry out acts that are authorised expressly or implicitly by the employer. Similarly, where their actions are so closely connected with the employment as to be incidental to it, although prohibited and unauthorised by the employer, employees act 'in the course of employment'. However, if an employee's action is so outside the scope of employment that it was not something the employee was hired to do ('on a frolic of his own'), then the employer is not liable. In *Lister v Hedley Hall Ltd* [2001], the employers were held vicariously liable for a warden who sexually abused the claimants whilst they were in his care. According to the House of Lords, the correct approach is to ask whether the employee's wrongdoing was so closely connected with his or her employment that it would be fair and just to hold the employer liable. It should be noted that the doctrine of vicarious liability discussed in chapter 5, 'Discrimination at work', used to be based on tort law but no longer is.

The statutory definitions of 'employee' and 'worker'

Section 230(1) Employment Rights Act 1996 (ERA) defines an **employee** as 'an individual who has entered into or works under (or, where the employment has ceased, worked under) a contract of employment'.

Section 230(2) ERA states that a **contract of employment** is 'a contract of service or apprenticeship, whether express or implied, and (if it is express) whether oral or in writing'. A contract of service is the old-fashioned term for a contract of employment.

A **worker** is defined more broadly by s 230(3) ERA as an individual who has entered into, or works under, a contract of employment or 'any other contract, whether express or implied and (if it is express) whether oral or in writing, whereby the individual undertakes to do or perform personally any work or services for another party to the contract whose status is not by virtue of the contract that of a client or customer of any profession or business undertaking carried on by the individual'. This definition is used for claims which fall within this statute but other Acts of Parliament have their own definition of 'worker'; and EU law has its own autonomous definition of 'worker'.

The courts' and tribunals' approach to identifying employees

The intention of the parties

Because there is no statutory definition of a contract of service we have to consider the criteria used by the tribunals and courts to identify who is an employee. It is clear that the intention of the parties cannot be the sole determinant of employment status as this would make it too easy to contract out of protective legislation, especially when the employers have much more bargaining power than do individuals and when they can buy in advice from 'armies of lawyers': see in particular *Autoclenz Ltd v Belcher* [2011] (SC), noted below.

Massey v Crown Life Assurance [1978] 1 WLR 676

A branch manager with an insurance company chose to change his status from employee to self-employed for financial reasons, although he continued in the same job. Two years later the company terminated the contract and he brought an unsuccessful claim for unfair dismissal. Lord Denning MR summed up the Court of Appeal's approach:

If the true relationship of the parties is that of master and servant under a contract of service, the parties cannot alter the truth of that relationship by putting a different label on it ... On the other hand, if the parties' relationship is ambiguous and is capable of being one or the other, then the parties can remove that ambiguity, by the very agreement itself which they make with one another.

'Master and servant' are nowadays 'employer and employee'.

The courts' and tribunals' approach to identifying employees

Thus, the parties' views as to their relationship can be important if there is any ambiguity. However, it is the operation of the contract in practice that is crucial rather than its appearance and the courts and tribunals will not endorse 'sham' arrangements. In *Autoclenz Ltd v Belcher* [2011] the Supreme Court held that in order to find that a contract is in part a sham it was not necessary to show that both parties intended to paint a false picture as to the true nature of their obligations. The relative bargaining power of the parties must be taken into account in deciding whether the terms that were documented truly represent what was agreed.

 Looking for extra marks?

Point out that whether the tribunals and courts should give any weight to the declared intentions of the parties or look solely at the contractual terms and how they operate in practice is a highly contentious issue.

Control

Historically, control was treated as the touchstone of an employment relationship. The position today is more complex in that an element of control is necessary but not sufficient to establish employee status (see 'Mutuality of obligation' and 'Personal service'). Subject to statutory and common law constraints, employers can still exercise considerable control over their workers.

Looking for extra marks?

Point out that the key question here is whether there is a contractual right to control and not whether, in practice, the worker has day-to-day control over his or her own activities.

Mutuality of obligation

Another important factor that the tribunals and courts have used to decide whether or not a contract of employment exists is that of mutuality of obligation between the employer and the individual.

> **Carmichael v National Power plc [2000] IRLR 43**
>
> The House of Lords upheld the decision of the employment tribunal. The case was about whether two tour guides had contracts of employment and were therefore entitled under s 1 ERA 1996 to a written statement of particulars of the terms of their employment. The House of Lords accepted that they worked on a casual 'as and when required' basis. An important issue was that there was no requirement for the employer to provide work or for the individual to perform it. Indeed, the court heard that there were a number of occasions when the applicants had declined offers of work. According to the court, the law was that there had to be an 'irreducible minimum of mutual obligation' (per Lord Irvine) that was 'necessary to create a contract of service' (nowadays a contract of employment). There needed to be an obligation to provide work and an obligation to perform that work in return for a wage or some form of remuneration.

✅ *Looking for extra marks?*

Point out that tribunals are entitled to find that a 'right to refuse work' clause was not genuine.

However, this focus on whether there is an ongoing commitment deflects us from the crucial question of whether casual staff can be regarded as employees *during the periods they are at work*. The question of whether there is continuity of service (see chapter 11) is an entirely separate one.

Cornwall County Council v Prater [2006] IRLR 362

The Court of Appeal accepted that a home tutor was an employee under a succession of teaching engagements, notwithstanding that there was no obligation to undertake any particular assignment and the local authority had no obligation to offer more work. There was mutuality of obligation in each individual teaching engagement such as to make it a contract of employment. The argument that there has to be a continuing obligation to provide more work and an obligation on the worker to do that work was not accepted.

Revision tip

You should not confuse the issue of employment status with the question of continuity of service (see chapter 11 for this concept).

Personal service

It is also crucial to employment status that the individual is required to perform his or her service in person. In *Express and Echo Publications v Tanton* [1999], a contract allowed a worker to provide a substitute if he was not available. According to the Court of Appeal, this prevented the worker from being an employee because there was no obligation to do the work personally. However, in *MacFarlane v Glasgow City Council* [2000], this approach was not applied to gymnasts working for a local authority who were able to provide substitutes for any shift that they were unable to work. In this case the local authority paid the substitutes directly and the gymnasts could only be replaced by others on the council's approved list. On this basis *Tanton* was distinguished.

The 'gig economy'

Gig economy jobs are nothing new. Musicians have for many years played at gigs and they have been classified as self-employed; therefore, they have few rights: see 'Reasons for distinguishing employees from other types of worker', above. What is new is the delivery of those who do jobs to customers via internet platforms, often through an app. It is thought that some 1.3 million now work in the gig economy, some out of choice, some not. Certainly the gig economy is one reason why unemployment figures did not balloon after the Great

The courts' and tribunals' approach to identifying employees

✳✳✳✳✳✳✳✳✳✳

Recession, as the rise of self-employment in low-paid jobs. Firms which deliver such people to customers include Uber, Deliveroo, and those involved in logistics on behalf of firms such as Amazon, eg CitySprint. These are often seen as 'disruptors', breaking the old ways of doing things by undercutting well-established firms such as black taxis and minicab services. One way in which these disruptors can save money is to put those who work for them on contracts for services. This means among other things that those who drive for Uber or deliver food for Deliveroo do not receive the National Minimum or Living Wage and do not receive holiday or sickness pay. Arguably the business model of firms such as Uber is that it is only by not providing rights given to employees or workers that they can thrive; Uber says otherwise.

From 2016 this form of economy has been discussed at length and cases have been brought against gig economy companies in order to move those who work for them from being self-employed (as their contract states) to the category of being workers for employment law purposes. It cannot be said that there is new law being made but the issues have captured the public's attention. Currently the leading case is *Uber BV v Aslam* (2017) where the Employment Appeal Tribunal (EAT), approving the employment tribunal (ET) (that judgment is worth reading), held that Uber drivers were not self-employed but workers, despite the 'label' in their contracts. Uber drivers were under the control of Uber; for example, they had to accept at least 80% of jobs when their app was switched on and were the subject of sanctions for cancellations. This case is scheduled to go to the Court of Appeal in early 2018. Similar is *Pimlico Plumbers Ltd v Smith* (2017) in the Court of Appeal. This case will go to the Supreme Court in February 2018. The court rejected a leapfrog appeal by Uber which would have led to both cases being heard together. It will be good for that court to settle the issue once and for all. It is expected that the court will follow its own decision in *Autoclenz* (see 'The intention of the parties') and will stress that gig economy cases turn on their own facts. An illustration of a gig economy case applying its own facts is *IWGB Union & RooFoods Ltd* (2017), which involves Deliveroo, where the Central Arbitration Committee (CAC) dealing with a request for statutory recognition (see chapter 12) held that union members were not workers but truly self-employed on the basis that Deliveroo riders did not have to perform their services personally but could employ others as substitute riders, and indeed could give up on the delivery half way through. There was no fetter on the right to use a substitute. The lack of personal service was emphasised by the CAC as being the touchstone of self-employment. Indeed, a good part of the decision is devoted to the fact that one rider employed three riders (he took 15–20% of their pay). How could it be that he was a worker? There was no element of personal service, a hallmark of a worker. The CAC noted, however, that the right to hire a substitute would seem to be inconsistent with the training Deliveroo gives its riders. 'Deliveroo loses visibility, and therefore assurance over who is delivering services in its name, thereby creating reputational risk, and potentially a regulatory risk, but that is a matter for them.' The decision is of importance in the area of statutory recognition, which does not cover the self-employed. However, decisions of the CAC are not binding on employment tribunals or other fora determining employment law issues—indeed, decisions of the CAC are not binding on later CAC panels.

The courts' and tribunals' approach to identifying employees

✳✳✳✳✳✳✳✳✳✳

The government's attention has been drawn to the drawbacks for those working in the gig economy such as the lack of a safe income. The disadvantages for the government include the shrinking of the tax and national insurance base. The Prime Minister commissioned Matthew Taylor to write a report on the issue. *Good Work: The Taylor Report on Modern Working Practices* came out in July 2017, and a response from the government was expected in late 2017 but that deadline was not met. At the time of writing (January 2018) the response is expected in early 2018. Among the report's proposals are establishing a new category of dependent workers (covering in particular those whose contract states that they are self-employed but who work totally or very largely for one company) and a default presumption that those who work are 'workers' for the purposes of employment law, ie the burden of proving self-employment will be on the employers. Other ideas include the government enabling class actions for these dependent workers in order to avoid multiply single claims on the same point and employment tribunals being given the power to issue punitive sanctions against employers who are repeat offenders in misclassifying workers as self-employed.

Agency workers

So far we have seen that individuals, including both homeworkers and casual staff, can be regarded as employees if there is sufficient mutuality of obligation and control over them when they are working. Indeed, unless the relationship is dependent solely upon the true construction of a written contract, whether a person is engaged under a contract of employment is a question of fact for a court or tribunal to determine. We now turn to the position of agency workers.

Dacas v Brook Street Bureau [2004] IRLR 358

This case provides authority for the proposition that, when an issue is raised about the employment status of an applicant, a tribunal must consider whether there is an implied contract between parties who have no express contract with one another. Formal written contracts between the applicant and the agency and between the agency and the end-user, the client, relating to the work to be done for the end-user do not necessarily preclude the implication of a contract of employment between the applicant and the end-user. In this case Ms Dacas was held not to be an employee of the agency for the purposes of claiming unfair dismissal. There was, unfortunately for the worker, no appeal on the ground that the end-user was the employer. Therefore, she could not bring a claim despite working for the end-user for several years.

By way of contrast, in *Cairns v Visteon Ltd* [2007] a contract of employment existed with the agency and the EAT felt that it was not necessary to imply a contract with the end-user. To imply a contract of employment by conduct it is necessary to show that the conduct of the parties is consistent only with there being a contract of employment between them.

> **James v London Borough of Greenwich [2008] IRLR 302**
>
> In the leading authority it was emphasised that the real issue in agency worker cases is whether a contract should be implied between the worker and the end-user rather than whether an irreducible minimum of mutual obligations exists. The Court of Appeal also pointed out that the implication of a contract of employment between the worker and the end-user is not inevitable in a long-term agency situation.

The **Agency Worker Regulations 2010**, based on EU law, introduced the principle of equal treatment for agency workers after they have been in 'the same role' with the same hirer for a qualifying period of 12 continuous calendar weeks. **Regulation 5** gives agency workers the right to the same 'basic working and employment conditions' as they would have been entitled to if they had been engaged directly by the hirer. The Regulations do not affect English law on whether an agency worker is employed by the end-user.

 ✅ *Looking for extra marks?*

Focus on the latest decisions of the Court of Appeal as its approach has changed in recent years.

Zero hours contracts

Such contracts are ones which provide that an employer is under no obligation to offer work and a person who works under one of them is under no obligation to accept any work offered. It may happen, for example, that the person who works gets no money in one week but in the next week they may work 35 hours. Such contracts may upset family life as well as not provide a secure income (with problems such as acquiring and paying mortgages); on the other hand, for students and pensioners, for instance, they may be a good way of topping up finances. The David Cameron government decided not to abolish the status but to reduce its disadvantages for those who work by ruling out contractual terms which purport to stipulate that those who work on zero hours contracts must not work for any other company: **Exclusivity Terms in Zero Hours Contracts (Redress) Regulations 2015 (SI 2015/2021)**. This statutory instrument does not deal with the employment status of those on zero hours. However, as with those in the gig economy (see 'The "gig economy"'), status depends on the normal tests.

Employee shareholders

Section 205A ERA 1996, as inserted by the **Growth and Infrastructure Act 2013**, creates the status of **employee shareholder**. Such persons receive between £2,000 and £50,000 paid up shares in the company but relinquish their general right to claim unfair dismissal, the statutory rights to a redundancy payment and to request flexible working, and certain statutory rights in relation to time off for training. In addition, employee shareholders are required to give 16 weeks' notice of their intention to return to work after maternity, adoption, or **paternity leave** rather than the standard eight weeks' notice.

The statute obliges the company to provide individual employee shareholders with a written statement of particulars which specifies:

1. that the employee shareholder will not have the statutory rights just described;

2. the notice periods which apply in relation to a return to work after maternity, adoption, or paternity leave;

3. whether any voting rights are attached to the shares and whether they carry any rights to dividends;

4. whether, if the company was wound up, the employee shares would confer any right to participate in the distribution of assets;

5. if the company has more than one class of shares, explain how any employee shareholder rights differ from the equivalent rights that attach to the shares in the largest class;

6. whether the employee shares are redeemable and, if so, at whose option;

7. whether there are any restrictions on the transferability of the employee shares and, if so, what they are.

An employee shareholder agreement cannot be implemented unless, before it is concluded, the individual has received advice about the terms and effect of the proposed agreement and seven days have elapsed since the advice was given: in other words, there is a cooling-off period. In addition, the company must reimburse any reasonable costs incurred in obtaining this advice whether or not the individual becomes an employee shareholder. Finally, employees have the right not to suffer a detriment on the ground that they have refused to accept an employee shareholder contract and a dismissal for this reason will be automatically unfair (see chapter 9).

This status has been rarely adopted and the government withdrew its tax advantages but did not formally abolish it. The expectation is that it will wither away.

 Key cases

Cases	Facts	Principle
Autoclenz Ltd v Belcher [2011] IRLR 820	Car valeters were required to sign contracts which stated that they were engaged 'from time to time on a sub-contract basis'.	In order to find that a contract is in part a sham it was not necessary to show that both parties intended to paint a false picture as to the true nature of their obligations.

Exam question

Cases	Facts	Principle
Carmichael v National Power plc [2000] IRLR 43	Tour guides who worked on a casual 'as and when required' basis claimed that they were employees.	For a person to be an employee there needs to be an obligation on the employer to provide work and an obligation on the individual to perform that work in return for a wage or some form of remuneration.
Express and Echo Publications v Tanton [1999] IRLR 367	The individual's contract allowed him to provide a substitute worker if he was not available.	It is inconsistent with a contract of employment that a person can provide a substitute. There must be an obligation to do the work personally.
Lister v Hedley Hall Ltd [2001] IRLR 472	A warden sexually abused the claimants while they were in his care.	The correct approach to vicarious liability in tort law is to ask whether the employee's wrongdoing was so closely connected with his or her employment that it would be fair and just to hold the employer liable.
Massey v Crown Life Assurance [1978] 1 WLR 676	A branch manager voluntarily changed his status from employee to self-employed but claimed unfair dismissal when his contract was terminated.	If the true relationship of the parties is that of employer and employee under a contract of service, the parties cannot alter the truth of that relationship by putting a different label on it.

 Exam question

Problem question

For five years Bruce worked for Manfoot plc as a specialist shoemaker in their factory. He was allowed to choose the hours he worked and was paid according to the number of shoes he produced. At the beginning of last month, Bruce asked his manager, George, if he could stop working in the factory at the end of the month and start working from home. George said that he would be happy to arrange this. On the first day of the month Bruce started working from home and signed a document which declared him to be self-employed. Subsequently, he took delivery of materials and handed over finished shoes to the company's collector every week. Payments were made on the basis of £8 per finished shoe, there being no deductions of any kind.

Advise Bruce as to whether or not he is an employee for the purpose of exercising his rights under the **ERA 1996**.

See the Outline answers section in the end matter for help with this question.

Concentrate Q&As

For more questions and answers on employment law, see the *Concentrate Q&A: Employment Law* by Roseanne Russell.

Go to the end of this book to view **sample pages**.

#2
Contracts of employment

Key facts

- Employment contracts are a species of contracts in general; common law contract rules such as illegality, offer, acceptance, consideration, and illegality therefore apply to them.

- Express terms normally take precedence over other terms apart from those implied by statute.

- One form of express terms is covenants in restraint of trade.

- Not later than two months after the start of employment the employer must supply a written statement of particulars of employment. This right applies to employees only. During the currency of this book the period may be reduced to one week and the right extended to workers. These proposals come from the Taylor review of modern working practices mentioned in chapter 1.

- This statement does *not* constitute a contract of employment; it is merely the employer's version of what has been agreed.

- Terms of a contract may be derived from collective agreements as well as (in theory) being individually negotiated. (In practice, because of inequality of bargaining power, it is employers and their 'armies of lawyers' who impose terms.)

- Substantive terms from a collective agreement may be incorporated into an employee's contract of employment expressly or impliedly, or as a result of custom and practice (rarely via the doctrine of agency).

- Works rules are normally determined by the employer and can be expressly or impliedly incorporated into a contract of employment.

- Custom and practice, which by definition must be reasonable, certain, and 'notorious' (ie well known) can be used to fill gaps in the employment relationship.

- Terms can be implied in the contract of employment by statute.

- Terms can also be implied by the common law if they are consistent with the express terms. They may, however, modify the width of express terms.

Introduction

A **contract of employment** is like any other contract in the sense that it is subject to the general principles of contract law. This means that the parties are free to negotiate the terms and conditions that suit them so long as they remain within the constraints imposed by statute and the common law. In practice, a significant proportion of the workforce does not negotiate on an individual basis and is engaged on such terms and conditions as are laid down in currently operative **collective agreements**, ie agreements between managements and unions.

Illegality

One aspect of the common law that has been relied on, particularly where an **employee** attempts to enforce statutory rights, is the principle that courts and tribunals will not enforce an illegal contract.

Colen v Cebrian (UK) Ltd [2004] IRLR 210

According to the Court of Appeal, where illegality is alleged the burden of proof is on the party making the allegation to show that the contract had been entered into with the object of committing an illegal act or had been performed with that objective. If the contract was unlawful at formation or the intention was to perform it unlawfully, the contract is unenforceable. However, if at the time of formation the contract was perfectly lawful and it was intended to be performed lawfully, the effect of some act of illegal performance is not automatically to make the contract unenforceable. If the contract is performed illegally and the person seeking to enforce it takes part in the illegality, that may render the contract unenforceable at his or her instigation. Yet not every illegal act participated in by the enforcer will have that effect. Where the enforcer has to rely on his or her own illegal action, then the tribunal or court will not assist. But if he or she does not have to do so, the question is whether the method of performance and the degree of participation in the illegality is such as to make the contract illegal.

Much of the case law involves attempts to evade income tax. In *Enfield Technical Services Ltd v Payne* [2007], the Employment Appeal Tribunal (EAT) stated that it does not consider that the authorities 'support the proposition that if the arrangements *have the effect* of depriving the Revenue of tax to which they were in law entitled then this renders the contract unlawful ... there must be some form of misrepresentation, some attempt to conceal the true facts of the relationship, before the contract is rendered illegal ...'. (Emphasis added.)

Sources of terms

Revision tip

Students are frequently asked to identify and discuss the sources of terms in contracts of employment.

Express terms

Apart from statutorily implied terms, which cannot be undermined by contract, **express terms** normally take precedence over other sources, ie common law implied terms and custom and practice. Express terms are those that are expressly stated to form part of the contract. Such terms may be in writing or oral. Note that covenants in restraint of trade must be in writing.

Covenants in restraint of trade

Restrictive covenants are express contractual terms which normally apply post-employment, but may apply during employment. During employment the employers may rely on an express term of faithful service (also known as fidelity) and the duty of fidelity, an implied term: see 'Terms implied by the common law'. Post-employment there is no implied term of fidelity. Covenants must be, unlike other express terms (unless Parliament otherwise ordains), *in writing*. Their aim is to prevent what is called illegitimate competition from the **employee** or former employee. There are several different types. The following are the main ones.

- **Preventing ex-employees from using trade secrets, highly confidential information, which they acquired during employment.** This type of covenant prevents ex-employees using data in their new employment to undercut their former employers by not going through the expensive processes of research and development. If such conduct is not stopped, former employees can undercut their former employers to the latter's grave economic disadvantage. Among the cases are examples of trade secrets such as methods of copying written materials and pharmaceutical formulae. The law draws a line between trade secrets and the employee's own skill and experience as well as between trade secrets and normal ways of doing business. Potentially such a covenant can be worldwide and can be long-lasting. They can endure to the time when the trade secret is no secret anymore, as occurs when the matter is published or put on the market or becomes the subject of a patent (which by definition is open to everyone, though it cannot be used by anyone except the patent holder).

- **Preventing ex-employees from dealing with their former clients and customers.** This type of covenant is directed at stopping former employees from soliciting their former contacts from transferring their custom to the employee's new firm. The law stresses that there must be influence over the clients or customers: mere contact is insufficient. For example, it may be that a hairdresser has such influence over customers that clients will move to the business where he or she now is to the financial detriment of the former employers. This type of covenant is often expressed as cover a certain territory, eg within a radius of so many metres or kilometres from the office or other place where the former employee used to work and is often expressed to last for a certain length of time.

- **Preventing 'team moves'.** This occurs when a former employee tries to attract former colleagues to join his or her new employer, bringing with them trade secrets and influence over clients.

The law on covenants in restraint of trade, the *doctrine of restraint of trade*, is purely common law and is not restricted to employees. For example, it applies to independent contractors, partners, and directors. It can be summarised in the following way. If the covenant does not survive testing against these rules stated below, it is rendered unenforceable (not illegal or void). Whether a covenant is valid is assessed at the date when it was entered into, not the date when the ex-employee allegedly broke the contractual term. Therefore, covenants should be amended as the employee moves up the hierarchy, and consideration for the new contractual term should be given in the normal way. The assessment as to enforceability of the clause is done by the civil courts. This is one part of employment law which does not fall within the jurisdiction of the employment tribunals.

Tests to validate a covenant

The following comprise the tests by which a covenant is adjudged to be enforceable or not.

1. Such a covenant is valid only it protects legitimate business (often known as 'proprietary') interests. In terms of the three varieties of covenants mentioned above these are trade secrets, 'trade connections' (a phrase connoting the influence over customers), and the stability of the workforce.

2. The covenant must be interpreted. If the employers aided by armies of lawyers draft over-wide covenants, courts rule these covenants to be unenforceable, and they will not carve out a shorter period of time or a narrower territory than the one sought to be enforced in order to preserve the enforceability of the covenant as written. There is one exception to this, known as the *doctrine of severance* or 'blue pencilling'. This means that a covenant which is too wide to be enforceable may be saved if the court can strike out a word or words without altering the grammatical sense. For example, if one has customers only in Sheffield but the covenant is expressed to cover the whole of South Yorkshire, then the covenant falls: the employers have tried to enforce an overbroad covenant and in so doing the whole clause is rendered

unenforceable. If, however, the clause is drafted differently, it may survive. For example, if the clause is not written as applying to South Yorkshire but to 'Sheffield, Barnsley, Doncaster, and Rotherham', where the three other towns mentioned are within South Yorkshire, then the punctuation and words ', Barnsley, Doncaster, and Rotherham' can be excised, leaving only 'Sheffield', which is grammatically correct. In this way a covenant which very much looks too wide to be enforceable can be saved. As can be seen, much depends on the drafting of the covenant.

3. Once any blue pencilling is done, the clause must be construed in its factual matrix, ie taking into account its background circumstances. This process is sometimes known as the *doctrine of construction*. Take, for instance, a milkman. A covenant prevents him after employment from working for employers who sell dairy products. What happens if he goes to work in a shop which sells dairy products such as cheese? The court will construe the covenant in light of its factual matrix. The former employee worked solely as a milkman: it was in that capacity that he acquired customers; he did not serve cheese to customers in a shop. Therefore, the covenant is read as applying only to working as a milkman for a rival firm and not as serving dairy products in a shop.

4. Once the covenant has been construed, the covenant must be tested as to whether it is *reasonable between the parties*. This is when the clause will be struck down if the employers have attempted to insert an overbroad phrase into the covenant. For example, if the employers seek to stop their former employee from approaching her former clients for a year, whereas any influence the ex-employee had over such customers would have died out within six months, the clause is unenforceable. Similarly, if as in one case the former employer's clients are based within a 20-mile radius of their Banbury office, but they seek to enforce a covenant of 25 miles from that office, again they have tried to protect too much territory and the clause is unenforceable. As stated earlier, the courts cannot carve out an area or duration which would pass this test of reasonableness between the parties.

Tillman v Egon Zehnder Ltd [2017]

A recent Court of Appeal decision exemplifies the test of reasonableness between the parties. In *Tillman v Egon Zehnder Ltd* [2017] the employers sought to prevent their former employee from being 'directly or indirectly engaged in or [being] concerned in any business carried on in competition with' them. This covenant was aimed at preventing the former employee from re-establishing her 'trade connection' with her former clients now that she was working for a rival firm. The court held that it was on the facts reasonable for there to be a worldwide restraint. However, it was unreasonable that the former employee could have no involvement at all in a competing business. A very small shareholding suffices as to being 'concerned in' a competing business. Since the courts cannot reword unreasonable covenants, the whole covenant fell. Longmore LJ said:

It may be said to be unattractive that Ms Tillman can rely on the theoretical width of the post-termination covenant to include a shareholding when she does not intend to acquire any shareholding in any competitor and wants to work for a competitor which she could have been restrained from doing if the clause were more carefully drafted. But the law avoids contracts in unreasonable restraint of trade is based on ... wide public policy ... In those circumstances the merits of individual cases must inevitably take second place.

5. For all **workers** except employees there is an extra test: is the covenant reasonable in the public interest? However, for employees that test is subsumed under the test here discussed of reasonableness between the parties.

   (a) The covenant must apply to the alleged breach. For example, if the clause is expressed as preventing a former employee from 'carrying on a business' which is a rival to the former employers, that covenant does not apply to the ex-employee who is working solely as an employee in the rival business.

   (b) If the covenant has survived these tests, it will still fall if the former employers have wrongfully dismissed the employee. The authority is *General Billposting Co Ltd v Atkinson* [1909] (HL). For wrongful dismissal, see chapter 8.

   (c) Though this rule is not, it seems, always adhered to, there must be consideration for the addition of a covenant to an existing contract. The rule, as stated earlier, is that covenants are to be assessed for enforceability at the time they are entered into. The employee may well rise in the hierarchy of the firm and the original covenant will become inapplicable on the facts, eg an employee joining as a salesperson may become the manager of all salespeople in the UK: a covenant restricted to the area in which the employee originally worked is useless to prevent her from working in the territory in which she now works. Therefore, covenants should be redrafted, or at least checked, on each promotion. Simply working under the contract as amended is insufficient: without consideration the clause is unenforceable.

Re-Use Collections Ltd v Sendall [2015]

In this case the High Court held that a covenant should be struck down because the employee had not received consideration for the covenant which was in an amended contract of employment. Although he had had a pay rise and a bonus around the time of the new covenant, these were not referable to that event; and their receipt was not conditional on his agreeing to the covenant.

Not all cases are to this effect, but a sensible lawyer would ensure that there is consideration, which a student knows can be one penny or a rose at midsummer.

If the covenant is enforceable, then the ex-employers will seek to enforce it. A covenant is a contractual term. Therefore, the remedies for breach or anticipated breach of contract, normally damages, are available. However, in a restraint of trade situation they are seeking to prevent the former employee from taking trade secrets to the new employer, to prevent him or her bringing their clients to the new employer, or to prevent him or her enticing former colleagues to join the new employer. In this case the remedy is an injunction. However, the period in the covenant (eg six months after termination of the contract of employment) runs from the date of breach, not from the date of hearing the claim; in normal circumstances the full case will not be heard until after that period has elapsed. Courts will not grant a permanent injunction which is otiose, ie it cannot apply to the facts because the contractual barring period has elapsed. The employers' remedy of choice is an *interim* injunction, one given without the full trial hearing. Unlike normal interlocutory hearings for an interim injunction, the court at this point does investigate the merits of the case, and do not enquire merely whether the ex-employers have a good case for the award of a remedy. An interim injunction gives the employers what they want, eg stopping their ex-employee from delivering trade secrets to the new employer while still enforcing only the words of the covenant.

The written statement

Sections 1 and 2 Employment Rights Act 1996 (ERA) provide that not later than two months after the start of employment of a person whose employment continues for a month or more, the employer must supply written particulars of key terms of employment. This is also known as a written statement or a **s 1** statement. The following information must be given to employees individually. However, according to **s 2(2)** and **(3) ERA**, in relation to the matters mentioned in 6, 7, 9, and 15 below, it is sufficient to make the information reasonably accessible to them by means of a document to which they are referred.

1. The identity of the parties.

2. The date on which the employee's period of continuous employment began (taking into account any employment with a previous employer which counts towards that period). See chapter 11 for continuity.

3. The scale or rate of remuneration, or the method of calculating remuneration, and the intervals at which remuneration is paid (see chapter 3).

4. Any terms and conditions relating to hours of work and normal working hours (see chapter 7 on the impact of the **Working Time Regulations 1998**).

5. Any terms and conditions relating to holidays and holiday pay (see chapter 7 on the impact of the **Working Time Regulations**).

6. Any terms and conditions relating to incapacity for work due to sickness or injury. This includes any provision for sick pay.

7. Any terms and conditions relating to pensions and pension schemes.

8. A note stating whether a contracting-out certificate is in force (contracting out was abolished on 6 April 2016 when the new-style state pension came into effect).

9. The length of notice that the employee is entitled to receive and is obliged to give (see chapter 8).

10. The title of the job or a brief description of the employee's work.

11. Where the employment is temporary, the period for which it is expected to continue or, if it is for a fixed term (a set period such as five years), the date when it is to end.

12. The place of work or, if the employee is required or permitted to work at various places, an indication of the employer's address.

13. Any collective agreements that directly affect the terms and conditions of employment, including, where the employer is not a party, the persons by whom they were made.

14. Where the employee is required to work outside the UK for more than a month, the period of work outside the UK, the currency in which payment will be made, any additional pay and benefits to be provided by reason of the work being outside the UK, and any terms and conditions relating to the employee's return to the UK.

15. Any disciplinary rules applicable to the employee and any procedure applicable to the taking of disciplinary decisions (including dismissal) relating to the employee.

16. The name or description of the person to whom employees can apply if they are dissatisfied with any disciplinary decision or seek to redress a grievance. The statement must indicate the manner in which any such application should be made.

17. Any further steps consequent upon an application expressing dissatisfaction over a disciplinary decision (including dismissal) or grievance (see chapter 9).

If there are no particulars to be entered under any of these headings, that fact must be mentioned in the written statement. Section 7A ERA provides that the information required can be supplied in the form of a written statement, a contract of employment, or a letter of engagement.

 Looking for extra marks?

Demonstrate your awareness that it is good practice to provide employees with detailed particulars rather than the statutory minimum.

Changes cannot be made to a contract of employment without the consent of the employee but, where there is a change in any of the details required by the written statement found in s 1 (also called 'written particulars' or the 'section 1 statement'), s 4 ERA provides that written notification must be given to the employee within one month.

Revision tip

Remember that the statement issued does not constitute a contract or even conclusive evidence of its terms but is merely the employer's version of what has been agreed. Indeed, in *Robertson v British Gas* [1983], the Court of Appeal decided that a statutory statement could not even be used as an aid to the interpretation of the contract. Changing a contract of employment's terms requires consent.

Where an employee is given a complete but incorrect statement, ie some of the particulars are wrong in that they do not reproduce what was agreed between the parties, the employee can complain to an employment tribunal (ET), which has the power to confirm, amend, or replace the particulars. If there is no written statement or an incomplete one is issued, s 11

Sources of terms

✳✳✳✳✳✳✳✳✳✳

ERA obliges the tribunal to determine what the missing particulars are. When the tribunal has decided what particulars should have been included, s 12(2) ERA deems the employer to have provided the employee with a statement containing those particulars. The sanction on an employer who fails to supply a suitable statement is that, in any of the proceedings listed in Sch 5 Employment Act 2002, a tribunal is obliged to make or increase an award by a minimum of two weeks' pay (or a maximum of four weeks' pay if that is considered just and equitable). In addition, s 12A Employment Tribunals Act 1996 allows ETs to impose a financial penalty on employers where there has been a breach of employment rights and the ET thinks that 'the breach has one or more aggravating features'. Normally the penalty must not be less than £100 or more than £5,000 but regard must be had to the employer's ability to pay and there is a 50% discount if payment is made within 21 days.

Currently the written statement must be provided only to employees (see chapter 1 for the definition of 'employee' and 'worker'). However, there is a proposal in the Taylor Report on modern working practices (2017), noted in chapter 1, that the right should be extended to workers and that the period of giving the statement should be reduced from two months to one week. The government has promised to consider the recommendations of the Taylor review.

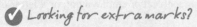 *Looking for extra marks?*

Demonstrate that you know the differences between the contract of employment and the written terms of employment.

Collective agreements

Terms may be derived from **collective agreements** as well as being individually negotiated. Collective agreements are construed by giving meaning to the words used in the factual context, often called the 'factual matrix', known to the parties at the time of agreeing the contract. It is possible to conclude a collective agreement that is legally enforceable, although this is not normally the wish of either party: there is, in contract parlance, no intention to create legal relations. Parliament has made a couple of collective agreements legally binding; in particular, those made by the union for prison officers is contractually binding.

Individual employees derive the legal right to claim the terms and conditions that have been negotiated on their behalf via the process of incorporation. By this mechanism collectively agreed terms become legally binding as part of the individual contract of employment. The simplest way of ensuring that substantive terms are incorporated into an employee's contract is by an express provision to this effect. Frequently, collective agreements will be expressly incorporated because they are referred to in a s 1 ERA 1996 statement of particulars (see 'Express terms and statements of particulars'). Equally, it is possible for terms to be incorporated from a collective agreement by implication or custom and practice, although this is less desirable because of the uncertainties involved. Implied incorporation occurs when employees have specific knowledge of the collective agreement and there is conduct that demonstrates that they accept the agreement and are willing to work under it. Terms will only be incorporated if they are appropriate ('apt') for insertion into an individual contract and, in *Malone v British Airways* [2011], the Court of Appeal stated that the touchstone for incorporation is whether a provision impacts on working conditions.

✔ Looking for extra marks?

You should point out that it is the task of tribunals and courts to ascertain the contractual intention of the employer and employee in relation to the legal enforceability of particular terms in a collective agreement.

Revision tip

Remember not to confuse the issue of legal enforceability *between the parties to the collective agreement* (unions and employers) with the enforceability of its terms via the process of incorporation into individual contracts of employment as between employees and employers.

Workforce agreements

The **Working Time Regulations 1998** and the **Maternity and Parental Leave Regulations 1999** are examples of where it is possible for 'relevant' agreements to be reached that enable employers to agree variations to the Regulations directly with their employees or their representatives. These 'relevant' agreements can be reached via a process of bargaining. Where there are no collective agreements, employers can reach **workforce agreements** with their employees or their representatives.

An agreement is a workforce agreement if:

* it is in writing;
* it has effect for a specified period not exceeding five years;
* it applies to all the relevant members of a workforce or all the relevant members who belong to a particular group;
* it is signed by the representatives of the group; and
* copies of the agreement are readily available for reading prior to the signing.

Works rules

The essential difference between collective agreements and works rules lies not so much in their subject matter but in the fact that the contents of the latter are unilaterally determined by the employer. Both can be expressly or impliedly incorporated into individual contracts of employment using the mechanisms previously described.

Sources of terms

✱✱✱✱✱✱✱✱✱✱

Custom and practice

Custom and practice is no longer a particularly important source of law, although it may still be invoked occasionally to fill gaps in the employment relationship: *WA Goold (Pearmak) Ltd v McConnell* [1995]. To do so, a custom or practice must be definite, reasonable, and 'notorious', ie generally applied in the area or trade in question: *Sagar v H Ridehalgh & Son Ltd* [1930]. If these criteria are met, the fact that the particular employee against whom the custom is applied is ignorant of its existence appears to be of no consequence.

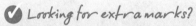

✅ Looking for extra marks?

Get to know the requirements for the existence of custom and practice.

Terms implied by statute and regulations

There are a number of examples of statutes and regulations implying terms into contracts of employment.

1. Terms and conditions awarded by the Central Arbitration Committee. Under s 185 Trade Union and Labour Relations (Consolidation) Act 1992 (on disclosure of information) these terms operate as part of the contract of employment of each worker affected.

2. The sex equality clause (see chapter 3).

3. The National Minimum Wage Act 1998 (see chapter 3).

4. The Working Time Regulations 1998 (see chapter 7). In addition to dealing with holidays, these provide, subject to opting out and exceptions, for maximum hours to be worked in various situations and occupations.

Terms implied by the common law

There are two distinct types of common law implied terms:

*   **terms implied in fact**—where there is a gap in the contract of employment it is possible to imply a term if a court or tribunal can be persuaded that it is necessary to do so in the circumstances of the particular case;

*   **terms implied in law**—these are terms that are regarded by the courts and tribunals as being inherent in all contracts of employment. They are sometimes called 'incidents of employment' or duties.

Terms implied in fact: it is a basic principle, though at times broken, that a contractual term can be implied only if it is consistent with the express terms of the contract. However, despite the increased use of written contracts and statements, it is not unusual for the parties to discover that they have failed to provide for a particular contingency. If there is a dispute over something that is not expressly dealt with in the contract of employment, a court or tribunal may be asked to insert a term to cover the point at issue. The party wishing to rely on an implied term must satisfy a court or tribunal either that such a term was so obvious that the parties did not think it necessary to state it expressly (the 'officious bystander' test) or that such a term was necessary to give 'business efficacy' (*The Moorcock* [1889] test) to the relationship.

Duties of the employer

To pay wages

This is the most basic obligation of employers and is normally dealt with by an express term. However, in certain circumstances the parties are not entirely free to determine the amount of remuneration payable, eg when the National Minimum Wage (and from 1 April 2016, the National Living Wage for those aged 25 and over) applies or if the sex equality clause operates. (Pay issues are considered in chapter 3.) In *Burns v Santander plc* [2011], the EAT confirmed that workers who are ready and willing to perform their contracts but are unable to do so by reason of sickness or other unavoidable impediment are entitled to **wages**.

To provide work (sometimes)

Employers are generally not obliged to provide work and most employees who receive their full contractual remuneration cannot complain if they are left idle. Nevertheless, in certain circumstances the failure to provide work may amount to a breach of contract:

- if a person's earnings depend upon work being provided, eg when payment is by the piece (eg sewing up garments) or the worker is on commission;
- where the lack of work could lead to a loss of publicity (as in the case of an actor) or affect the reputation of an employee; or
- where an employee needs to practise in order to preserve his or her skills, eg an accountant.

William Hill Organisation Ltd v Tucker [1998] IRLR 313

The Court of Appeal held that the employer had an obligation to provide work when the work was available. This was partly because of the need to practise and partly because there was a contractual obligation on the employee to 'work those hours necessary to carry out his duties in a full and professional manner'.

To cooperate with the employee

One of the effects of the unfair dismissal provisions (see chapter 9) has been that the courts and tribunals have displayed a willingness to accept that employers have a positive duty to ensure that the purposes of the contract are achieved. Thus in *Malik v BCCI* **[1997]** the House of Lords confirmed that employers must not destroy the mutual trust and confidence upon which cooperation is built without reasonable and proper cause.

Although each case depends on its particular set of facts, some examples of situations in which employers have been held to be in breach of this implied term are:

- changing the terms of a transferred employee's bridging loan to his or her detriment;
- the operation by an employer of a business in a dishonest and corrupt manner which damaged an innocent employee's reputation, as in *Malik* itself;
- an employer's discretion under a mobility clause being exercised in a way that made it impossible, eg for family reasons, for the employee to comply with a contractual obligation to move (see *United Bank Ltd v Akhtar* [1989]);
- employees not being afforded a reasonable opportunity to obtain redress of a grievance;
- a false accusation of theft on the basis of flimsy evidence;
- reprimanding an employee in public or before colleagues;
- the persistent attempt by an employer to vary an employee's conditions of service without a term in the contract permitting such variation;
- without reasonable cause, denying the employee the opportunity given to everyone else of signing a revised contract with enhanced redundancy payments;
- a serious failure over a period of time to make **reasonable adjustments** to accommodate a disabled person (see chapter 4 for such adjustments);
- failing to notify an employee on **maternity leave** of a vacancy for which she would have applied had she been aware of it.

Scally v Southern Health and Social Services Board **[1991] IRLR 522**

The House of Lords on appeal from Northern Ireland accepted that in certain circumstances it will be necessary to imply an obligation on the employer to take reasonable steps to bring a contractual term to the employee's attention. Such a duty will arise when:

- the contractual terms have not been negotiated with individuals but result from collective bargaining or are otherwise incorporated by reference; and
- a particular term makes available to employees a valuable right contingent upon action being taken by them to avail themselves of its benefit; and
- employees cannot in all the circumstances reasonably be expected to be aware of the term unless it is drawn to their attention.

Looking for extra marks?

Draw attention to the fact there is still no general duty on employers to advise employees of their rights.

To take reasonable care of the employee

According to *Paris v Stepney Borough Council* [1951] in the House of Lords, the tort law standard of care that the law demands is that which 'an ordinary prudent employer would take in all the circumstances'. In *White v Holbrook Ltd* [1985], the Court of Appeal indicated that if a job has risks to health and safety that are not common knowledge but about which an employer knows or ought to know, and against which he or she cannot guard by taking precautions, then the employer should tell anyone to whom employment is offered what those risks are if, on the information then available, knowledge of those risks would be likely to affect the decision of a sensible prospective employee about accepting the offer. Thus the common law accepts that employers should be held liable only if they fail to safeguard against something that was reasonably foreseeable. Once an employer knows of a source of danger, or could have been expected to know of it, it is necessary to take all reasonable steps to protect employees from risks that have hitherto been unforeseeable. The duty is to assess the likelihood of injury and to weigh the risk against the cost and inconvenience of taking effective precautions to eliminate it. Employers owe a personal duty of care to each of their employees, having proper regard to the employee's skill and experience, etc.

This general duty in both contract and tort can be subdivided into the following headings:

Safe premises

In *Latimer v AEC Ltd* [1953], a factory was flooded owing to exceptionally heavy rainfall. A layer of oil and grease was left on the floor, which the employers attempted to cover with sawdust. However, this was not spread across the entire factory floor and an employee slipped in an area which was uncovered. It was held by the House of Lords that the employers had taken reasonable precautions and they could not be expected to close down their factory in order to avoid what was a fairly small risk of injury.

Safe plant, equipment, and tools

This heading is self-explanatory.

Safe system of work

Under this heading are included all the matters that relate to the manner in which the work is performed: job design, working methods, the provision of protective clothing, training, and supervision. Since the case of *Walker v Northumberland County Council* [1995], it has been accepted that employers have a duty not to cause their employees psychological damage by the volume or character of the work that they are required to perform.

Duties of the employer

 Looking for extra marks?

Point out that courts and tribunals will need to distinguish between signs of stress and signs of impending harm to health.

Competent and safe colleagues

Employers are required to take reasonable steps to ensure that employees do not behave in a way that is a source of danger to others, such as playing practical jokes.

 Looking for extra marks?

Examiners will be impressed if you demonstrate awareness that there are also a number of key statutes and statutory instruments (some based on EU law) in the area of health and safety, for example the **Health and Safety at Work etc Act 1974**. (This area is not normally covered in employment law courses.)

There is generally no duty to provide references

The rule is that there is no duty to provide references. However, if one is provided, tort law on liability for economic loss as a result of negligent misstatement applies. The employer will also be liable for the tort of discrimination (see chapters 4 and 5) if she provides references to, say, women but not men, black people but not white people.

> **Spring v Guardian Assurance plc [1994] IRLR 460**
>
> The claimant argued that a reference provided by a former employer was a breach of an implied term in the contract of employment that any reference would be compiled with all reasonable care. The House of Lords concluded that an employer has a tortious duty to take reasonable care in compiling a reference by ensuring the accuracy of the information upon which it was based.

Subsequently the courts have taken the view that the duty is to provide a reference that is in substance true, accurate, and fair and this will usually involve making a reasonable enquiry into the factual basis of any statements made. The provider of a reference must not give an impression that is unfair or misleading overall, even if the component parts of the reference are accurate. According to the Court of Appeal in *Jackson v Liverpool City Council* [2011], accuracy and truth relate to the facts, whereas fairness goes to the overall balance and any opinion stated in the reference.

 Looking for extra marks?

Point out that employers may be liable for economic loss if the contents of any emails are negligently prepared.

Duties of the employee

To cooperate with the employer

This duty has two aspects: to obey lawful and reasonable orders and not to impede the employer's business. In this context the obligation to carry out lawful orders has two distinct aspects. First, it means that employees are not required to comply with an order if to do so would break the law, as when an employed accountant is ordered to falsify invoices. Secondly, it also means that employees are not obliged to carry out instructions that fall outside the scope of the contract, eg to put themselves in danger of being hanged, as occurred in one case.

 Looking for extra marks?

Point out that, despite the common law, employees may be fairly dismissed for refusing to follow instructions that may be outside their contractual obligations (see chapter 9).

To take reasonable care

Employees must exercise reasonable skill and care in the performance of their contracts. For example, they must drive carefully to avoid knocking over colleagues at the workplace.

 Looking for extra marks?

Indicate your awareness that **s 7 Health and Safety at Work etc Act 1974** requires employees to take reasonable care of themselves and others who may be affected by their acts and omissions at work.

Fidelity (or faithful service)

Employees must avoid putting themselves in a position whereby their own interests conflict with the duties that they owe their employer. Thus, employees must not accept any reward for their work other than from their employer. Therefore, receiving a bribe (sometimes called a secret commission) is a breach of this duty. There is no general implied obligation on employees to disclose their own misconduct and whether there is a duty to report the misconduct of fellow employees depends on the individual contract of employment and the circumstances. In *Item Software v Fassihi* **[2004]**, the Court of Appeal suggested that senior employees, here a director with a contract of employment, have a duty to disclose both their own wrongdoing and that of others.

There are two particular aspects of the duty of fidelity that need to be examined: (1) the obligation not to compete with the employer; and (2) the obligation not to disclose confidential information.

Duties of the employee

✽✽✽✽✽✽✽✽✽✽✽✽

The obligation not to compete with the employer

The intention to set up in competition with the employer is not in itself a breach of the implied duty of loyalty. Normally ex-employees are entitled to make use of the skills and knowledge that they have acquired, and are allowed to compete with a former employer provided they do not rely on confidential information (see 'The obligation not to disclose confidential information'). However, this is not the position if there is an express clause written into the contract of employment that restrains competition by employees when they leave. Such restrictive covenants (noted at 'Covenants in restraint of trade') will be enforced by the courts (cases are heard only in the civil courts, not in employment tribunals) only if they provide protection against something more than competition alone, if they are shown to be reasonable in the circumstances, and if they are not contrary to the public interest. The reasonableness of the restraint is to be assessed as at the date the contract was made. Non-competition clauses in a contract may be reasonable to protect the employer's proprietary interests in the customer connections that have been built up by the departing employees and non-solicitation clauses should not be too broad.

Practical example: It will often be an unreasonable restraint of trade to stop employees or ex-employees soliciting even the most junior of employees.

The obligation not to disclose confidential information

The following principles were enunciated by the Court of Appeal in *Faccenda Chicken Ltd v Fowler* [1986]. First, an individual's obligations are to be determined by the contract of employment and, in the absence of any express term, the employee's obligations in respect of the use and disclosure of confidential information are the subject of implied terms. Secondly, while the individual remains in employment the obligations are included in the implied term that imposes a duty of fidelity on the employee. The extent of this duty varies according to the nature of the contract and would be broken if an employee copied a list of the employer's customers for use after the employment ended, or deliberately memorised such a list. Thirdly, the implied term that imposes an obligation on the employee as to his or her conduct after the employment has terminated is more restricted than that imposed by the duty of fidelity during employment. The obligation not to use or disclose information might cover secret processes of manufacture or designs, or any other information of a sufficiently high degree of confidentiality as to amount to a trade secret. However, this obligation does not extend to information which is only 'confidential' in the sense that any unauthorised disclosure to a third party *while the employment subsisted* would be a breach of the duty of fidelity. Fourthly, in order to determine whether any particular item of information falls within the implied term thus preventing its use or disclosure after the employment has ceased, it is necessary to consider all the circumstances of the case including, for example, whether the employer has taken reasonable steps to safeguard the confidential material.

☑ **Looking for extra marks?**

Show awareness of two further points. First, in an appropriate case a court has power to grant injunctions, both interim and permanent, against ex-employees to restrain them from fulfilling contracts already concluded with third parties. Secondly, while the Data Protection Act 1998 imposes additional constraints on an employee's ability to disclose information, Pt IVA ERA protects workers who make certain disclosures in the public interest (see 'Public interest disclosures' next).

Public interest disclosures

The purpose of Pt IVA ERA is to protect individuals who make certain disclosures of information in the public interest. The worker is protected even if the reasons for disclosure are mixed: the disclosure need not be wholly because the worker believes on reasonable grounds that it is in the public interest: *Parsons v Airplus International Ltd* [2017]. Section 43A ERA defines a 'protected disclosure' as a qualifying disclosure that is made to the persons mentioned in ss 43C–43H ERA. According to s 43B(1), there is a qualifying disclosure if a worker—protection is not restricted to employees—reasonably believes that the information is in the public interest and tends to show one or more of the following: (1) a criminal offence; (2) a failure to comply with any legal obligation; (3) a miscarriage of justice; (4) danger to the health and safety of any individual; (5) damage to the environment; or (6) the deliberate concealment of information tending to expose any of the matters listed here. Section 43C(1) ERA protects workers who make qualifying disclosures to their employer or to another person who is responsible for the matter disclosed. According to s 43C(2) ERA, workers are to be treated as having made disclosures to their employer if they follow a procedure that the employer has authorised, even if the disclosure has been made to someone else, such as an independent person or organisation. Section 43D ERA enables workers to seek legal advice about their concerns and to reveal to their adviser the issues about which a disclosure may be made. Section 43E ERA protects workers in government-appointed organisations if they make a disclosure to a Minister of the Crown. Section 43F(1) ERA protects workers who make disclosures to a person prescribed for the purpose by the Secretary of State. Section 43G ERA enables workers to make a protected disclosure in other limited circumstances and s 43H ERA deals with disclosures about exceptionally serious wrongdoing.

Whistle-blowing is about the public interest: disclosure about private interests are not covered, as the government made plain in 2013 when it amended the wording of the statute to include reference to the 'public interest' in s 43, thereby reversing earlier case law. How far does the public interest extend? The case which was reversed involved one person complaining about terms in his contract of employment. After the 2013 amendment, the Court of Appeal held in *Chesterton Global Ltd v Nurmohamed* [2017] that disclosure of wrongdoing by a company which affected some 100 managers, whereby profitability of a certain office was allegedly being suppressed in order to reduce commission due to those managers (and thereby pay more to shareholders), was in the public interest despite the number affected being only around 100. Such a disclosure was on the facts one which the whistle-blower reasonably believed was in the public interest and was therefore a qualifying disclosure. The court said that the public interest was not a matter of numbers and that what is public and what is private are not mutually exclusive spheres.

Whether there is a protected disclosure or not depends on an objective test, not on whether or not the employers believe it to be protected: *Beatt v Croydon Health Services NHS Trust* **[2017] (CA)**.

Section 47B(1) and **(1A) ERA** give workers the right not to be subjected to any detriment for making a protected disclosure and impose **vicarious liability** if a worker suffers a detriment at the hands of a co-worker and the employer did not take all reasonable steps to prevent this happening. **Section 103A ERA** makes it automatically unfair to dismiss employees on the grounds that they have (at any time) made such a disclosure (see chapter 9). No qualifying period of service is required. Finally, you should note that there is no limit on the compensation that can be awarded by an ET if s 103A ERA applies. Compensation is available for stigma damages, ie the whistle-blowing may make it impossible for the worker to get a new job. The amount is the money the worker would have received had her prospects of employment not been ruined: *Small v The Shrewsbury and Telford Hospitals NHS Trust* **[2017] (CA)**. However, an award for detriment or dismissal can be reduced by up to 25% if it appears to an ET that a disclosure was not in good faith.

There is a duty on prescribed persons to report on whistle-blowing.

 ✳ Key cases

Cases	Facts	Principle
Colen v Cebrian (UK) Ltd [2004] IRLR 210	The employers alleged that the claimants' contracts were tainted with illegality because the way commission was allocated amounted to a fraud on the Revenue.	Where illegality is alleged, the burden of proof is on the party making the allegation to show that the contract had been entered into with the object of committing an illegal act or had been performed with that objective.
Faccenda Chicken Ltd v Fowler [1986] IRLR 69	It was alleged that a sales manager had used confidential information when he set up a rival business.	The circumstances in which an employee can be prevented from disclosing confidential information are set out under 'The obligation not to disclose confidential information'.

Cases	Facts	Principle
Malik v BCCI [1997] IRLR 462	The claimant employees alleged that they had suffered damage as a result of the way in which the bank had conducted business prior to its collapse.	Employers must not destroy the mutual trust and confidence upon which cooperation is built without reasonable and proper cause.
Paris v Stepney Borough Council [1951] AC 376	A partially sighted employee suffered an injury which resulted in a further loss of vision.	The tortious standard of care that the law demands is that which 'an ordinary prudent employer would take in all the circumstances'.
Scally v Southern Health and Social Services Board [1991] IRLR 522	The claimants suffered losses as a result of the employer's failure to inform them about their right to purchase added years of pension entitlement.	In certain circumstances it will be necessary to imply an obligation on the employer to take reasonable steps to bring a contractual term to the employee's attention.

(?) Exam questions

Problem question

Mildred has been employed for many years as the 'personal secretary' to Mr Smith. Her terms and conditions state that she may be required to undertake any tasks 'that are within her capabilities and appropriate to her post'. Owing to an increased workload in the department, Mildred has been asked to take on some further secretarial duties for two other senior employees and to cover the switchboard every other lunchtime.

Mildred has refused to take on the extra duties, arguing that they are outside the scope of her contract. During one heated debate about the matter with Mr Smith, he banged his fist on her desk and shouted abusively at her in full view of other staff. Mildred wants to keep her job and is thinking of lodging a formal grievance.

Discuss the legal issues that arise in this situation.

See the Outline answers section in the end matter for help with this question.

Essay question

Individual express terms are not the main source of terms in contracts of employment.

Discuss.

Exam questions
✱✱✱✱✱✱✱✱

 Online Resources

To see an outline answer to this question log on to www.oup.com/lawrevision/

 Concentrate Q&As

For more questions and answers on employment law, see the *Concentrate Q&A: Employment Law* by Roseanne Russell.

Go to the end of this book to view sample pages.

#3
Pay

- An employer may be required to pay wages even if there is no work for the employee to do.

- A deduction from wages or a payment by the employee to the employer is unlawful unless required or authorised by statute or the worker has agreed to it.

- Employers may be entitled to restitution of overpayments made to an employee owing to a mistake of fact but not a mistake of law.

- Employers must give their employees an itemised pay statement.

- Part II Employment Rights Act 1996 (ERA) deals with the protection of wages.

- The National Minimum Wage Act 1998 (NMWA) provides a minimum hourly wage for workers. Lower rates apply to younger workers and Pt 6 National Minimum Wage Regulations 2015 (NMW Regs) describes those who do not qualify at all. The government introduced the National Living Wage for those aged 25 and over with effect from 1 April 2016.

- The hourly rate is calculated by adding up the total remuneration, less deductions, and dividing by the total number of hours worked during a pay reference period.

- The Equality Act 2010 lays down three routes to equal pay between women and men.

- Employers have a defence if they prove that there is a material difference between the woman's pay and the man's.

- With effect from spring 2018, employers with more than 250 employees are subject to a duty to report their gender pay gap.

****

Wages and unauthorised deductions

Section 27(1) ERA defines 'wages' as 'any sum payable to the **worker** in connection with his employment'.

The duty to pay wages is a fundamental obligation of employers and is normally dealt with by an **express term**. The general rule is that wages must be paid if an **employee** is available for work, but everything will depend on whether there is an express or **implied term in fact** (see the previous chapter) in the contract that deals with the matter. According to ss 13(1) and 15(1) ERA, deductions from wages or a payment by the employee to the employer are unlawful unless required or authorised by statute, for example PAYE or social security contributions, or the worker has agreed to it.

Wages includes holiday pay and commission earnings that are payable after an employee has left. According to *Farrell Matthews & Weir v Hansen* [2005], it also includes discretionary bonus payments where the employee has been told that he or she will receive the payments. It should be noted that in this context the word 'discretion' might relate to whether to pay, its calculation, or amount. Before payment of 'wages', the employer is entitled to deduct an amount to repay any advances that have been given to the employee.

The worker must give oral or written consent to the deduction before it is made and s 13(2) ERA provides that where the agreement constitutes a term of the **contract of employment** it must be in writing and drawn to the employee's attention (or its effect must have been notified to the worker in writing). To satisfy the requirements of ERA 1996 there must be a document that clearly states that a deduction is to be made from the employee's wages and that the employee agrees to it.

If a tribunal is not persuaded on the evidence that a deduction was authorised by a provision of the employee's contract, the individual is entitled to be paid the money deducted. Thus in *IPC Ltd v Balfour* [2003], the Employment Appeal Tribunal (EAT) held that a reduction in pay following the unilateral introduction of short-time working amounted to an unauthorised deduction.

Practical example: If the contract of employment allows the employer to change the hours or shift patterns of an employee, then the employer would be entitled to adjust pay levels to reflect those changes.

For these purposes there is no valid distinction between a deduction and a reduction of wages. Under s 13(3) ERA, the issue is whether, for whatever reason, apart from an error of computation, the worker is paid less than the amount of wages properly payable. However, employers who take a conscious decision not to make a payment because they believe that they are contractually entitled to do so are not making an error of computation. Although s 13(4) ERA refers to an 'error of any description', it does not include an error of law. Where there is a dispute over the justification for a deduction, it is the employment tribunal's task to resolve it.

You should note that payments in lieu of notice are not wages within the meaning of the ERA if they relate to a period after the termination of employment. According to the House of Lords' decision in *Delaney v Staples* [1992], the legislation requires wages to be construed as payments in respect of the rendering of services during employment. Thus, the only payments in lieu covered by the legislation are those in respect of 'garden leave' because these are viewed as wages owed under a subsisting contract of employment. In the same case, the Court of Appeal accepted that non-payment of wages constitutes a deduction for these purposes, as does the withholding of commission and holiday pay.

Section 23 ERA stipulates that a complaint that there has been an unauthorised deduction must normally be lodged with an employment tribunal (ET) within three months of the deduction being made. If the complaint is well founded, the tribunal must make a declaration to that effect and must order the reimbursement of the amount of the deduction or payment to the extent that it exceeded what should lawfully have been deducted or received by the employee. In addition, s 24 provides that a worker may be compensated for financial losses suffered. Section 12A Employment Tribunals Act 1996 (ETA 1996) allows ETs to impose a financial penalty on employers where there has been a breach of employment rights and the ET thinks that 'the breach has one or more aggravating features'. Normally the penalty must not be less than £100 or more than £5,000 but regard must be had to the employer's ability to pay and there is a 50% discount if payment is made within 21 days.

 Looking for extra marks?

Point out to the examiner that *Avon County Council v Howlett* [1993] provides authority for the proposition that employers may be entitled to restitution of overpayments made to an employee owing to a mistake of fact but not a mistake of law.

Practical example: An overpayment that arose as the result of a misunderstanding of the NMWA 1998 would be irrecoverable.

Employees may, if dishonest, commit theft if they fail to notify the employer of an accidental overpayment. Section 16(1) ERA makes specific provision for the recovery of overpayments and tribunals cannot enquire into the lawfulness of a deduction for this purpose.

Pay statements

Under s 8 ERA employers must give their employees an itemised pay statement. The statement must contain the following particulars:

* the gross amount of wages or salary;

- the amount of any variable or fixed deductions and the purposes for which they are made; and

- the net wages or salary payable and, where the net amount is paid in different ways, the amount and method of payment of each part payment.

Such a statement need not contain separate particulars of a fixed deduction if it specifies the total amount of fixed deductions and each year the employer provides a standing statement of fixed deductions that describes the amount of each deduction, its purpose, and the intervals at which it is made. If no pay statement is issued, an employee may refer the matter to an ET to determine what particulars ought to have been included. Where a tribunal finds that an employer failed to provide such a statement or the statement does not contain the required particulars, the tribunal must make a declaration to that effect. Additionally, where it finds that any unnotified deductions have been made during the 13 weeks preceding the application, it may order the employer to pay compensation to the employee. Section 12(4) ERA provides that this refund cannot exceed the total amount of unnotified deductions. However, s 12A ETA 1996 allows ETs to impose a financial penalty on employers where there has been a breach of employment rights and the ET thinks that 'the breach has one or more aggravating features'. Normally the penalty must not be less than £100 or more than £5,000 but regard must be had to the employer's ability to pay and there is a 50% discount if payment if made within 21 days.

The common law right to sick pay

In the absence of an express term in the contract of employment, the correct approach to finding out if the employer has a duty to pay wages to an employee absent through sickness is to look at all the facts and circumstances to see whether such a term can be implied: *Mears v Safecar Security Ltd* [1982] (CA).

Such a term may be implied from the custom or practice in the industry or from the knowledge of the parties at the time the contract was made. The nature of the contract will have to be taken into account and, on occasions, it will be permissible to look at what the parties did during the period of the contract. Only if all the factors and circumstances do not indicate what the contractual term is will it be assumed that wages should be paid during sickness. If such a term is implied, it is likely to provide for the deduction of sums received under social security legislation.

> **Howman & Sons v Blyth [1983] IRLR 139**
>
> It was held that the reasonable term to be implied in respect of duration in an industry where the normal practice is to give sick pay for a limited period only is the term normally applicable in the industry. The Employment Appeal Tribunal (EAT) did not accept that where there is an obligation to make payments during sickness, in the absence of an express term to the contrary, sick pay is owed as long as the employment continues.

In recent years the courts have intervened to ensure that employees' entitlements to disability benefits under health insurance schemes have not been frustrated by a strict interpretation of the employment contract.

> **Adin v Sedco Forex International [1997] IRLR 280**
>
> An employee's contract of employment included provisions for short-term and long-term disability benefits. It also contained a clause that allowed the employer, at its sole discretion, to terminate the contract for any reason whatsoever. The Court of Session, the Scottish equivalent of the Court of Appeal, concluded that because the right to these benefits was established in the contract of employment, the employer could not take them away by dismissing the employee.

 ✅ Looking for extra marks?

Demonstrate your awareness that workers may be entitled to statutory sick pay in certain circumstances.

The National Minimum Wage (NMW) and the National Living Wage (NLW)

The NMWA 1998 provides a minimum hourly wage for workers.

According to s 54(3) NMWA, a 'worker' is someone working under a contract of employment or any other contract under which an individual undertakes to do or perform in person any work or service for another.

From 1 April 2016, the government introduced with great flourish a NLW for those aged 25 and over. The NLW has a target of £9.00 per hour by 2020. The rates from 2018 are as follows:

- NLW: £7.83;
- over 21 but under 25 NMW: £7.38;
- over 18 but under 21 NMW: £5.90;
- 16–17 year olds NMW: £4.20;
- apprentices NMW: £3.70. This is for apprentices under 19 and those over 19 who are in the first year of their apprenticeship. Otherwise, the rates above apply.

You should note that these rates are reviewed annually in April and that tips and any allowances paid by the employer to the workers in relation to their work cannot be used to offset the fact that an individual's basic hourly rate is less than the NMW or NLW. Although it is possible to reduce other rates of pay, eg commission and payment by results in order to increase the basic rate without contravening the legislation, doing so might result in the employer being guilty of an unlawful deduction of wages in contravention of s 13(1) ERA.

Part 6 NMW Regs describes those who do not qualify for the NMW or NLW at all. These include:

- a worker who is participating in a scheme designed to provide him or her with training, work, or temporary work, or which is designed to assist him or her to obtain work;
- a worker who is attending higher education up to first degree level or a teacher-training course, and who, before the course ends, is required as part of the course to attend a period of work experience not exceeding one year; and
- a homeless person who is provided with shelter and other benefits in return for performing work.

Part 6 NMW Regs also excludes those who work and live in the employer's household and who are treated as members of the family.

Workers who, by arrangement, sleep on the employer's premises may be entitled to payment for all the hours that are required to be spent there. This rule has been controversial for more than a decade and is one of the areas which may well come under attack post-Brexit. In *Scottbridge Ltd v Wright* [2003], a night-watchman was required to be on the premises between 5 pm and 7 am each night. Apart from some minor duties, he was mainly required to be present in case of intruders. He was provided with sleeping facilities and allowed to sleep during the course of the night. The Court of Session confirmed that he was entitled to be paid at least the NMW rate for the specific hours that he was required to be at work. It was up to the employer to provide him with work and the fact that he was not required to do any did not nullify his entitlement to be paid. Similarly, 'on call' hours can be taken into account for such hours as the worker is awake for the purposes of working. This rule has led to financial problems in the adult social care sector which are, at the time of writing (January 2018), ongoing. The government temporarily lifted this regulation in this particular sector, and only this one, and the situation is now that any back pay must be provided by 31 March 2019. Enforcement by Her Majesty's Revenue and Customs resumes then. The main problem remains chronic underfunding of local government, which pays for such care. There is a case on this topic, *Focus Care Agency Ltd v Dunkley* [2017] (EAT), which is scheduled to be heard by the Court of Appeal in March 2018. One effect of this law if upheld will be firms withdrawing from this area of care and possible insolvencies, not exactly desirable outcomes for the aged or disabled residents.

British Nursing Association v Inland Revenue [2002] IRLR 480

The employers were a national organisation providing emergency 'bank' nurses in homes and other institutions. Part of the work involved a 24-hour per day telephone booking service. This service was carried on at night by employees working from home. The duty nurse would take the diverted call and contact the appropriate person to do the work requested. The duty nurse was paid an amount per shift. The issue was whether this person was 'working' within the meaning of the **NMW Regs** when they were not actually receiving or making phone calls. The Court of Appeal endorsed the EAT's view that, in deciding when a worker is working for the purposes of the **NMW Regs**, an ET should look at the type of work involved and its different elements to see if it could be described properly as work. Aspects to be examined include:

- the nature of the work;
- the extent to which the workers are restricted when not performing the particular task;
- the mutual obligations of employer and worker, although the way in which remuneration is calculated is not conclusive; and
- the extent to which the period during which work is being performed is readily ascertainable.

Thus, the duty nurses in this case were held to be working throughout their shift and entitled to payment.

Regulation 7 provides that the hourly rate is calculated by adding up the total remuneration, less reductions, and dividing by the total number of hours worked during a pay reference period. A pay reference period is one month or a shorter period if a worker is usually paid more frequently. **Regulation 9** stipulates that the total remuneration in a pay reference period is calculated by adding together:

- all money paid by the employer to the worker during the reference period;
- any money paid by the employer to the worker in the following reference period that is in respect of work done in the current reference period;
- any money paid by the employer to the worker later than the end of the following pay reference period in respect of work done in the current reference period and for which the worker is under an obligation to complete a record and has not done so; and
- the cost of accommodation, calculated in accordance with **reg 14**.

Chapter 2 sets out the deductions that can be made from this figure.
These include:

- any payments made by the employer to the worker in respect of a previous pay reference period;
- in the case of non-salaried work, any money paid to the worker in respect of periods when the worker was absent from work or engaged in taking industrial action;
- in the case of time-work, the difference between the lowest rate of pay and any higher rates of pay paid during the reference period;
- any amounts paid by the employer to the worker that represent amounts paid by customers in the form of service charge, tips, gratuities, or cover charge that are not paid through the payroll; and
- the payment of expenses.

The calculation of the hours worked can also be complicated, with Pt 5 establishing four categories: salaried hours work, time-work, output work, and unmeasured work.

Revision tip

Remember that s 28 NMWA reverses the normal burden of proof by inserting a presumption that the worker both qualifies for the national minimum wage and is underpaid.

Section 9 NMWA and reg 59 allow the Secretary of State for Business, Energy and Industrial Strategy to require employers to keep and preserve records for at least three years. Sections 10 and 11 NMWA give workers the right to inspect these records if they believe, on reasonable grounds, that they are being paid at a rate less than the NMW. Following the receipt of a 'production notice', the employer must provide the records within 14 days and make them available at the worker's place of work or some other reasonable place. Failure to produce the records or to allow the workers to exercise their rights can lead to a complaint at an ET. In these circumstances the tribunal can make an award of up to 80 times the NMW. If a worker has been remunerated, during the reference period, at a rate less than the NMW, then there is a contractual entitlement to be paid the amount underpaid.

Her Majesty's Revenue and Customs (HMRC) has the task of ensuring that workers are remunerated at a rate that is at least equivalent to the NMW. Sections 13–17 NMWA give HMRC wide powers to inspect records and enforce the legislation. If it is discovered that workers are not being paid the NMW, ss 19–19H NMWA empowers HMRC to issue enforcement notices requiring payment of the NMW together with arrears and a financial penalty, payable to the government not to the aggrieved worker. That financial penalty was increased to a maximum of £20,000 per worker in April 2016. The tribunal may impose a penalty of twice the hourly rate recommended for as long as the lack of compliance takes place. In addition, s 12A ETA 1996 allows ETs to impose a financial penalty on employers where there has been a breach of employment rights and the ET thinks that 'the breach has one or more aggravating features'. Normally the penalty must not be less than £100 or more than £5,000 but regard must be had to the employer's ability to pay and there is a 50% discount if payment if made within 21 days. Finally, s 23 NMWA protects workers who suffer detriment as a result of asserting in good faith their right to the NMW, to inspect records, or to recover underpayments.

Equality of terms including pay between men and women

The Equality Act 2010 provides three routes by which women may achieve equal contractual terms with men (or men achieve equal pay with women). This law is not restricted to 'pay' but from the start (the Equal Pay Act 1970) applied to all contractual terms. Where there is a claim for equal contractual terms between persons with other 'protected characteristics'

Equality of terms including pay between men and women

(eg race, as where a Japanese company pays Japanese workers more than British ones), that claim is one under discrimination law: see the next two chapters. Similarly, if the claim relates to a non-contractual matter (eg a pre-employment interview, promotion during employment, a post-employment reference), then the claim is one for breach of discrimination law (see the next two chapters) and this is so even when the claim is one where a woman is using a man as a comparator. For other differences between equal contractual claims and discrimination ones, see chapter 5. The 2010 statute uses the heading of 'Equality of terms' and that phrase is used in this book. Normally it will be a woman bringing a claim using a male comparator and this section is written with that in mind, but note that the law is symmetrical, ie a man can use a female comparator. It should be stressed that this law is concerned with equality between men and women; it is not about fair pay. Therefore, if the female claimant should be paid more than her male comparator(s), the tribunal cannot so order. It is restricted to equal pay and does not have jurisdiction over disproportional pay: *Murphy v Bord Telecom Eireann* [1988] (ECJ).

The three routes to equal pay: s 65 Equality Act 2010.

- 'Like' work. This is defined as covering both exactly the same work and work where there is no difference 'of practical importance' between the woman's job and the man's. For example, in *Capper Pass Ltd v Lawton* [1989] (EAT) the differences were not of practical importance when a female chef cooked for 10–20 directors at lunchtime and several men cooked for some 350 workers throughout the day. Compare *Eaton Ltd v Nuttall* [1977] (EAT) where the man's job entailed more responsibility than the woman's. The EAT held that the differences were of practical importance.

- Work rated as equivalent. This occurs when the employers have voluntarily undertaken a 'job evaluation study' (JES), which gives equal value to the woman's and man's jobs 'in terms of the demands made on a person by reference to factors such as effort, skill and decision-making': s 80(5) Equality Act 2010.

- Work of equal value. This is when the ET or an independent expert ranks the woman's and man's jobs equally 'by reference to factors such as effort, skill and decision-making': s 65(6) Equality Act 2010. This method was not in the Equal Pay Act 1970 but was incorporated into English law in 1983, much to the chagrin of the then Prime Minister, as a result of infringement proceedings brought by the European Commission against the UK government.

Hayward v Cammell Laird Ltd [1988] AC 894 (HL)

This case remains the landmark authority. The woman was a cook; she compared herself against three men, a joiner, a painter, and a thermal insulation engineer (a 'lagger'). Her pay per hour was less than the men's but she had free meals, paid lunch breaks, two more days holiday a year, and better sick pay. The Lords held that each individual term had to be compared, not the overall job package; on that basis she won her claim. Note that the men could use her victory to claim equality of terms as to, eg, contractual sick pay using her as a comparator.

Equality of terms including pay between men and women
****

In all cases the law applies to workers, not just employees, and the female worker has a free choice of male comparators: *Ainsworth v Glass Tubes & Components Ltd* [1977] (EAT). However, unlike discrimination law, equality of terms law requires an 'actual' and not a 'hypothetical' comparator (see chapter 5). The female worker must choose an actual male worker who works for the same employer at the same establishment or works for an associated employer or who works at a place where 'common terms' apply to both the female and male worker. At the time of writing, ASDA is strongly contesting that common terms apply to some 7,000 mainly female workers in the shops and mainly male workers in distribution centres. This is the first large equal value case involving the private sector. If ASDA lose, it is estimated that £100 million will be due to the female workers in the stores. Other private sector claims are in the pipeline: until now claims involving large numbers of claimants have involved public authorities such as local councils and the NHS.

Leverton v Clwyd County Council [1989] AC 706 (HL)

This case exemplifies 'common terms'. The female claimant was a nursery nurse and the male was a clerical officer; both were employed by the defendants. It was held that 'common terms' applied across both jobs and it was immaterial that she had 70 days' holiday a year and he had only 20 and that her working week was 32½ hours and his was 37.

A woman can compare her terms using male predecessors and successors in her job: *Macarthys v Smith* [1980] (ECJ) and s 64(2) Equality Act 2010 respectively.

The employers' defence: s 69(1) Equality Act 2010

Even when the two jobs are equal using one of the three methods of determining that issue, employers have a defence if they prove a 'material difference' between the woman's job and the man's. The burden of proof is on them. They have to prove that they have acted using a 'proportionate means of achieving a legitimate aim'. There is no closed list of such material differences but case law is helpful.

Rainey v Greater Glasgow Health Board [1987] AC 224 (HL)

The women were prosthetists working for the NHS; the men were prosthetists working privately. The men earned more than the women. To attract the men into the NHS, the defendants maintained the men's pay when they recruited them. The women and men were now working side by side doing the same job. The House held that the employers had a defence, that of a material difference between the women's pay and the men's. Using the terminology now used the employers had successfully proved that they had used proportionate means to achieve a legitimate aim.

Other major authorities upholding material differences include:

* *NAAFI v Varley* [1977] (EAT): long service, higher output, better qualifications, different locality (eg London weighting allowance);

- *Snoxell v Vauxhall Motors Ltd* [1978] (EAT): pay protection of male moved from heavy work to lighter work undertaken by women in the workforce. This pay protection, also called 'red circling', must cease after a reasonable period; and

- *Waddington v Leicester Council for Voluntary Service* [1977]: extra responsibility.

Cases where the employers' defence have failed include:

- *Enderby v Frenchay Health Authority* [1994] (ECJ): separate pay bargaining for men and women where the men's union exercised its industrial muscle more than the women's with the effect that the men earned more than the women did;

- *Kelly v Minister for Justice, Equality and Reform* [2013] (CJEU) (on a reference from Ireland): 'good industrial relations' did not justify paying (largely) female civilian administrative officers less than (largely) male administrative officers who were members of the police.

Procedural and remedial matters in equal contractual terms claims

The time limit for bringing a claim is six months from the last day of employment unless the employers have deliberately concealed a fact on which the worker could have relied or the worker was suffering from a disability (eg mental illness). There is, unlike in discrimination claims, no additional 'just and equitable' extension to this period of six months. If the worker wins her case, statute deems her contract to include a 'sex equality clause', which modifies her contract to make it the same as that of the male comparator. Breach of this imposed term is remedied by a declaration or damages or both. Damages are assessed on the tort basis and the limitation period is the normal contractual one of six years. There is no power, unlike in discrimination claims, to award damages for injured feelings.

Why is this law important?

Using the median figure and comparing all working women against all working men and excluding overtime and bonuses, women earn 19.2% less than men per hour. If one compares full-time female workers against full-time male ones, again excluding overtime and bonuses, women earn 9.4% less. If the private sector alone is looked at, that figure rises to 17.2%. All figures are taken from the latest publication, the House of Commons Women and Equalities Committee's Second Report of Session 2015–16, *Gender Pay Gap*, HC 584, 22 March 2016, which in turn is based on the Office for National Statistics, *Annual Survey of Hours and Earnings*, November 2015. Current figures show a slight narrowing of the pay gap. In 2017, the gap was 9.1% according to the Office for National Statistics' report, *Understanding the Gender Pay Gap in the UK*, January 2018. In fact, men tend to receive bonuses and overtime payments more than women and it is arguable whether these extra payments should be taken into account when determining equal contractual terms. The gender pay gap rises with age and between 50 and 59 reaches 27.3%. On the other hand, women aged 22–29 earn more than men using the median hourly rate. In the jargon for these women, there is a 'negative pay gap'. For women aged 30–39 the difference is minimal. Sometimes the pay gap is 'negative'; that is, in some sectors of the economy women earn more than men per hour, and the same is true of part-time female workers when compared against part-time male workers. Contrariwise, the gap is 35% or more between part-time female workers and full-time male workers. The difference also varies across the UK with the gap being at its highest in London. Since women outperform men at school and university, there are some who would not change the law because in time women will, they believe, obtain at least equal pay in all age groups. The then Prime Minister announced on 14 July 2015 that the pay gap will be closed 'in a generation'. Recent news releases have brought this issue to the fore.

What are the causes of the difference in hourly pay?

Almost all the factors noted below are ones involving the structure of the labour market, not conscious or even unconscious, discrimination.

- Many women work part-time because the majority of unpaid work caring for children and parents is performed by women and part-time work is often low paid in comparison with full-time work. 58% of carers in the last census, 2011, were female. The median hourly wage for full-timers was £13.29 in 2016 but for part-timers £8.44. Since 41% of women work part-time but only 12% of men do, the effect of low-pay part-timers is to increase the gender pay gap. If one looks at only female pay, full-timers earn 32% (!) per hour more than men. This is called the 'part-time pay penalty'.

- Many women work in jobs which are occupationally segregated, ie ones where the vast majority of workers are female. Where there is such concentration, pay tends to be less than in jobs normally performed by men. In industrial relations terminology, these are the 'Five C' jobs: cleaning, catering, cashiering (eg working on the tills at supermarkets), caring, clerical. Equal contractual terms law could be aligned with discrimination which does permit hypothetical comparators.

- Some economists (in particular, Professor Len Shackleton of the University of Buckingham) postulate that women choose jobs with less commuting, fewer unsocial hours, less danger, and that these jobs are underpaid in comparison with jobs with longer commutes, more unsocial hours, and more danger.

- There may be discrimination but this is hard to judge. Simply saying that taking all the above into account leaves a percentage unaccounted for does not mean that that remainder must be the result of discrimination. The general view is that discrimination as to equality of terms is the factor which least explains the gender pay gap.

Ways of addressing the gender pay gap include the following:

- making almost all jobs open to **flexible working**: doing so would be the default position;

- encouraging men to undertake more childcare and eldercare, eg through an increase in the rate at which shared parental leave (SPL) is paid (currently, April 2018, shared parental pay is a little over £140 a week)—the government promises to review SPL in 2018—and through non-transferable leave for the second parent, whether male or female;

- increasing the NMW and the NLW: most recipients are female;

- more free childcare;

- enforcing the law on no discrimination against women who return to work after maternity: they are often treated so badly by their employers that they leave and enter less remunerative work. The Equality and Human Rights Commission (EHRC) estimates that some 30,000 returnees per year are discriminated against;

- extending the right to request flexible working to all employees, not just as it is now all employees with more than 26 weeks' continuous employment;

- ending gendered educational and career choices (eg hairdressing apprentices are almost all female, and in adult social care 82% are female); and

- bringing back equal pay questionnaires, which were abolished on 6 April 2014, despite 83% of respondents to a government consultation wishing them to be retained.

Gender pay gap reporting

The government introduced equal pay audits for the private sector and the third sector (non-profit-making organisations) where over 250 workers are employed: Equality Act 2010 (Gender Pay Gap) Regulations 2017. (The public sector in England is subject to similar duties by amendment to the public sector equality duty; the public sector in Wales as well as in Scotland is already subject to stronger duties under the specific obligations applying to the public sector as a result of devolution.) Provision for private companies was originally found in s 78 Equality Act 2010 but the previous government but one, the Coalition, refused to bring the law into force. The government changed its mind shortly after the 2015 election. See s 147 Small Business, Enterprise and Employment Act 2015 which required the government to make regulations on mandatory gender pay reporting within 12 months of the Act being passed. These audits should not be confused with the equal pay audits which an ET may order employers to undertake after they lose an equal contractual terms claim. These were introduced by the Enterprise and Regulatory Reform Act 2013, inserting s 139A into the Equality Act 2010. For discussion of s 139A, see 'A word about the s 139A equal pay audits'.

The s 78 audits apply to employees who work in Great Britain and whose contract is governed by the law of a part of the UK. 'Pay' in this context covers basic pay, paid leave, maternity pay, shift premia, and the like but excludes overtime pay, expenses, benefits in kind, and redundancy payments. The audits cover both median and mean pay as well as the mean bonus pay between men and women employees and the proportion of male and female employees who received bonus pay; and employers have to publish numbers of male and female employees in each salary quartile. April 2017 is the first date of collection of the information and April 2018 is the start of annual publication online.

This information must be published in English on the employer's UK website, which must be searchable, and the information must remain on that website for at least three years. Where the material concerns a company, a director must append a signature confirming its accuracy. The information also has to be uploaded on a website designated by the appropriate Secretary of State. However, there is no need to analyse employees by age or part-time or full-time status, which undermines the usefulness of this attempt at transparency; and there is no legal sanction found in s 78: the government expected the provisions to be self-enforcing (ie shareholders, the public, and workers will complain to the company, which will lose at least some of its reputation). However, the EHRC has at the time of writing (January 2018) issued a draft of the enforcement regime it intends to use (*Closing the Gap: Enforcing the Gender Pay Gap Regulations*, December 2017), and consultation on those provisions is taking place. The EHRC proposes that it attempts resolution outside the law with the employers first. If that does not work, it will issue a compliance notice; if the employers do not comply with that notice, unlimited fines are available in the courts.

Moreover, restricting coverage to firms with over 250 employees excludes 99% of all employees! The TUC proposes to reduce this minimum to 150, which is in line with the public sector equality duty. The European Commission recommends a maximum of 50, and in Finland the figure is 30. Much will depend on how much narrative, which is not required but is encouraged by the government, employers will write, eg if an organisation has no gender pay gap is that because it employs no women? Reporting the gender pay gap is not the same as remedying it. The government promises to review this reporting obligation within five years of implementation.

A word about the s 139A equal pay audits

ETs have power to impose equal pay audits on employers who have broken equal contractual terms law. There are exceptions: new businesses, micro-businesses (fewer than ten employees), where there is no reason to think that the employers will breach the law in future. Employers must publish the audit on their website for three years. The penalty for complete or partial non-compliance is a fine of up to £5,000, but the tribunal must take into consideration the employer's ability to pay. The fine paves the way for equal contractual terms claims and for further fines. It is probable that these mandatory pay audits will not have much impact because workers are deterred from bringing all claims including ones for equal pay now that there are fees for ET claims and hearings. There was a drop from 7,928 equal pay claims from the first quarter of 2013 to 1,236 in the same period in 2014, a decrease of 84% and no one thinks that the amount of unequal pay has decreased by 84% in that time. The abolition of fees in the summer of 2017 by the Supreme Court in the stunning decision of *R (Unison) v Lord Chancellor* [2017] is expected to increase employment law claims such as these vastly. First figures after the decision show a 64% increase in claims: see the Ministry of Justice's statistics for the period July–September 2017 issued on 14 December 2017.

 Key cases

Cases	Facts	Principle
Avon County Council v Howlett [1993] 1 All ER 1073	There was a dispute about the circumstances in which an employer was entitled to recover an overpayment made to an employee.	Employers may be entitled to restitution of overpayments owing to a mistake of fact but not a mistake of law.
British Nursing Association v Inland Revenue [2002] IRLR 480	There was dispute about when a person should be regarded as working for the purposes of calculating the minimum wage.	In deciding when a worker is working for the purposes of the **NMW Regulations**, an ET should look at the nature of the work; the extent to which the worker's activities are restricted when not performing the particular task; the mutual obligations of the parties, although the way in which remuneration is calculated is not conclusive; and the extent to which the period during which work is being performed is readily ascertainable.
Farrell Matthews & Weir v Hansen [2005] IRLR 60	It was claimed that there had been no unauthorised deduction because a bonus was described as discretionary.	The word 'wages' includes discretionary bonus payments where the employee has been told that he or she will receive the payments.
Hayward v Cammell Laird Shipbuilders Ltd [1988] AC 894	A female cook compared her basic hourly pay with that of three men: a joiner, a painter, and a thermal insulation engineer.	She won her equal pay case, despite her overall job package being better than the one the males had. The Lords held that each individual contractual term had to be compared, not the overall wage for the job.
Rainey v Greater Glasgow Health Board [1987] AC 224	The NHS recruited male prosthetists from private practice; the men worked alongside female prosthetists who were already working for the NHS. The men retained the salary which they had earned in private practice, which was more than the women earned.	The House of Lords held that the NHS's pay protection policy constituted a material factor defence to an equal pay claim within what is now the **Equality Act 2010**. They had proved that they had the defence because they had (what is now termed) a 'proportionate means of achieving a legitimate aim'. The aim was to bring more prosthetists in to the NHS and paying the new staff more than the old was on the facts a proportionate means of doing so.

Exam questions

****

(?) Exam questions

Problem question

Alex is an information technology specialist who accepted a two-month contract to work abroad. It was his understanding that the cost of his accommodation would be reimbursed by his employer. After performing his duties for a week, Alex discovered that his employer was not prepared to pay for his accommodation so he returned home. When the employer refused to pay him for the week he had worked, Alex alleged that he had suffered an unauthorised deduction under Pt II ERA.

Advise Alex.

See the Outline answers section in the end matter for help with this question.

Essay question

The great contribution made by the introduction of a national minimum wage is that no one in the country can receive less than the prescribed rate.

Discuss.

 Online Resources

To see an outline answer to this question log on to www.oup.com/lawrevision/

 Concentrate Q&As

For more questions and answers on employment law, see the *Concentrate Q&A: Employment Law* by Roseanne Russell.

Go to the end of this book to view **sample pages**.

#4
Discrimination: the protected characteristics

Key facts

- The **Equality Act 2010** replaced the **Sex Discrimination Act 1975**, the **Race Relations Act 1976**, the **Disability Discrimination Act 1995**, and the **Equal Pay Act 1970**.

- The **Equality Act 2010** also replaced Regulations concerned with stopping discrimination on the grounds of age, religion or belief, and sexual orientation.

- The **Equality Act 2010** protects people from discrimination in relation to nine protected characteristics.

- The Act also protects people from discrimination by association with someone who has one of the protected characteristics (eg where the claimant is a **worker** who cares for a disabled child) and from discrimination by perception (eg discrimination because of sexual orientation includes discrimination against those one perceives to be gay even if they are not).

- The Act tries to reconcile the potential conflict between protecting religious beliefs and protecting lesbian, gay, bisexual, and transgender people from discrimination.

Introduction

Sections 4–12 Equality Act 2010 list the nine protected characteristics with which the Act is concerned. The **protected characteristics** are age, disability, gender reassignment, marriage and civil partnership, pregnancy and maternity, race, religion or belief, sex, and sexual orientation.

Looking for extra marks?

Remember that the Equality Act is quite new, so many of the cases or articles that you read will refer to the previous legislation: there is still a need to be familiar with the Sex Discrimination Act, the Race Relations Act, etc.

Age

A person belonging to a particular age group is protected. Age group means persons of the same age or persons of a range of ages, so an age group could be the 'over 50s' or just '50-year-olds' or '21-year-olds'. The statute is not solely about protecting the young or the old.

The Equal Treatment in Employment and Occupation Directive (2000/78/EC) is intended to lay down a general framework for combating discrimination in relation to a number of grounds, including that of age. This is, according to Art 3, in relation to conditions for access to employment, access to vocational training, employment, working conditions, and membership of employers' or workers' organisations. The approach is the same as other measures in relation to disability, sexual orientation, religion or belief. The Directive aims to introduce the 'principle of equal treatment' into all these areas, including age. As a result the UK adopted the Employment Equality (Age) Regulations 2006 (the Age Regulations). These have been replaced by the provisions of the Equality Act 2010.

Revision tip

The Equality Act 2010 replaced all of the Age Regulations except for the part which referred to the default retirement age. This default retirement age was abolished in 2011, so employers can now impose a retirement age only if they are able to objectively justify it. Objective justification in both English and EU law requires the employers to demonstrate to the civil law standard of proof that they have 'a proportionate means of achieving a legitimate aim'.

As with the other statutes and regulations, protection is offered against **direct and indirect discrimination**, **harassment**, and **victimisation**. The definition of direct and indirect discrimination is the same as for all the other unlawful grounds of discrimination (see chapter 5). Unlike all other forms of discrimination, it is permissible to directly discriminate on the grounds of age in some circumstances. There is a requirement to show that the less favourable treatment is a 'proportionate means of achieving a legitimate aim' (s 13(2)). The defendant employers must prove that the difference is 'objectively justified'.

Hampton v Lord Chancellor [2008] IRLR 258

This case concerned someone who held the judicial position of Recorder. He complained that he had been retired at the age of 65, when for other members of the judiciary it was 70. The employer claimed retirement at 65 was necessary to maintain a flow of new candidates for judicial appointments. The employment tribunal did not accept that this was a proportionate means of achieving a legitimate aim.

Exceptions

Schedule 9, Pt 2 Equality Act 2010 deals with the exceptions to the anti-discrimination principle. In respect of age, **para 9** provides, for example, that applicants who would become **employees** can be excluded from protection if they are older than the employer's normal retirement age or, if the employer does not have such an age, 65 years.

Homer v Chief Constable of West Yorkshire Police [2012] UKSC 15

In this case the employer imposed a requirement for a law degree for candidates who wished to be promoted. It was claimed that this amounted to indirect age discrimination against older workers as this might be more challenging for them to achieve in time before their retirement date. The Supreme Court agreed.

The other exceptions include the National Minimum Wage and the National Living Wage, certain benefits based on length of service (eg pay, which results in those with longer service with their employers earning more than those with less service, despite their performing exactly the same job), retirement, the provision of enhanced redundancy payments (which are calculated according to age bands), and the provision of life assurance to retired workers.

Revision tip

Compare the treatment of age discrimination with the other unlawful grounds and point out that there are more exceptions to age discrimination in the Equality Act than in relation to any of the protected characteristics.

Service-related pay and benefits may include salary scales, holiday entitlement, company cars, etc, all or some of which may be related to length of service. Without some action, benefits linked to length of service may amount to age discrimination as younger people who have not served the time required may suffer detriment. **Schedule 9, para 10** provides that an employer may award benefits using length of service as the criterion for selecting who should benefit from the award. There is no need to justify any differences related to service of less than five years. Where it exceeds five years, it needs to fulfil a business need of the undertaking 'for example, by encouraging the loyalty or motivation, or rewarding the experience, of some or all of his workers'.

Age

✳✳✳✳✳✳✳✳✳✳✳✳

> ### Rolls Royce v Unite the Union [2009] IRLR 576
>
> This case concerned two **collective agreements** relating to redundancy: one for staff and one for works employees. The agreed matrix for redundancy showed five criteria for redundancy selection purposes—achievement of objectives; self-motivation; expertise/knowledge; versatility/application of knowledge; wider contribution to the team. In addition there were extra credits given for each year of service. The question was whether this could be justified even though it discriminated against younger workers with less service. The Court of Appeal held that this was a proportionate means of achieving a legitimate aim.

✔ Looking for extra marks?

Think about why it is deemed necessary to allow an exception for length of service. The argument is that having pay scales of a certain length is justified to recognise experience and, perhaps, seniority. It can also be argued that workers who have been with an employer for five years should receive some preferential treatment compared to those that have just joined an organisation.

There is also a general exemption concerning the National Minimum Wage and the National Living Wage so that employers can pay the lower rate for those under 21 and under 18 years and a higher one for those over 25 without it amounting to age discrimination (**Sch 9 para 11**). The intention of the lower age bands is to help younger workers to find jobs by making them more attractive to employers. One question is whether such a measure is a proportionate response to the problem.

Retirement

The UK, in implementing the **Framework Directive**, at first adopted a default retirement age of 65 years. This was abolished in 2011 but there still remains the possibility of an employer-justified retirement age. If an employer wishes to have a compulsory retirement age, then the employer must show that it is for a legitimate aim and that retirement is a proportionate (appropriate and necessary) means of achieving that aim.

> ### Seldon v Clarkson Wright and Jakes [2012] UKSC 16
>
> This case concerned a solicitor who was forced to retire at the age of 65. The Supreme Court accepted that this was a proportionate means of achieving the firm's legitimate aims, which were concerned with sharing out professional employment opportunities fairly between the generations and limiting the need to expel partners by way of performance management for incompetence, thus preserving the dignity of the employee.

✔ Looking for extra marks?

Make the point that the default retirement age was introduced at the same time as the Regulations which made age discrimination in employment unlawful. As compulsory retirement is in itself age discriminatory, it seemed a strange policy to adopt. The default retirement age was abolished in 2011.

The introduction of the default retirement age was the subject of a challenge by the charity Age UK.

> ### *R (on the application of Age UK) v Secretary of State for Business* [2009] IRLR 1017
>
> The most important question in this case, which went to the European Court of Justice, was whether the default retirement age was a proportionate means of achieving a legitimate aim. The High Court held that this was so on the facts, but if the government had not been carrying out a review or had tried to introduce it in 2009 (rather than 2006) then the court would have arrived at a different decision.

Revision tip

The issue of an employer-justified retirement age was discussed in *Seldon* and the House of Lords held that it was possible to justify compulsory retirement if this was a proportionate means of achieving a legitimate aim.

Disability

The **Framework Directive on Equal Treatment in Employment and Occupation (2000/78/EC)** includes measures to combat discrimination on the grounds of disability 'with a view to putting into effect in the Member States the principle of equal treatment'. By EU law, a disability is a limitation on the worker's capacity caused by a long-term physical, mental, or psychological impairment which hinders the worker's full and effective participation in the workplace by rendering her not able to participate in professional life on an equal basis with other workers. A recent application of this definition occurs in *Ruiz Conjero v Ferroser Servicios Auxiliares SA* [2018] in the Court of Justice of the European Union. It is, the Court held, for the national court to determine whether the alleged disability, here physical disability of the spine caused by obesity, amounted to a disability within the EU definition.

Article 5 provides that employers have a duty of 'reasonable accommodation'. This means that employers are obliged to take steps, when needed, to ensure that a person with a disability could have access to, participate in, have advancement in, and undergo training. The only possible exception to this duty, according to the Directive, is if this places a 'disproportionate burden' on the employer. This duty is called 'reasonable adjustments' in English law. This is discussed under 'Duty to make reasonable adjustments', below. There is no equivalent protection for other protected characteristics, though it has often been suggested that the characteristic of religion or belief should also be subject to a duty of reasonable adjustments. Also applying in the context of disability only is the claim for **disability-related discrimination**. An example of this form of discrimination is *Land Registry v Houghton* [2015]. Five employees with disabilities were excluded from a bonus scheme because they had received a sickness absence warning. The employer had already made reasonable adjustments which delayed the operation of the issuance of such warnings to workers with disabilities. However, since the issuing of that notice led to an automatic disqualification from the bonus scheme, that constituted unfavourable treatment relating to the disability. It should be noted that (1) with regard to this cause of action, there is no need for a comparison with an 'able' worker—simply unfavourable treatment, not necessarily less favourable treatment; and (2) there is no need for unfavourable treatment 'because of' the disability: it is sufficient that the unfavourable treatment was related to the disability, a looser link than the 'but for' test.

Revision tip

The Directive permits, in certain circumstances, positive discrimination in favour of the disabled worker or applicant by imposing this duty of reasonable accommodation. A worker without a disability cannot obtain a reasonable adjustment.

Meaning of disability

Section 6(1) Equality Act 2010 provides that a person has a disability if he or she has a physical or mental impairment that has a substantial and long-term adverse effect on his or her ability to carry out normal day-to-day activities. This is different from the EU version, cited in 'Disability', above. (All the examples given in this chapter are taken from the Guidance to the **Equality Act**.)

Practical example: A man works in a warehouse, loading and unloading heavy stock. He develops a long-term heart condition and no longer has the ability to lift or move heavy items of stock at work. Lifting and moving such heavy items is not a normal day-to-day activity. However, he is also unable to lift, carry, or move moderately heavy everyday objects, such as chairs, at work or around the home. This is an adverse effect on a normal day-to-day activity. He is likely to be considered a disabled person for the purposes of the Act.

The requirements are, therefore, that, first, there must be a physical or mental impairment; secondly, the impairment must have a substantial adverse effect; thirdly, it must also have a long-term adverse effect; and, finally, this adverse effect must relate to the ability to carry out normal day-to-day activities.

Revision tip

Certain conditions are not treated as impairments for the purposes of the Act. These include addictions to alcohol, nicotine, or any other substance, unless the addiction was originally the result of medically prescribed drugs or treatment; a tendency to set fires (pyromania), to steal (kleptomania), or to physically or sexually abuse other persons; exhibitionism and voyeurism; seasonal allergic rhinitis (hay fever), although it can be taken into account where it aggravates other conditions; severe disfigurement that results from tattooing or piercing.

In *Goodwin v The Patent Office* [1999], the Employment Appeal Tribunal (EAT) held that the legislation required the employment tribunal to look at the evidence by reference to four different conditions or questions: (1) whether the applicant has a mental or physical impairment; (2) whether the impairment affects the applicant's ability to carry out normal day-to-day activities; (3) whether the adverse effect is 'substantial'; (4) whether the adverse effect was long-term.

> **Hewett v Motorola Ltd [2004] IRLR 545**
>
> The complainant was diagnosed as having autism in the form of Asperger's Syndrome. He argued that, without medication or medical treatment, his memory would be affected and he would have difficulties in concentrating, learning, and understanding. The EAT held that one had to have a broad view of the meaning of understanding and that any person who had their normal human interaction affected might also be regarded as having their understanding affected. What is 'normal' may be best defined as anything that is not abnormal or unusual.

There is also an important issue concerning 'associative' discrimination, ie whether a person who is not disabled herself, can claim to be protected by association with a person with a disability.

> **Attridge Law v Coleman [2010] IRLR 4**
>
> This case concerned a legal secretary who had a son suffering from disabilities. She alleged that she had suffered discrimination under the **Disability Discrimination Act 1995 (DDA 1995)** as a result of being a carer for her disabled son. She was not disabled herself. She argued that the **Framework Directive** offered protection from discrimination on 'the grounds of disability' and that the **DDA 1995** should be construed broadly so as to implement this, and thus provide her with protection. The issue was referred by the tribunal to the European Court of Justice. The Court of Justice (Case C-303/06) agreed and held that the Directive did not only apply to those who are themselves disabled.

As a result of this case the Equality Act 2010 has defined direct discrimination in such a way as to include others who may suffer discrimination because of their association with someone who has a protected characteristic such as disability.

Duty to make reasonable adjustments

The employer also discriminates against a disabled person if the employer fails to comply with a duty to make **reasonable adjustments** in relation to the disabled person (s 20).

The duty to make adjustments has three requirements:

- a requirement, where a provision, criterion, or practice of A's puts a disabled person at a substantial disadvantage in relation to a relevant matter in comparison with persons who are not disabled, to take such steps as it is reasonable to have to take to avoid the disadvantage;

- a requirement, where a physical feature puts a disabled person at a substantial disadvantage in relation to a relevant matter in comparison with persons who are not disabled, to take such steps as it is reasonable to have to take to avoid the disadvantage;

- a requirement, where a disabled person would, but for the provision of an auxiliary aid, be put at a substantial disadvantage in relation to a relevant matter in comparison with persons who are not disabled, to take such steps as it is reasonable to have to take to provide the auxiliary aid.

This obligation applies to applicants for employment as well as to existing workers. There is no requirement that the employers incur unreasonable costs in making the adjustment: *Corry v Merseyrail Electrics* [2015]. The claimant was an epileptic and the sole adjustments for his working at railway stations were that he would never work alone and that he should never work near the track. The EAT held that these adjustments were not reasonable because they could not always supply a worker to work alongside him and sometimes he would have to be rostered to small stations where help would not be available immediately. There is, however, no obligation placed upon the employer if the employer does not know, or could not have reasonably been expected to know, that the applicant or employee had a disability. This was the situation in *Secretary of State for Work and Pensions v Alam* [2010], where the EAT held that the employers were excused from the provisions concerning the duty to make reasonable adjustments because they did not know of the disability and, although they might reasonably have been expected to know about it, the employers could not have reasonably been expected to know that this would put the employee at a substantial disadvantage compared to a non-disabled person.

Revision tip

It is really worth mastering the concept of the duty to make reasonable adjustments as it is difficult to imagine a question about disability discrimination that does not include it.

The question of whether an employer had made sufficient arrangements in the light of their knowledge is one of fact for the employment tribunal.

Ridout v TC Group [1998] IRLR 628

This case concerned an applicant with a rare form of epilepsy who may have been disadvantaged by the bright fluorescent lighting in the interview location. The EAT held that no reasonable employer could be expected to know, without being told, that the arrangements for the interview might place the applicant at a disadvantage. The **DDA 1995** (now the **Equality Act 2010**) 'requires the tribunal to measure the extent of the duty, if any, against the assumed knowledge of the employer both as to the disability and its likelihood of causing the individual a substantial disadvantage in comparison with persons who are not disabled'.

Archibald v Fife Council [2004] IRLR 651

This case concerned an employee of Fife Council who was employed as a road sweeper. As a result of a complication during surgery she became virtually unable to walk and could no longer carry out the duties of a road sweeper. Over the next few months she applied for over 100 jobs within the council but she always failed in a competitive interview situation. Eventually she was dismissed as the redeployment procedure was exhausted. The House of Lords held that the **DDA 1995**, to the extent that the provisions of the Act required it, permitted and sometimes obliged employers to treat a disabled person more favourably than others. This may even require transferring them to a higher level position without the need for a competitive interview.

Gender reassignment

A person has this protected characteristic if the person is proposing to undergo, is undergoing, or has undergone a process (or part of a process) for the purpose of reassigning the person's sex by changing physiological or other attributes of sex. A man transitioning to a woman and a woman transitioning to a man both share the characteristic of **gender reassignment**. Section 7(2) provides that all transsexual people are included. There is no need for any surgery.

Practical example: A person who was born physically male decides to spend the rest of his life living as a woman. He declares his intention to his manager at work, who makes appropriate arrangements, and she then starts life at work and at home as a woman. She eventually decides to start hormone treatment and after several years she goes through gender reassignment surgery. Throughout this process she would have the protected characteristic of gender reassignment for the purposes of the **Equality Act 2010**.

Marriage and civil partnership

This applies to those who are married or in a civil partnership; living together is not enough. Examples of those who would not have this characteristic are a person who is only engaged to be married, or a person who has divorced his or her partner or had the civil partnership dissolved.

 ✅ Looking for extra marks?

Make the point that, in contrast to persons in a marriage or civil partnership who are protected from discrimination on those grounds, single people are not protected from discrimination on the grounds that they are single. Given the steady decline in the numbers of people getting married, this distinction may not seem appropriate.

In considering issues between a married couple, outdated assumptions that the man is the breadwinner might also amount to unlawful sexual discrimination against the woman in the marriage. In *Coleman v Sky Oceanic Ltd* [1981], two competing travel firms employed one member each of what became a married couple. There was a concern about confidentiality of each business's information. The two companies consulted and decided to dismiss the female because the man was assumed to be the breadwinner. Such an assumption, according to the Court of Appeal, was an assumption based upon sex and amounted to discrimination under the relevant legislation (at the time this was the **Sex Discrimination Act 1975**).

Pregnancy and maternity

This protects people from discrimination on the grounds of pregnancy or any illness arising from that pregnancy. There is no requirement for a comparator when trying to show discrimination (s 18). It also applies to taking or exercising rights under the **maternity leave** provisions contained in the Act (see chapter 6).

> **Mayr v Bäckerei und Konditorei Gerhard Flockner OHG [2008] IRLR 387**
>
> This case concerned a woman who was undergoing in vitro fertility treatment. She claimed that she was protected as a pregnant woman. At the time of her dismissal, her fertilised extracted ova had not yet been transferred to her uterus. The European Court of Justice held that she could not yet claim to be pregnant, but that she might have a sex discrimination claim as only a woman could undergo this treatment.

Section 73 Equality Act 2010 provides for the inclusion of a maternity equality clause into every woman's terms of work. **Section 74** sets out what this means in relation to a woman's pay whilst she is on maternity leave.

A maternity equality clause:

- is designed to ensure that any increase in pay (before or during maternity leave) is taken into account when calculating her maternity leave pay;
- operates to ensure that pay, including any bonus, is paid to the woman at the time she would have received it had she not been on maternity leave;
- provides that any pay increase that she would have received had she not been on maternity leave is taken into account on her return to work.

Practical example: Early in her maternity leave, a woman receiving maternity-related pay becomes entitled to an increase in pay. If her terms of employment do not already provide for the increase to be reflected in her maternity-related pay, then the employer must recalculate the maternity pay to take into account the increase.

Special protection

The period during pregnancy and maternity leave is a specially protected one. The dismissal of a female worker on account of pregnancy can only affect women and therefore constitutes direct sexual discrimination (see *Dekker* Case C-177/88 [1991]). In *Brown v Rentokil Ltd* Case C-394/96 [1998]) the European Court of Justice considered the dismissal of a female employee who was absent through most of her pregnancy and was dismissed under a provision of the **contract of employment** that allowed for dismissal after 26 weeks' continuous absence through sickness. The Court held that **Arts 2(1)** and **5(1) Equal Treatment Directive**: 'preclude dismissal of a female worker at any time during her pregnancy for absences due to incapacity for work caused by an illness resulting from that pregnancy'.

This protection does not just apply to permanent employees, but will also apply to others. In *Patefield v Belfast City Council* [2000], for example, a contract worker was replaced by a permanent employee whilst she was on maternity leave. The fact that the employer could have replaced her at any time when she was actually working was not relevant. Of importance was that she was replaced whilst on maternity leave and the employer was, therefore, liable for direct sex discrimination.

Revision tip

You need to read these provisions as part of studying parental rights (see chapter 6) as the protection given during pregnancy and maternity needs to be considered in the context of the protection and support that is given to parents.

P & O Ferries Ltd v Iverson [1999] ICR 1088

This case concerned a woman who was stopped from going to sea once she reached week 28 of her pregnancy. Pregnancy was one of a number of lawful reasons for stopping an individual going to sea, but it was the only one for which, with this employer, there was no pay. All the other reasons, including sickness, resulted in suspension with pay. The fact that this was not available to pregnant women was held to be discriminatory.

For further material on this subject, see chapter 6 on parental rights.

Race

European Council Directive 2000/43/EC implementing the principle of equal treatment between persons irrespective of racial or ethnic origin is an important European initiative in tackling race discrimination in Europe. The purpose of the Directive, contained in **Art 1**, is to lay down a framework for combating discrimination on the grounds of racial or ethnic origin, with a view to putting into effect in the Member States the principle of equal treatment. **Article 2** is concerned with the meaning of direct and indirect discrimination.

Its scope, of course, is wider than just employment, but those areas that are related to employment are also similar to the **Equal Treatment in Employment Directive** (which, as previously stated, is concerned with discrimination on the grounds of age, disability, religion or belief, or sexual orientation).

Pregnancy and maternity
****

> ### Centrum voor Gelijkeid van Kansen v Firma Feryn Case C-54/07 [2008] IRLR 732
>
> One of the directors of the respondent company made a statement to the effect that, although the company was seeking to recruit, it could not employ 'immigrants' because its customers were reluctant to give them access to their private residences for the duration of the works. The European Court of Justice held that such a statement concerning candidates of a particular ethnic or racial origin constituted direct discrimination under **Art 2(2)(a) Directive 2000/43/EC**. Such a public declaration was clearly likely to dissuade some candidates from applying for jobs with the employer.

Race includes colour, nationality, and ethnic or national origin. Those who have any of these characteristics can be described as a 'racial group' (s **9 Equality Act 2010**).

Practical example: Examples of 'race' might include colour as being black or white; nationality being British or, say, Australian; ethnic or national origins could include being from a Roma background or of Chinese heritage; a racial group could be 'black Britons'.

Mandla v Dowell Lee [1983], which is not an employment case but which does apply in employment law, resulted from a school refusing to change its school uniform policy to allow the wearing of turbans. This stopped a boy's application to join the school, because his father wished him to be brought up as a practising Sikh, which for males in turn required the wearing of a turban. The boy's father complained to the Commission for Racial Equality (now the Equality and Human Rights Commission), which took up the case that finally went to the House of Lords. In order to establish that racial discrimination had taken place, in terms of the Act, it was necessary for Sikhs to be defined as a racial group.

> ### Mandla v Dowell Lee [1983] IRLR 209
>
> The House of Lords decided that there were a number of conditions to be met before a group could call itself an ethnic group. These were:
>
> 1. a long shared history, of which the group is conscious as distinguishing it from other groups, and the memory of which it keeps alive;
> 2. a cultural tradition of its own, including family and social customs and manners, often but not necessarily associated with religious observance.
>
> In addition to those two essential characteristics, the House ruled that the following characteristics are also relevant:
>
> 1. either a common geographical origin or a descent from a small number of common ancestors;
> 2. a common language, not necessarily peculiar to the group;
> 3. a common literature peculiar to the group;
> 4. a common religion different from that of neighbouring groups or from the general community surrounding it;
> 5. being a minority or being an oppressed or a dominant group within a larger community.
>
> Such a group could include converts to it or persons who have married into it.

This definition did not extend to Rastafarians. In *Dawkins v Department for the Environment* [1993], an applicant for a job was turned away because he was a Rastafarian and would not comply with a requirement for short hair. His complaint of discrimination was rejected by the Court of Appeal on the grounds that Rastafarians could not be defined as a racial group within the definition of s 3(1) **Race Relations Act 1976 (RRA 1976)**. They did not fulfil the criteria laid down in *Mandla v Dowell Lee* because they did not have a long shared history and could not be compared as a racial group to the Jamaican community or the Afro-Caribbean community in England. It is likely, now, that they would have a claim under the religion or belief parts of the **Equality Act 2010**.

R (E) v Governing Body of JFS [2010] IRLR 136

This case concerned the admissions policy of the Jewish Free School in London. Like *Mandla v Dowell Lee*, this is not an employment case but it does apply to employment law. An applicant was refused admission because the school did not recognise him as a Jew, even though he had a Jewish father and a mother who had converted to Judaism. Orthodox Jewish belief was that Jewishness came from the matrilineal line, ie the need for the mother to be Jewish. The Supreme Court held that discrimination on the grounds of ethnic origin was not limited to discrimination on the basis of membership of an ethnic group as in *Mandla* but also to discrimination on the basis of ethnic origins. The matrilineal test was one based on ethnic origins and so constituted discrimination on that basis.

Revision tip

When looking at cases on discrimination prior to the adoption of the **Equality Act 2010**, you will find that the tribunals and courts were able to rely on race cases in considering sex discrimination claims, and vice versa, as the provisions of the **Sex Discrimination Act 1975** and the **RRA 1976** were very similar, though not the same (eg lavatories could be set aside for women or men but not for white women and black women).

It is possible for a person to be unfavourably treated on racial grounds even if the claimant is not a member of the group being discriminated against. In *Weathersfield v Sargent* [1999], a person of white European ancestry was instructed to discriminate against black and Asian people in hiring out vehicles. She resigned and claimed **constructive dismissal** (see chapter 8, 'Constructive dismissal', for the meaning of constructive dismissal) on the grounds that she had been unfavourably treated on racial grounds. The Court of Appeal held that it was appropriate to give a broad meaning to the expression 'racial grounds'. It was an expression that should be capable of covering any reason or action based on race.

During the currency of this book it is expected that the government will extend 'race' to cover 'caste'. The **Enterprise and Regulatory Reform Act 2013** amends the **Equality Act 2010** to require the government to make law prohibiting discrimination because of caste. A consultation as to whether the statute should expressly cover 'caste' finished in September 2017. At the time of writing, January 2018, no legislation has been adopted and some case law supports the proposition that caste is already included within 'race'. Clarification in a statue would be good. For more consideration of race and sex discrimination, see chapter 5.

Religion or belief

According to s 9 Equality Act 2010, 'religion' means any religion or lack of religion; 'belief' means any philosophical belief or lack of such belief. The Guidance from the European Court of Human Rights states that atheism or humanism would be included as beliefs, but not 'adherence to a particular football team'. For an example, see *GMB v Henderson* [2015] where strong left-wing democratic socialist beliefs were held by the EAT to fall within the protection of the Equality Act 2010.

***Azmi v Kirklees Metropolitan Borough Council* [2007] IRLR 484**

This case concerned a school support worker who was a devout Muslim. She was used to wearing a long dress and a veil that covered all her head and face apart from her eyes. After much consultation, she was instructed not to wear the veil in school as it restricted the visual signals that children would normally receive from a person not wearing a veil. Her claim of direct discrimination failed because she was held not to have been treated less favourably compared to another person, who was not a Muslim, but who had her face covered: this comparator would have been dismissed too.

 ✔ *Looking for extra marks?*

Think about and research the potential conflict between the desire to protect those who wish to practise their religion and the desire to protect people on the basis of sexual orientation.
If a person is barred from working for a religious organisation because they are gay, they are being discriminated against because of their sexual orientation, but, at the same time, there is a requirement to respect the beliefs of the religious body.

There is perhaps a difficulty with outward manifestations of religious belief, as shown in *Eweida v British Airways plc* [2013].

***Eweida v British Airways plc* [2013] IRLR 231**

This concerned a person who was a devout practising Christian, who regarded the cross as a central image of her beliefs. She worked as a member of the airline's check-in staff and believed it was a mandatory part of her religion to wear the cross in a place where it could be seen. She was forbidden to wear it in this manner and complained that she had been subjected to indirect discrimination because of her religious belief. The European Court of Human Rights (Fourth Section) held that the applicant succeeded in her claim that her employers had breached Art 9 European Convention on Human Rights. The employers had interfered with her right to wear a religious symbol as a manifestation of her faith and that interference was not proportionate. While the employers had a legitimate objective in that their dress code was part of their corporate image, the banning of a small cross was disproportionate:

> Ms Eweida's cross was discreet and cannot have detracted from her professional appearance. There was no evidence that the wearing of other, previously authorised, items of religious clothing, such as turbans and hijabs, by other employees, had any negative impact on British Airways' brand or image. Moreover, the fact that the company was able to amend the uniform code to allow for the visible wearing of religious symbolic jewellery demonstrates that the earlier prohibition was not of crucial importance.

Religious requirements relating to sex, marriage, etc, and sexual orientation

There is a perceived need to make an exception to some of the Act's provisions in relation to organised religion. Clearly there is an important issue for some organised religions in relation to the gender of some of the employees and in relation to the sexual orientation of employees. The Act tries to deal with this by accepting that in some very limited situations it will be permissible to discriminate on the grounds of sex and/or sexual orientation.

Schedule 9 Pt 1 para 2 Equality Act provides that a person does not contravene the non-discrimination at work provisions if a person (A) applies one of the following requirements:

1. a requirement to be of a particular sex;
2. a requirement to be a transsexual person;
3. a requirement not to be married or a civil partner;
4. a requirement not to be married to, or the civil partner of, a person who has a living former spouse or civil partner;
5. a requirement relating to circumstances in which a marriage or civil partnership came to an end;
6. a requirement related to sexual orientation;

if A can show that:

1. the employment is for the purposes of an organised religion;
2. the application of the requirement engages the *compliance or non-conflict principle*; and
3. the person to whom A applies the requirement does not meet it (or A has reasonable grounds for not being satisfied that a person meets it).

In this section the *compliance principle* means if the requirement is applied so as to comply with the doctrines of the religion. The *non-conflict principle* occurs when, because of the nature or context of employment, the requirement is applied so as to avoid conflicting with the strongly held religious convictions of a significant number of the religion's followers.

Thus it is possible to make an exception to the principle of non-discrimination if it is needed to comply with the doctrines of a religion or to avoid conflicting with the strongly held religious beliefs of the followers of that religion. Examples are given in the Guidance showing the narrowness of the exception.

Practical example: The requirement that a Catholic priest be unmarried and a man.

- It is unlikely to permit a requirement that a church youth worker who primarily organises sporting activities is celibate if he is gay, but it might apply if the church worker mainly taught Bible classes.
- It would not apply to a rule that required a church accountant to be celibate if he is gay.

Sex

****

There is also an exception for employers with an ethos based on religion or belief (Sch 9 Pt 1 para 3). The employer does not contravene the non-discrimination at work provisions by applying a requirement to be of a particular religion or belief, having regard for the ethos and the nature or context of the work, if:

- it is an **occupational requirement**;
- the application of the requirement is a proportionate means of achieving a legitimate aim; and
- the person to whom A applies the requirement does not meet it (or A has reasonable grounds for not being satisfied that a person meets it). This repeats the provisions contained in legislation prior to the Equality Act 2010 and has a very narrow limited effect. The Guidance gives the example of an organisation being able to justify it for the role of the head of the organisation, but not for other administrative posts within that organisation.

Sex

Section 11 Equality Act provides that references in the Act to the protected characteristic of sex mean being a man or a woman; men share this characteristic with other men and women with other women.

The Equal Opportunities and Equal Treatment Directive (2006/54/EC) provides, in Art 1, that its purpose is 'to ensure the implementation of the principle of equal opportunities and equal treatment of men and women in matters of employment and occupation'. Article 2 states that, for the purposes of the Directive, discrimination includes:

- harassment and sexual harassment, as well as any less favourable treatment based on a person's rejection of or submission to such conduct;
- instruction to discriminate against persons on grounds of sex;
- any less favourable treatment of a woman related to pregnancy or maternity leave within the meaning of Directive 92/85/EC.

One issue was whether this was positive discrimination in favour of women in terms of access to work (see chapter 5). This was tested in *Marschall* [1998].

Marschall v Land Nordrhein-Westfalen **Case C-409/95 [1998] IRLR 39**

The complainant was a male comprehensive school teacher who had applied for promotion to a higher grade. He was told that an equally qualified female applicant would be given the position as there were fewer women than men in the more senior grade. The European Court of Justice considered previous judgments that concluded that the **Equal Treatment Directive** did not permit national rules that enabled female applicants for a job to be given automatic priority. The Court distinguished between those measures that were designed to remove the obstacles to women and those measures that were designed to grant them priority simply because they were women. The

---

latter measures conflicted with the **Equal Treatment Directive**. There was a difference between measures concerned with the promotion of equal opportunity and measures imposing equal representation. This situation appears unchanged despite **Art 157(4) Lisbon Treaty** which states: 'With a view to ensuring full equality of practice between men and women in working life, the principle of equal treatment shall not prevent any Member State from maintaining or adopting measures for providing for specific advantages in order to make it easier for the under-represented sex to pursue a vocational activity or to prevent or compensate for disadvantages in professional careers.'

Although the legislation has as a primary purpose the removing of discrimination between men and women, it does not necessarily require the same treatment as between men and women. The aim is to ensure that one gender is not treated less favourably than another. For example, an employer may have a dress code which permits women but not men to have long hair or which has a rule that backroom (not customer-facing) staff must wear a tie if male. This is discussed below.

Revision tip

Remember that, although the primary purpose of the Equality Act 2010, in relation to sex, is to protect women from discrimination, it also has the effect of protecting men from discrimination on the grounds of sex.

One area of contention in the employment field has been the imposition of dress codes that might be different for men and women.

Smith v Safeway plc [1996] IRLR 457

A male employee was dismissed because his ponytail grew too long to keep under his hat. The store had a code that required men to have hair not below shirt-collar level, but female employees were permitted to have hair down to shoulder length. Phillips LJ stated that:

I can accept that one of the objects of the prohibition of sex discrimination was to relieve the sexes from unequal treatment resulting from conventional attitudes, but I do not believe that this renders discriminatory an appearance code which applies a standard of what is conventional.

The result was that the court held that the employer was imposing a dress code that reflected a conventional outlook and that this should not be held to be discriminatory.

Sections 158 and **159 Equality Act 2010** now contains provisions relating to positive discrimination (see chapter 5).

For more consideration of race and sex discrimination, see chapter 5.

Sexual orientation

Sexual orientation means a sexual orientation towards people of the same sex (applying to gay men and lesbians), the opposite sex (applying to heterosexuals), or either sex (bisexuals).

Key cases

✴✴✴✴✴✴✴✴✴✴

Thus a man and a woman attracted to people of the opposite sex share a sexual orientation as do men only attracted to men and women who are only attracted to women.

As mentioned under 'Religion or belief', there is a potential for conflict with the provisions of the Equality Act 2010 in relation to the protection of religion or belief. One example of this issue can be found in *Ladele* [2013].

Ladele v London Borough of Islington [2013] IRLR 231

Ms Ladele was a registrar of births, deaths, and marriages in Islington. She was a strongly committed Christian and believed that marriage should be an exclusive and life-long union between a man and a woman. In December 2005 the **Civil Partnership Act 2004** came into force and Ms Ladele was expected, as part of her job, to register civil partnerships between same-sex couples. She refused to do this and brought a claim against the council relying upon the religion or belief regulations (now in the **Equality Act 2010**). She lost her claim because the council's aim, as accepted by the European Court of Human Rights, was to provide an efficient service and it wished to respect the homosexual community in the same manner as the heterosexual community. The court held that the council had a legitimate aim and the means of achieving that aim were proportionate.

 (✴) Key cases

Cases	Facts	Principle
Archibald v Fife Council [2004] IRLR 651	This case concerned an employee of Fife Council who was employed as a road sweeper. As a result of a complication during surgery, she became virtually unable to walk and could no longer carry out the duties of a road sweeper. Over the next few months she applied for over 100 jobs within the council but she always failed in a competitive interview situation. Eventually she was dismissed as the redeployment procedure was exhausted.	The House of Lords held that the **DDA 1995** (now the **Equality Act 2010**), to the extent that the provisions of the Act required it, permitted and sometimes obliged employers to treat a disabled person more favourably than others. This may even require transferring them to a higher level position without the need for a competitive interview.
Centrum voor Gelijkeid van Kansen v Firma Feryn Case C-54/07 [2008] IRLR 732	One of the directors of the respondent company made a statement to the effect that, although the company was seeking to recruit, it could not employ 'immigrants' because its customers were reluctant to give them access to their private residences for the duration of the works.	The European Court of Justice held that such a statement concerning candidates of a particular ethnic or racial origin constituted direct discrimination under **Art 2(2)(a) Directive 2000/43**. Such a public declaration was clearly likely to dissuade some candidates from applying for jobs with the employer.

Cases	Facts	Principle
Ladele v London Borough of Islington [2013] IRLR 231	Ms Ladele was a registrar of births, deaths, and marriages in Islington. She was a strongly committed Christian and believed that marriage should be an exclusive and life-long union between a man and a woman. In December 2005 the **Civil Partnership Act 2004** came into force and Ms Ladele was expected, as part of her job, to register civil partnerships between same-sex couples. She refused to do this and brought a claim against the council relying upon the religion or belief regulations (now in the **Equality Act 2010**).	She lost her claim because the council's aim, as accepted by the European Court of Human Rights, was to provide an efficient service and a wish to respect the homosexual community in the same manner as the heterosexual community. The Court held that the council had a legitimate aim and the means of achieving that aim were proportionate.
Mandla v Dowell Lee [1983] IRLR 209	A school refused to change its school uniform policy to allow the wearing of turbans. This stopped a boy's application to join the school, because his father wished him to be brought up as a practising Sikh, which in turn required the wearing of a turban.	The House of Lords decided that there were a number of conditions to be met before a group could call itself a racial group (see main text).
Seldon v Clarkson Wright and Jakes [2012] UKSC 16	This case concerned compulsory retirement and whether it was possible for an employer to do this even though the default retirement age has now been abolished.	It is possible to have an employer-justified retirement age providing that there is a legitimate aim and that the means of achieving this aim are proportionate.

 Exam questions

Problem question

Dodgy Car Rentals Ltd is a car hire company that runs a fleet of cars available for hire by the public, sometimes with a driver. Mr Dodgy is the owner and managing director. One of his sales executives is Mrs Nice, who is a white female.

Mr Dodgy had a very unhappy holiday in the Caribbean and, as a result, instructs Mrs Nice not to hire cars to potential customers with a Caribbean accent. She is very upset about this, refuses to carry out the instructions, and resigns.

The company also has a policy that all its drivers must have very short hair. This has the effect of putting off Mona from applying, as she has shoulder-length curly hair. She did not discover this rule until she attended her interview.

Exam questions
✳✳✳✳✳✳✳✳✳

Mr Singh was turned down for a driver's job when he explained that his religion did not allow him to cut his hair.

Advise Mrs Nice, Mona, and Mr Singh about their rights in relation to employment with this firm.

See the Outline answers section in the end matter for help with this question.

Essay question

Religious groups ought not to have to employ gay people if their religious beliefs do not accept homosexuality. (Fictitious quote.)

Discuss.

 Online Resources

To see an outline answer to this question log on to www.oup.com/lawrevision/

 Concentrate Q&As

For more questions and answers on employment law, see the *Concentrate Q&A: Employment Law* by Roseanne Russell.

Go to the end of this book to view **sample pages**.

#5

Discrimination at work, prohibited conduct, and enforcement

Key facts

- **Part 2 Ch 5 Equality Act 2010** applies the non-discrimination provisions to work.

- Applicants for jobs must not be asked about their health or disability in the recruitment process.

- The question traditionally asked in sex and race discrimination cases is 'Would the complainant have received the same treatment from the defendant but for his or her sex or race?' This is known as the 'but for' test.

- Prohibited conduct means direct and indirect discrimination, harassment, and victimisation. Segregation on racial grounds is also prohibited.

- There is a different definition of discrimination for the protected characteristic of pregnancy and maternity.

- There is no minimum period of employment needed before one can make a discrimination claim.

- Compensation is unlimited. The other remedies are recommendations and declarations.

- For equal contractual terms law as between men and women, see chapter 3. The law in this chapter applies to non-contractual matters, whether pre-employment or post-employment, and indeed during employment provided that the issue is a non-contractual one such as promotion. For example, if a bonus is a matter of contract and men receive it but women do not, that is an issue dealt with in chapter 3 because it involves a contractual term which differs between men and women; however, if the bonus is not a contractual matter, it falls within this chapter.

Discrimination at work

Section 39 Equality Act 2010 concerns workers, ex-workers, and applicants and provides that an employer must not discriminate against (or victimise) a person in the arrangements made in deciding who should be offered employment, the terms of that employment, or not offering employment at all. Similarly an employer is forbidden from discriminating against any of her **workers** in relation to the terms of their employment, opportunities for promotion, transfer or training (or any other benefit, facility, or service), dismissals, or subjecting **employees** to any other detriment.

The 2010 statute originally had a provision forbidding **harassment** by third parties (such as customers, eg a person being looked after in a care home and suppliers) but that was repealed by the Coalition government in October 2013. There are, however, other ways of protecting workers in these situations such as the tort of negligence and the implied term of trust and confidence.

Revision tip

Remember that, except for those who do not qualify, such as those who work wholly outside Great Britain, there are no restrictions imposed, such as a minimum length of continuous service or an upper age limit, to stop an individual making a complaint of discrimination.

The Court of Appeal held in *Bain v Bowles* [1991] that an act of discrimination had taken place when a UK magazine refused to accept an advertisement for a housekeeper/cook based in Tuscany, Italy. The advertisement was placed in the magazine by a single man. The journal's reason for refusing it was that it accepted advertisements for overseas positions only where the employer was a woman and that this was a way of protecting young females from exploitation. The court decided that this approach was unacceptable. The motive (whether bad or good), in accordance with the decision in *James v Eastleigh Borough Council* [1990], was not a valid justification for discrimination.

Martins v Marks & Spencer plc [1998] **IRLR 326**

This case concerned an applicant of Afro-Caribbean ethnic origin who unsuccessfully applied four times for a post as a trainee manager with Marks & Spencer. She settled a race discrimination claim on the last occasion and as part of the arrangement was allowed to take a selection test and was given an interview. She failed her selection interview with poor marks. The employment tribunal had found the selection panel 'biased' in its treatment of the candidate. This, the Court of Appeal decided, was not a meaningful conclusion. The real questions were, first, whether they were treating this candidate less favourably than they would treat another candidate in the same circumstances; and, secondly, whether one could infer that this less favourable treatment was on racial grounds. The Court of Appeal found that there was insufficient evidence for this less favourable treatment.

Asking applicants about health

Section 60 Equality Act 2010 concerns enquiries about disability and health in recruitment. A person to whom an application for work is made (A) must not ask about the health of the applicant (B) before offering B work or, where A is not in a position to offer work, before including B in a pool of applicants from whom A intends (when in a position to do so) to select a person to offer work to. A contravention of this is enforceable as an unlawful act under Pt 1 Equality Act 2010. A does not contravene a relevant disability provision merely by asking about B's health, but A's subsequent conduct in reliance on this information may be a contravention. There are a number of exceptions listed in s 60(6). 'Work' has a wide meaning and includes employment and contract work (s 60(9)).

Looking for extra marks?

Consider the issue of not being allowed to ask questions about health and disability. At the same time an employer is excused from the need to make **reasonable adjustments** if the employer does not know about a disability or might reasonably not be expected to know. Employers need to be very careful in collecting this information and what actions are taken as a result.

Prohibited conduct

The Equality Act 2010 defines the conduct that is prohibited in relation to the nine **protected characteristics** (see chapter 4).

Direct discrimination

Section 13(1) describes **direct discrimination** in the following way:

> A person (A) discriminates against another (B) if, because of a protected characteristic, A treats B less favourably than A treats, or would treat, others.

Thus, direct discrimination occurs where, because of one of the protected characteristics, a person is treated less favourably than someone who does not share that characteristic is treated or would be treated. This would cover situations where there has been a generalised stereotypical assumption that people in a particular group possess or lack certain characteristics.

Practical examples: All examples in this chapter are taken from the official Guidance to the Equality Act published by the Equality and Human Rights Commission and available on its website, equalityhumanrights.com.

- If an employer recruits a man rather than a woman because she assumes that women do not have the strength to do the job, this would amount to direct sex discrimination.
- If an employer rejects a job application from a white man whom he wrongly thinks is black, because the applicant had an African-sounding name, this would constitute direct race discrimination based upon the employer's mistaken perception.

Direct sex discrimination

If one takes sex discrimination as an example, one can see that the two essential features of direct discrimination, in relation to sex, are, first, that it takes place because of sex (which is a protected characteristic) and, secondly, that it takes place when a person is treated less favourably than a person of the other sex is treated or would be treated. Thus a comparative model of justice is used. The treatment given to A is relative to the treatment given to the comparator B.

The question traditionally asked by the tribunals and courts is: 'Would the complainant have received the same treatment from the defendant but for his or her sex?' This 'but for' test can be applied where the treatment given derives from the application of gender-based criteria and where the treatment given results from the selection of the complainant because of his or her sex. Thus, when a local authority gave free use of its swimming pools to persons of pensionable age, a male of 61 years who has not reached pensionable age is discriminated against in comparison with a woman who reached it at the age of 60 years, the then pension age for women (*James v Eastleigh Borough Council* [1990]). There need be no intention to discriminate and motives, good or bad, are not relevant.

R v Birmingham City Council, ex parte Equal Opportunities Commission [1989] IRLR 173

The local authority offered more places in selective secondary education to boys than girls. (This is a school case but such authorities apply to employment law.) This was held by the House of Lords to be treating those girls less favourably on the grounds of their sex and the fact that the local authority had not intended to discriminate was not relevant. In the absence of an actual comparator, the tribunal will need to construct a hypothetical one.

Revision tip

Remember that the provisions on direct discrimination are mirrored in relation to all the protected characteristics, so that interpretations concerning one characteristic can be applied to the others, with some exceptions, eg direct age discrimination can be justified: it is the sole protected characteristic which can be. For example, the test to be applied in race discrimination cases is the same as that applied in sex discrimination claims. The tribunal will need to ask the question whether the complainants would have received the same treatment but for their race. This question needs to be asked when a choice is to be made between a racial and a non-racial explanation offered by the complainant.

The Guidance also states that the definition of direct discrimination is broad enough to include those treated less favourably because of their association with someone who has the characteristic or because the victim is thought ('perceived') to have it. The provision in the **Equality Act 2010** is worded wide enough to cover both discrimination by association and discrimination by perception. This was shown to be the case for associated discrimination in *Coleman v Attridge Law* [2008], where the European Court of Justice interpreted EU law as extending protection from discrimination to those associated with an individual, rather than to just the individual alone. In this case, a mother of a child with a disability claimed successfully that she was protected by the then **Disability Discrimination Act 1995** (now the **Equality Act 2010**) even though she was not herself disabled. She had been obliged to take a lot of time off work to look after her child.

There are some special rules concerning different protected characteristics.

- **Section 13(2)** provides that direct discrimination in relation to age can be justified if shown to be a proportionate means of achieving a legitimate aim. Age is the only protected characteristic for which it is possible to justify direct discrimination.

- **Section 13(3)** makes it clear that treating a person with a disability more favourably than a non-disabled person does not amount to discrimination against a person who does not have a disability. Therefore, those with disabilities can gain advantages over those without, and those without cannot in turn gain those advantages. The easiest example for university students is giving extra time in examinations to candidates who have dyslexia; those who do not have this disability cannot compare themselves against those with it and gain that extra time.

- In the case of sex discrimination, no account is to be taken of any special treatment given to a woman in connection with pregnancy or childbirth (s 13(6)).

✅ Looking for extra marks?

Think about the three exceptions just listed and remember to include them in your answers. The first one concerns age and shows how age is treated differently from the other protected characteristics. The second is about disability and ensures that there are no complications arising from treating a person with a disability more favourably than others who do not have one. The third exception ensures that special treatment can be given to women in connection with pregnancy or childbirth without it amounting to discrimination against men who do not receive this special treatment.

Combined discrimination: dual characteristics

Section 14 Equality Act 2010 as originally enacted introduced, in a limited way, protection from direct discrimination on multiple grounds. Multiple discrimination or intersectional discrimination occurs when a person is discriminated against on more than one protected characteristic. The Act limited this to two characteristics. An example is discriminating against a Muslim woman, not because she is a woman (which would be sexual discrimination) or because she is a Muslim (which would be religious discrimination), but because she is a Muslim woman; the employer does not discriminate against Muslim men or against non-Muslim women.

The Coalition government refused to implement this provision. This means that individuals will continue to be able to complain about discrimination only in relation to one protected characteristic at a time.

Indirect discrimination

Indirect discrimination is defined, in s 19(1), as:

> A person (A) discriminates another (B) if A applies to B a provision, criterion or practice which is discriminatory in relation to a relevant characteristic of B's.

It occurs (see s 19(2)) when a policy that applies in the same way for everybody has an effect that disadvantages people with a particular protected characteristic. Where a particular group is disadvantaged in this way, a person in that group is indirectly discriminated against if he or she is put at a disadvantage, unless A can show that it is a proportionate means of achieving a legitimate aim. There is no need to show the reason why a certain group (eg members of a certain race or of a certain age) is disadvantaged in comparison with another; it is sufficient that one group *is* disadvantaged: *Naeem v Secretary of State for Justice; Essop v Home Office* [2017] *(SC)*. In *Essop*, the 49 claimants, all black, Asian, and minority ethnic (BAME) members, had failed their employers' core skills assessment. The BAME pass rate was 40.3% that of white persons. The reason for the difference could not be found. (This may sound unlikely but it did happen.) Lady Hale giving the sole speech stated that the disadvantage of the test's results for all BAME people, including those who passed the assessment, when compared to white people affected the claimants. Therefore, they, the claimants, had suffered disadvantage as required by the definition of indirect discrimination. What of those BAME candidates who had failed the examination because, for example, they did not turn up on time? This issue was discussed at length by counsel but was in fact easily resolved by Lady Hale. It did not matter, she said, whether the tribunal dealt with this issue as a matter of causation (they did not fail 'because of' their race) or at the justification stage (the employers proved that there were proportionate means of achieving a legitimate aim). The issue of justification was remitted to the employment tribunal.

Practical example: An example of indirect discrimination from the Act's Guidance is when a woman is forced to leave her job because her employer operates a practice that staff must work a shift pattern that she is unable to comply with because she needs to look after her children at particular times of day, and no allowances are made because of those needs. This would put women (who are more likely to be responsible for childcare than men) at a disadvantage in comparison with men, and the employer will have indirectly discriminated against the woman unless the practice can be justified by the employer showing that he has a legitimate aim and the means of achieving that aim are proportionate.

This provision does not apply to the protected characteristic of pregnancy and maternity, which has its own definition of discrimination (s 18 and see chapter 6).

Where a prima facie case of indirect discrimination has been established, the employer will have to satisfy the tribunal that the discriminatory provision, criterion, or practice was justifiable. In order to justify a provision, criterion, or practice (PCP) that has a disproportionate impact, the employer must demonstrate that the PCP is designed to meet a legitimate aim and that the means chosen are appropriate and necessary ('proportionate') to achieving that objective. The burden of proof is explicitly placed on the employers.

Allen v GMB [2008] IRLR 690

This case concerned a **collective agreement** between a local authority and a trade union. This agreement discriminated against female employees by agreeing to a lower pay increase than they were entitled to if there had been a complete implementation of a proper equal pay policy. This was done to protect the pay of other members, recognising that the local authority had limited resources. The Court of Appeal held that the aim was legitimate, but the means were not proportionate to achieving this aim. These 'means' included the manipulation of female members of the union and the provision, criterion, or practice could not therefore be justified.

Examples of indirect sex and race discrimination

Much of the case law on indirect discrimination comes from racial and sexual discrimination. The following provides a sample. These cases are, however, generalisable to the other protected characteristics which have the same definition of indirect discrimination. The process for deciding whether **indirect sex discrimination**, for example, has taken place is, therefore, to examine the PCP and assess, first, whether it would be discriminatory to a larger proportion of women than of men and is discriminatory against this particular woman, and, secondly, whether the application of the 'provision, criterion, or practice' cannot be justified by being a proportionate means of achieving a legitimate aim and the sex of the person to whom it is applied is not relevant. Each situation needs to be looked at on its own merits. Just because a policy might be gender-neutral in some situations, it does not follow that it will be so in all situations.

Ministry of Defence v DeBique [2010] IRLR 471

Ms DeBique joined the British Army as a result of a recruitment drive in her home state of St Vincent and the Grenadines. Some years later, she gave birth to a daughter and she subsequently arranged with her unit to work from 8.30 am to 4.30 pm during the week and not work at weekends. This caused problems and she was disciplined for being late on one occasion. Eventually she was told that she would have to make arrangements so that she could be available for duty on a 24/7 basis. She also experienced considerable problems because her potential child-carer was not allowed to come to the UK from St Vincent. She brought proceedings for indirect sex and race discrimination and successfully claimed that the army had applied a PCP (the need to be available 24/7) that would have a greater detriment to female soldiers compared to male ones.

The same rules apply in cases of racial discrimination, of course. The justification for any measure needs to be regardless of the colour, race, nationality, or ethnic or national origins of the persons concerned.

Prohibited conduct

✶✶✶✶✶✶✶✶✶✶✶

> **JH Walker Ltd v Hussain [1996] IRLR 11**
>
> An employer had banned employees from taking non-statutory holidays during its busy period of May, June, and July. Its justification for this was a business-related one. About half the company's production workers were Muslims of Indian ethnic origin. The holiday period ban coincided with an important religious festival when many of the employees traditionally took time off. Seventeen employees took the day off despite the ban. When they returned to work they were given a final written warning. The 17 employees successfully complained of indirect racial discrimination. The employment tribunal and the Employment Appeal Tribunal (EAT) held that the rule was discriminatory and that the business justification put forward was not adequate.

 ✅ Looking for extra marks?

Indirect discrimination applies to all the protected characteristics except for pregnancy and maternity. It is important to note that the Act provides for indirect discrimination for the protected characteristic of disability. This did not apply to legislation prior to 2010 and the amendment is aimed at limiting the effect of a House of Lords judgment in *LB of Lewisham v Malcolm* [2008]. This was a housing case that had the effect of limiting the application of the protection against **disability-related discrimination** in all other fields, including employment.

Harassment

Section 26(1) Equality Act 2010 provides that:

A person (A) harasses another (B) if—

(a) A engages in unwanted conduct related to a relevant protected characteristic, and

(b) the conduct has the purpose or effect of—

    (i) violating B's dignity, or

    (ii) creating an intimidating, hostile, degrading, humiliating or offensive environment for B.

There are three types of harassment, the first of which applies to all protected characteristics except for pregnancy and maternity, and marriage and civil partnership:

- A engages in unwanted conduct related to a relevant protected characteristic which has the purpose or effect of violating B's dignity, or creating an intimidating, hostile, degrading, humiliating, or offensive environment for B;

- A engages in any form of unwanted verbal, non-verbal, or physical conduct of a sexual nature that has that effect (s 26(2));

- because of B's rejection of or submission to conduct (whether A's or not) related to sex or **gender reassignment**, A treats B less favourably than B would have been treated if B had not rejected or submitted to the conduct (s 26(3)).

Account must be taken, in deciding whether the conduct has that effect, of the perception of B, the other circumstances in the case, and whether it is reasonable for the conduct to have that effect (s 26(4)).

At the time of writing (January 2018) the Court of Appeal in *Peninsula Business Service Ltd v Baker* is to decide whether the definition of harassment is restricted to those with a disability as defined above or whether it extends to those *perceived* to have a disability but do not. *Direct* discrimination does apply to such persons but it had been assumed because of the different wording of the harassment provision that it did not.

Practical example:

- A white worker who sees a black colleague being subjected to racially abusive language could have a case of harassment if the language also causes an offensive environment for her.
- An employer who displayed any material of a sexual nature, such as a topless calendar, may be harassing her employees where this makes the workplace an offensive place to work for any employee, female or male.

Ministry of Defence v Fletcher [2010] IRLR 25

This case, at the EAT, was about what compensation could be awarded in a harassment and **victimisation** case. It is a classic example, however, of the kind of harassment that an individual can be subject to. Kerry Fletcher was a lesbian who was subject to prolonged sexual harassment of a very unpleasant kind by her superior in the army. She complained about the treatment and was away from work on health grounds. During this period she was subject to a recommendation that she be discharged from the army on the grounds that she was 'temperamentally unsuitable'. She was awarded aggravated damages for the treatment that she had suffered. Aggravated damages compensated the claimant for injury to feelings when her distress was exacerbated by the circumstances in which the injury was caused or by the conduct of the defendant after the tort was committed. They are not penal damages. See 'Remedies: general' for compensation.

Victimisation

Section 27(1) Equality Act 2010 provides that:

A person (A) victimises another person (B) if A subjects B to a detriment because—

(a) B does a protected act, or

(b) A believes that B has done, or may do, a protected act.

'Protected act' means bringing proceedings under this Act; giving evidence or information in connection with any proceedings under the Act; doing any other thing for the purpose of or in connection with this Act; making an allegation that A or another person has contravened the Act (s 27(2)). Giving false information or evidence is not protected if the information or evidence given, or the allegation is made, in bad faith (s 27(3)).

The important change here, compared to previous legislation, is that victimisation is no longer treated as a form of discrimination. There is therefore no need for a comparator.

Practical example: Examples given in the Guidance include:

- a woman makes a complaint of sex discrimination against her employer. As a result, she is denied promotion. The denial of promotion would amount to victimisation;
- an employer threatens to dismiss a staff member because he thinks she intends to support a colleague's sexual harassment claim. This threat would amount to victimisation.

Revision tip

Remember that a complaint of victimisation on sex, race, or one of the other protected characteristics is different from a complaint of discrimination. The latter is about showing less favourable treatment on the grounds of, say, sex or race, whilst a victimisation claim is about showing a detriment suffered as a result of doing a protected act, such as making a discrimination complaint to an employment tribunal.

Lawful discrimination

Despite what has already been stated, discrimination may be lawful in certain circumstances:

Occupational requirements

There is a general exception to what might otherwise be unlawful direct discrimination at work. This is where being of a particular age, disability, race, religion or belief, sex, or sexual orientation, or not being a transsexual or married or in a civil partnership, may be a requirement for a particular job (an **occupational requirement**). It needs to be shown that, having regard to the nature or context of the work:

- it is an occupational requirement;
- the application of the requirement is a proportionate means of achieving a legitimate aim; and
- the person to whom the requirement is applied does not meet it (or the employer has reasonable grounds for not being satisfied that the person meets it) (Sch 9 Pt 1).

This was a similar exception to the provisions contained in legislation before the Equality Act 2010, except that this statute harmonises the arrangement across the protected characteristics and drops the wording for a *genuine* occupational requirement that was in the previous legislation. There is no difference in content: under the current statute the occupational requirement must still be a genuine one, even though the word 'genuine' is no longer found in the definition. The Act also makes clear that the occupational requirement must pursue a legitimate aim and the means of achieving that aim are proportionate (appropriate and necessary). It is for those seeking to rely on this exception that the burden of proof rests.

Practical example: Examples listed in the Guidance include:

- the need for authenticity or realism in an acting role which may require someone of a particular age, race, or sex (the example cited is the need for a black man to play the part of Othello);
- considerations of decency and privacy might require a public changing room or lavatory to be attended by someone of the same sex as the users of the facility;
- an organisation for deaf people might employ a deaf person who uses British Sign Language to act as a counsellor to other deaf people.

Lasertop Ltd v Webster [1997] IRLR 498

A male applicant failed to obtain an interview for a sales/trainee manager position with a women-only health club. The job entailed showing potential members around the club, including the changing rooms, saunas, sun-bed room, and toilet. The EAT concluded that the club could rely upon a (genuine) occupational qualification defence in such circumstances.

Glasgow City Council v McNab [2007] IRLR 476

This case concerned a teacher who was turned down for an interview as acting principal teacher of pastoral care in a Roman Catholic school. It was established that had he been a Roman Catholic, he would have been given an interview. The education authority failed to establish that being a Roman Catholic was a (genuine) occupational requirement as the post had not previously been covered by an agreement to reserve certain posts. The education authority also claimed that it was an employer that had an ethos based on religion or belief in accord with **reg 7(3) Employment Equality (Religion or Belief) Regulations 2003 (SI 2003/1660)** as it was responsible in part for schools that did have that ethos. This claim was also unsuccessful because such an authority, according to the EAT, could be one that had responsibility for schools with a number of different and possibly contradictory ethoses at the same time.

Revision Tip

Make a point of looking at the Code of Practice on employment on the website of the Equality and Human Rights Commission (EHRC). It will give you lots of examples of what might be an occupational qualification. There are probably fewer situations in relation to race (eg it may be non-discriminatory to use separate lavatories for men and women, but not for blacks and whites). These might include authenticity in drama or other entertainment that requires a person of a particular racial group or where the job involves working in a place where food and drink is served to the public and membership of a racial group is required for authenticity such as a Chinese or Indian restaurant.

Armed forces

Schedule 9 Pt 1 para 4 allows the armed forces to discriminate against women and transsexual people if this a proportionate means of ensuring the combat effectiveness of the armed forces. It also exempts the armed forces from the work provisions of the Act in relation to age and disability.

Positive action

Section 158 Equality Act 2010 allows generally for the taking of positive action measures to alleviate disadvantage suffered by people who share one of the protected characteristics but does not oblige employers to use positive action. It may be used only if the participation of persons who share a particular protected characteristic is 'disproportionately low' (s 158(1) (c)). This provision is limited in that it will need to be interpreted in accordance with EU law and decisions of the Court of Justice of the European Union (CJEU).

Section 159 then deals with positive action in relation to recruitment and promotion. This section applies if persons of a protected characteristic suffer a disadvantage connected to the characteristic or if participation in an activity by persons who share the protected characteristic is disproportionately low. Part 5 (work) does not prevent the employer from taking action with the aim of enabling or encouraging persons who share the protected characteristic to overcome or minimise that disadvantage or participate in that activity (s 159(2)). The action is treating the person (A) with the characteristic more favourably than another person without the characteristic (B) (s 159(3)). This applies only if:

- A is as qualified as B to be recruited or promoted;
- the employer does not have a policy of treating persons who share the protected characteristic more favourably in connection with recruitment and promotion; and
- taking the action is a proportionate means of achieving the aim referred to in sub-s (2).

Enforcement

Here we consider how a person may enforce their rights under the Equality Act 2010.

Burden of proof

Proving that discrimination has taken place can be very difficult. In order to assist complainants, s 136 provides that it will be the respondent's task to show that discrimination did not take place, rather than the respondent having to prove that it did. In any claim where a person is alleging discrimination, harassment, or victimisation under the Equality Act, the burden of proof may shift to the respondent. Section 136(2) provides that if there are facts from which the tribunal or court could decide, in the absence of any other explanation, that a person (A) contravened the provision concerned, the forum must hold that the contravention occurred. Section 136(3) provides that this does not apply if A is able to show that A did not contravene the provision. Thus, once the complainant has established the facts from which the tribunal could conclude that a contravention had taken place, the onus switches to the respondent to show that there was no such breach.

For a while in 2017 the EAT changed the law stated above. It held that there was no burden of proof on the claimant at any stage; instead, the employment tribunal had to decide on the whole facts whether or not there was discrimination: *Elofi v Royal Mail Group Ltd* [2017]. This heresy was quickly expunged by the Court of Appeal in *Ayodele v Citylink Ltd* [2017] and the law remains that there are two stages: the first must be satisfied by the claimant and then the burden switches to the employer.

Practical example: A man of Chinese ethnic origin applies for a promotion at work but is not given an interview for the job. He finds that a number of white colleagues were given interviews despite having less experience and fewer qualifications. He brings a case for race discrimination before the employment tribunal and provides sufficient evidence to show that he had been treated less favourably because of his ethnic origin. It would then be up to his employers to prove that they had not discriminated against him in the promotion process.

 Looking for extra marks?

Consider the need for a shift in the burden of proof in discrimination cases. Often it is very difficult for a complainant to prove that the actions taken against him or her are the result of discrimination so, after he or she has established a prima facie case, it is then up to the employer to prove that the actions were taken for a non-discriminatory purpose. Without this shift in the burden of proof it might be almost impossible for many claimants to win their case.

Vicarious liability

Section 109 Equality Act 2010 makes employers vicariously liable for discrimination by their employees in the course of their employment. Employment law used to apply the tortious doctrine of **vicarious liability**. Employers are liable for the torts of their employees provided that the torts were committed in the course of their employees' employment. However, if the employees are 'on a frolic of their own', the employers are not liable. The effect of applying the tort law, however, was to make the worst acts of discrimination beyond the scope of discrimination law, the reverse of the policy behind the law. For example, if white workers branded a black worker with a heated screwdriver, as they did in the case next mentioned, the employers were not liable because the workers could not be said to be acting in the course of their employment. Indeed, since no worker is employed to bully or harass another, the effect of using tort law might be to exculpate all employers whenever discrimination had taken place in the workplace. The Court of Appeal in *Tower Boot Co Ltd v Jones* [1997] recognised the issue and created an employment law doctrine of **vicarious liability** in the field of discrimination law. As Waite LJ said, the phrase 'in the course of employment' should be read in such a manner as to advance anti-discrimination law without the constraints of tort law doctrine: the words should be given their everyday meaning. The law has been applied, for example, to work-related leaving celebrations but it does not extend to one police officer sexually assaulting another in the latter's own room (the latter is the ruling of the Court of Appeal in *Waters v Metropolitan Police Commissioner* [1997], a case which went to the House of Lords but not on this ground).

Vicarious liability

****

The doctrine is subject to the statutory defence available to employers who prove—note the burden of proof—that they took such steps as were reasonably practicable to prevent the discriminatory conduct (s 109(4)). It is not enough that the employers have a policy against discrimination: that policy must be applied. The actual discriminator is personally liable (s 110) and this liability applies even when the employers are able to use the s 109(4) defence.

Remedies: general

In a complaint to an employment tribunal the proceedings or complaint may not be brought after the end of three months starting with the date to which the complaint relates, unless the employment tribunal thinks that some other period is 'just and equitable' (s 123(1)). There used to be a mechanism for the complainant to obtain information by asking questions by using the prescribed form but the Coalition government abolished this long-standing (established 1975) statutory questionnaire. However, there is nothing to stop the claimant using questions. The questions and answers are admissible as evidence and the court or tribunal may draw inferences from a failure of the respondent to answer or from evasive or equivocal answers.

If the employment tribunal finds that there has been a contravention of a provision, then it may:

- make a declaration as to the rights of the complainant and the respondent in relation to the complainant; and/or
- order the respondent to pay compensation to the complainant. There is no statutory upper limit for compensation in discrimination claims or those concerned with a breach of the sex equality clause (see chapter 3): compensation is made on the tort basis and will normally include compensation for injured feelings and may include compensation for aggravated and/or exemplary damages; and/or
- make a recommendation.

The courts and tribunals have laid down guidelines (still called *Vento* bands after the Court of Appeal case from 2002 in which they were originally laid down) for compensation for injured feelings. From 11 September 2017 there are three bands:

1. between £25,200 and £42,000 for the most serious cases;
2. between £8,400 and £25,200 for the middle-ranking cases; and
3. between £800 and £8,400 for fairly minor one-off events.

The court or tribunal may exceed the top band in particularly bad cases.

These figures are contained in Presidential Guidance issued by the President of Employment Tribunals (England & Wales) and the President for Employment Tribunals (Scotland).

The extra ability to make an 'appropriate' recommendation was introduced by the Equality Act 2010 but was abolished by the Deregulation Act 2015. It was a recommendation that within a specified period the respondent took specified steps for the purpose of obviating or reducing the adverse effect of any matter to which the proceedings related, either on the complainant or more generally, such as the wider workforce. A tribunal could, for example, recommend the introduction of an equal opportunities policy, the retraining of staff, or the making public of the selection criteria for transfers and promotions. This remedy is now restricted to recommendations affecting the claimant herself. Therefore, it is of little use when, as so often will be the case, she has left the employment of the defendants.

(✳) Key cases

Cases	Facts	Principle
JH Walker Ltd v Hussain [1996] IRLR 11	An employer had banned employees from taking non-statutory holidays during its busy period of May, June, and July. Their justification for this was a business-related one. About half the company's production workers were Muslims of Indian ethnic origin. The holiday period ban coincided with an important religious festival when many of the employees traditionally took time off. Seventeen employees took the day off despite the ban. When they returned to work they were given a final written warning.	The 17 employees successfully complained of indirect racial discrimination. The employment tribunal and the EAT held that the rule was discriminatory and that the business justification put forward was not adequate.
Lasertop Ltd v Webster [1997] IRLR 498	This was a situation where a male applicant failed to obtain an interview for a sales/trainee manager position with a women-only health club. The job entailed showing potential members around the club, including the changing rooms, saunas, sun-bed room, and toilet.	The EAT concluded that the club could rely upon a (genuine) occupational qualification defence in such circumstances.
Ministry of Defence v DeBique [2010] IRLR 471	Ms DeBique joined the British Army as a result of a recruitment drive in her home state of St Vincent and the Grenadines. Some years later, she gave birth to a daughter and she subsequently arranged with her unit to work from 8.30 am to 4.30 pm during the week and not to work at weekends. This caused problems and she was disciplined for being late on one occasion. Eventually she was told that she would have to make arrangements so that she could be available for duty on a 24/7 basis. She also experienced considerable problems because her potential child-carer was not allowed to come to the UK from St Vincent.	She brought proceedings for indirect sex and race discrimination and successfully claimed that the army had applied a provision, criterion, or practice (the need to be available 24/7) that would have a greater detriment to female soldiers compared to male ones.

Exam questions

✶✶✶✶✶✶✶✶✶

Cases	Facts	Principle
Ministry of Defence v Fletcher [2010] IRLR 25	This case, at the EAT, was about what compensation could be awarded in a harassment and victimisation case. It is a classic example, however, of the kind of harassment that an individual can be subject to. Kerry Fletcher was a lesbian who was subject to prolonged sexual harassment of a very unpleasant kind by her superior in the army. She complained about the treatment and was away from work on health grounds. During this period she was subject to a recommendation that she be discharged from the army on the grounds that she was 'temperamentally unsuitable'.	She was awarded aggravated damages for the treatment that she had suffered.
R v Birmingham City Council, ex parte Equal Opportunities Commission [1989] IRLR 173	The local authority offered more places in selective secondary education to boys than girls.	This was held to be treating those girls less favourably on the grounds of their sex and the fact that the local authority had not intended to discriminate was not relevant. In the absence of an actual comparator, the court will need to construct a hypothetical one.

 (?) Exam questions

Problem question

The Bigfactory Company has been on a recruitment drive to fill some of its vacancies. Two of the candidates who have been turned down feel aggrieved and have come to you for advice on their legal rights.

Agnes was interviewed for a secretarial position. She is 52 years of age and has arthritis, which particularly affects one hand. She was turned down because, according to the company, she would not be able to keep up with all the typing that was required.

Delilah was interviewed for an admin position, but the room was very brightly lit. She has a problem with her eyesight, which makes it difficult for her to sit for long in bright lights. As a result, she felt that she did not perform well.

See the Outline answers section in the end matter for help with this question.

Essay question

Critically review recent reported cases in the UK courts and the CJEU, in relation to *two* of the following grounds:

- age;
- disability;
- race;
- religion or belief;
- sex;

(a)   sexual orientation.

Comment on and discuss how they add to our knowledge of the law on discrimination.

 Online Resources

To see an outline answer to this question log on to www.oup.com/lawrevision/

 Concentrate Q&As

For more questions and answers on employment law, see the *Concentrate Q&A: Employment Law* by Roseanne Russell.

Go to the end of this book to view **sample pages**.

#6

Parental rights

- A pregnant woman is entitled to paid time off for antenatal care. This right to time off has been extended to the father or mother's partner (male or female) but the leave is unpaid and only for two visits.

- Maternity leave is voluntary apart from the compulsory period which lasts for two weeks beginning with the day of the birth.

- Paternity leave, which is paid, is of two weeks' duration.

- An employee has the right to return to his or her job on terms and conditions no less favourable than those that would have applied if the employee had not taken maternity, adoption, parental, or paternity leave.

- Where an employee is pregnant, has given birth within the last six months, or is breastfeeding, the employer must assess the special risks faced by the woman in the workplace and take measures to avoid those risks.

- Shared parental leave came into force in 2015. Depending on the facts, this may supersede maternity leave (which remains the default position). Currently shared parental leave pay is a little over £140 a week.

- It is automatically unfair to dismiss an employee for reasons connected with pregnancy or the taking of maternity, adoption, parental, or paternity leave.

- Parents with child responsibilities are entitled to time off for parental leave for a maximum of 18 weeks for a child under 18.

- None of these tackles what is seen as the current major drawback of parental rights, the scarcity of affordable childcare. And none prevents the employer from providing better rights to employees than those detailed in this chapter. For example, employers may provide enhanced (ie contractual) maternity rights. At the time of writing (January 2018), men who are paid shared parental leave pay (around £140 a week) are seeking equality with women on enhanced maternity pay. At the time of writing, one case has been heard in the Employment Appeal Tribunal (EAT) and one case is scheduled to be heard there in early 2018. We await developments!

Maternity leave

EU law has played an important part in providing protection to women during their pregnancy and **maternity leave** period. The European Court of Justice (now the Court of Justice of the European Union, CJEU) regarded discrimination against pregnant women and those who have given birth or are breastfeeding as acts of sex discrimination that are in breach of Union laws on equal treatment and equal pay for women and men.

A refusal to employ results in **direct discrimination** when the reason for the refusal applies only to one sex, rather than to **workers**, without distinction, of both sexes. Only women can be refused employment because of pregnancy; so a decision not to employ someone because they are pregnant is directly discriminatory against the woman concerned. There is no need for a comparison against a man.

> ***Dekker v Stichting Vormingscentrum voor Jong Volwassenen Plus* Case C-177/88 [1991] IRLR 27**
>
> This case concerned a woman who had applied for a post of training instructor in a youth centre. She was pregnant when she applied and she informed the selection committee of this. The committee recommended her as the most suitable candidate, but the board of the youth centre declined to employ her. The reason given was that their insurer would not compensate them for payments that would be due to Ms Dekker during her maternity leave. The European Court of Justice (ECJ) concluded that the refusal to employ had been a reason connected with the pregnancy and that this was contrary to the Equal Treatment Directive. As only women can be refused employment because of pregnancy, the fact that there were no male candidates for the post was not relevant.

In *Pedersen* [1999], the ECJ held that a policy that stated that workers who are unfit for work because of illness would receive full pay, but that pregnant women off sick from work for an illness related to the pregnancy would not, was in breach of Art 141 EC Treaty (now Art 157 Treaty on the Functioning of the European Union (TFEU)) and the Equal Pay Directive. This developed further the view of the Court as expressed in *Brown v Rentokil* [1998], in which the ECJ held that the dismissal of a woman at any time during her pregnancy for absences caused by illness resulting from that pregnancy is direct discrimination on the grounds of sex contrary to the EU Equal Treatment Directive.

Maternity leave

✱✱✱✱✱✱✱✱✱✱✱

> ### Patefield v Belfast City Council [2000] IRLR 664
>
> This case concerned the replacement of a pregnant temporary worker with a permanent **employee** whilst the temporary worker was on maternity leave. This was held to be discrimination on the grounds of sex. The employer could have replaced her with a permanent replacement at any time before she went on leave. However, during maternity she was in a specially protected position.

Pregnancy and maternity is now one of the **protected characteristics** in the Equality Act 2010 (see chapter 4) and there is implied into every woman's terms of employment a maternity equality clause (s 73 Equality Act 2010). The Act protects women from **direct discrimination** (s 13(1)) in relation to pregnancy and maternity.

Unlike the other grounds of discrimination, there is no need for a comparator when claiming pregnancy discrimination. Thus, s 18(2) Equality Act 2010 defines direct discrimination in this context as:

A person (A) discriminates against a woman if, in the protected period in relation to a pregnancy of hers, A treats her unfavourably—

(a) because of her pregnancy, or

(b) because of illness suffered by her as a result of it.

Previous legislation (Sex Discrimination Act 1975) had contained the need for a comparator but this was changed in 2008 in response to criticism in *Equal Opportunities Commission v Secretary of State for Trade and Industry* [2007] The Employment Appeal Tribunal (EAT) stated that this provision impermissibly introduced a requirement for a non-pregnant comparator and that the statute needed to be reworded to remove this requirement. This subsequently occurred. The current statute is the Equality Act 2010.

The protected period provided for in s 18(2) begins with the pregnancy and finishes at the end of any maternity leave to which the individual is entitled. If there is no entitlement to maternity leave, then it finishes two weeks after the end of the pregnancy (s 18(5)).

Revision tip

Be aware of the role of EU law and have the ability to cite a number of relevant cases from the Court of Justice in any exam question on the subject.

The compulsory maternity leave period

An employer may not permit an employee to work during her **compulsory maternity leave** period. Compulsory maternity leave is a period of two weeks commencing on the day on which childbirth occurs. The period is to help the new mother recover. An employer who allows an employee to work during this period is subject to a fine (s 72(5) Employment Rights Act 1996 (ERA)). This period is not superseded by shared parental leave, if that is taken: see 'Shared parental leave' below.

The maternity leave period

Part VIII ERA consolidates law dating back to 1993 brought about by the **Pregnant Workers Directive 1985** and contains provisions for maternity rights that are further detailed in the **Maternity and Parental Leave Regulations 1999 (SI 1999/3312)** (the **MPL Regulations**) as amended. Women are now entitled to 52 weeks' maternity leave, which includes compulsory maternity leave (see 'The compulsory maternity leave period', above). Maternity leave of this length may prove difficult for small employers to accommodate. There is no qualifying period or minimum number of hours worked. The size of the employer is also irrelevant. The provisions detailed here are minima—contractual rights may be greater (but not less) than statutory ones.

The dates of statutory maternity leave are calculated as being periods before or after the 'expected week of childbirth'. **Regulation 2(1) MPL Regulations** defines the **expected week of childbirth** as the week, beginning with midnight between Saturday and Sunday, in which it is expected that childbirth will occur.

Under previous law there was a difference between ordinary and additional maternity leave. Now there is no difference and over time the terms 'ordinary' and 'additional' will fade away.

Regulation 4 MPL Regulations states that an employee is entitled to maternity leave if she satisfies certain conditions. These are that:

* no later than the 15th week before her expected week of childbirth she notifies (the notification need not be in writing) her employer of her pregnancy and the date on which she intends to start her maternity leave. If it is not reasonably practicable to inform the employer by this time, then the requirement is that notice must be provided as soon as is reasonably practicable;

* the employee must give these notices in writing if the employer so requests;

* the employer is able to request, for inspection, a certificate from a registered medical practitioner or a registered midwife stating the expected week of childbirth.

She need not inform her employer of her date of returning to work.

She cannot start leave before the 11th week before the expected week of childbirth. The leave will start if she has not given notice within four weeks of the expected week of childbirth and she is absent from work wholly or partly because of pregnancy.

Regulation 6 provides that if the maternity leave has not commenced:

* by the first day after the beginning of the fourth week before the expected week of childbirth on which the employee is absent from work wholly or partly because of pregnancy, or

* by the day on which childbirth occurs,

then the maternity leave will be deemed to have commenced on that day, provided that the employee notifies her employer, in writing if requested, as soon as reasonably practicable.

Maternity leave

The woman's contractual position is protected whilst on maternity leave. **Section 71(4) ERA** states that such an employee is:

- entitled to the benefit of the terms and conditions of employment that would have applied had she not been absent. This does not include terms and conditions relating to remuneration;
- bound by obligations arising under those terms and conditions;
- entitled to return from leave to the job in which she was employed before her absence, with her seniority, pension, and similar rights as if she had not been absent. She is also to return on terms and conditions not less favourable than those that would have applied if she had not been absent. This last right means that she is entitled to any pay increase she would have received had she not been on maternity leave.

Since 2008, these rights and obligations also apply to additional maternity leave. That is why nowadays there is no difference between the two.

✔ Looking for extra marks?

You might consider why only women are entitled to maternity leave. There are times when a man might wish to have the caring responsibility for a child. In *Ulrich Hofmann v Barmer Ersatzkasse* **Case C-184/83 [1984]** the ECJ was asked to consider a claim that the giving of leave to women alone did not accord with the terms of the **Equal Treatment Directive**. The claimant was a man who looked after a child whilst the mother returned to work as a teacher shortly after the birth. He was denied a claim for maternity benefit by the German social security service. The man's argument, in the legal proceedings that followed, was that the introduction of maternity leave was concerned not with the protection of the mother's health, but exclusively with the care that she gave to the child. If this argument were correct, it was said, then the leave should be available to either parent and become a form of parental leave. The ECJ rejected this approach and stated that the **Equal Treatment Directive** was not intended to 'settle questions concerned with the organisation of the family'.

Work during the maternity leave period

Regulation 12A provides that an employee may carry out up to ten days' work for her employer during her statutory maternity period (excluding the compulsory maternity period) without bringing her maternity leave period to an end. These days have come to be known as 'KIT' days, keeping in touch days. This is part of a policy designed to encourage employers and those on maternity leave to keep in touch with each other and, of course, to ease the moment of return to work. Any work carried out on any day constitutes a day's work and the work can include training or any activity designed for the purpose of keeping in touch with the workplace. This does not mean that the employer has the right to require this work or that the employee has a right to work. It clearly needs to be an agreed option, but one that many employers and those on maternity leave may be interested in using. The period spent working does not have the effect of extending the total duration of the maternity leave period.

The date of the return to work

To avoid confusion, an employer who has been notified under reg 4 about when an employee's maternity leave will commence, or has commenced, has an obligation to notify the employee of the date on which her additional maternity leave will end. This must be done within 28 days of the date on which the employer received notification of the commencement (reg 7(7)).

If the employee wishes to return early and not take her full entitlement of maternity leave, then she must give *eight* weeks' notice, in writing, of her intended return date. If she does not give the required notice, the employer may delay her return for up to eight weeks (reg 11). Where the employer has engaged a replacement for the absent woman, provided that person has been informed in writing that his or her employment will be terminated on the woman's return to work, the dismissal of the replacement will be regarded as having been for 'some other substantial reason' within the law of unfair dismissal (see chapter 9). This does not mean that such a dismissal will always be fair, because a tribunal will have to be satisfied that it was reasonable to dismiss in the circumstances. For instance, it might be unfair to dismiss if the employer had a vacancy that the replacement could have filled.

Webb v EMO Air Cargo (UK) Ltd [1994] ICR 770

This case concerned an applicant who was employed initially to cover for another employee who was to go on maternity leave. It was envisaged that the new employee would continue to be employed after the pregnant employee returned from her maternity leave. Shortly after starting work, the new employee discovered that she was also pregnant and the employer dismissed her. She complained of sex discrimination contrary to **s 1(1) Sex Discrimination Act 1975** (now **s 13(1) Equality Act 2010**). When the case reached the House of Lords, it was referred to the ECJ for a decision on whether the dismissal constituted sex discrimination. The Court held that it was contrary to the **Equal Treatment Directive** and that one could not compare a pregnant woman who was not capable of performing the task for which she was employed with a male who was absent through sickness and incapable therefore of carrying out his tasks. Pregnancy is not an illness; and unlike an illness it may be planned. (Note: it is estimated by Maternity Action that 60,000 women are dismissed each year for pregnancy-related reasons: R Dunstan, *Overdue: A Plan of Action to Address Pregnancy Discrimination Now* (2013), pp 18–20. Furthermore, some employers, particularly owners of small businesses, may refuse to employ women of child-bearing age because they do not expect them to work indefinitely for the firm.)

If, during maternity leave, it becomes clear that the employer cannot continue to employ the employee under her existing **contract of employment** by reason of redundancy, the employee is entitled to be offered any other suitable employment that may be available. The work to be done must be both suitable and appropriate in the circumstances, and its provisions as to the capacity and place of work and other terms and conditions should not be substantially less favourable than if she had continued to be employed under the previous contract (reg 10).

Shared parental leave

While this right is called 'shared parental leave' (SPL), it is not the 'parental leave' right noted under 'Parental leave', below. In reality it is shared maternity leave (see under 'Maternity leave'), and is dependent on the woman who has given birth surrendering part of her maternity leave. If she does not consent, she retains her right to maternity leave. Except for the two-week period of compulsory maternity leave (see 'The compulsory maternity leave period', above), the mother can share her maternity leave with her spouse or partner (whether in a civil partnership or not), hereinafter 'partner', male or female, provided both partners qualify for this right. If the partner does not qualify and the partners do not agree to split the maternity leave, the default position is that the mother has her maternity leave. Leaving aside the compulsory period, the mother has up to 50 weeks' maternity leave, and that is the period which is the subject of shared parental leave. Of the 52 weeks of maternity leave, 39 are subject to statutory maternity pay (90% of pay for the first six weeks, and a (low) set amount after then, currently a little over £140 a week, unless her employers pay enhanced maternity pay); the remaining weeks are unpaid. It is this calculation which applies to SPL pay. For example, if the woman gives up her maternity leave after four weeks, the partner gets the remaining two weeks of maternity pay at 90% of full pay and that full pay is the partner's full pay, not that of the woman who has given birth. One can see headaches for human resources departments when both people who are entitled to SPL are employed by different employers! The aim of SPL is to increase the amount of childcare provided by men and should incidentally over time reduce the gender pay gap. Whether SPL does have these effects is in part dependent on the uptake by men of the opportunity to share childcare. That is affected by the low sum paid as shared maternity leave pay (some £140 a week) and seemingly by the fact that unlike in Nordic countries there is no 'Daddies' leave' to be taken by fathers: if they do not use it, they lose it. The government expected that 2–8% of those men who could opt to take SPL would do so, but in fact take-up is around 1%. The Department for Business, Energy and Industrial Strategy promises to review this right in 2018, by which time the right should have bedded in.

The law, which came into force in April 2015, is the result of the **Children and Families Act 2014** (which also abolished additional paternity leave) and a host of associated regulations. It is complex and the following is the basic law. For a partner to obtain SPL, he (assuming that the partner is male) must have been continuously employed for 26 weeks before the 15th week before the expected date of childbirth and must be still employed in the week preceding the first week of SPL: see **reg 33(1) Shared Parental Leave Regulations 2014**. If the mother has the right to maternity leave, maternity allowance, or statutory maternity pay, her leave can be shared, but she too must comply with the same requirements as her partner (note that, however, maternity leave is a 'day one' right, ie it is not subject to the 26-week qualification period required for SPL). Once the mother relinquishes her right to maternity leave, the SPL provisions take effect. Both partners must send a notice of entitlement to take leave to their employers at least eight weeks before the SPL is intended to begin.

SPL can be shared between the partners and can be taken in one continuous period or, provided the employers consent—there is no limit on the type of reasons they must provide if they refuse consent—discontinuously in periods of not less than a week; it can be taken simultaneously by both partners or separately. It can be varied (as many times as the partners desire: reg 6) by at least eight weeks' notice and can be terminated by giving notice. Statutory shared parental pay (ShPP) is payable for the period which remains after the mother's 39-week entitlement to statutory maternity pay (SMP) expires. ShPP is paid at the same rate as SMP, currently (January 2018) £140.98 after the first six weeks of SMP have elapsed. Generally, the rate increases annually in April. This is not a large sum (though employers may give more contractually or ex gratia) and is one reason for the poor take-up of this right by fathers. The government expected that take-up would be between 2% and 8% (Department for Business, Innovation and Skills, 'Modern Workplaces: Shared Parental Leave and Pay Administration Consultation–Impact Assessment' (2013), p 4) but it has according to research by the Women's Business Council and My Family Care been 1% of all men (not, it should be noted, all eligible men) in SPL's first year of operation. It should be noted that SPL pay is *less* than the National Minimum Wage! Without a top-up from employers, it is hard to see that partners will be able to take leave concurrently, even though doing so may be in the best interests of the child. Moreover, many men fear that taking SPL will detrimentally affect their careers; and surveys demonstrate that about four-fifths of men are not aware of SPL. Another drawback on uptake by men is that some three-fifths of women think that women should be primary carers. Figures in the last two sentences are taken from a survey by Totaljobs in 2016. It is worth stating also that SPL does not apply to single parents. The government does not keep statistics on take-up of SPL, but has promised both to review the right to SPL in 2018 and to extend the right to grandparents. Consultation on grandparents' leave was scheduled for 2016 but nothing has happened by the time of writing (January 2018). Nevertheless, the expected year of implementation remains 2018.

At the time of writing, two cases have been heard but judgment is awaited in both as to whether paying enhanced maternity pay to the mother but not paying enhanced statutory SPL to the partner is discriminatory. Employment tribunal cases are divided whether or not paying ShPP at the same rate as maternity pay is sexually discriminatory against men. Judgments are anxiously awaited. One reason for the low take-up of SPL by partners is the low pay they receive (unless the employers enhance the payments, as some do): see the previous paragraph for this criticism. The government's position is that any difference in pay is not sexually discriminatory but they may be proved wrong.

Similar to maternity leave's up to ten 'KIT' days (see 'Work during the maternity leave period', above), employees on SPL may take up to 20 Shared Parental Leave in Touch ('SPLiT') days in order to keep in touch with their employers and vice versa.

Time off for antenatal care

Irrespective of the length of service or the number of hours she works, a pregnant woman who, on the advice of a registered medical practitioner, midwife, or health visitor, has made an appointment to receive antenatal care, has the right not to be *unreasonably* refused time off during working hours to enable her to keep the appointment. Antenatal care is not

Shared parental leave

✷✷✷✷✷✷✷✷✷

defined but it may include, for example, parenting and breathing classes. Apart from the first appointment, the woman may be required to produce a certificate and some documentary evidence of the appointment for the employer's inspection. A woman who is permitted such time off is entitled to be paid for her absence at the appropriate hourly rate (s 56(1) ERA).

If reasonable time off is refused or the employer has failed to pay the whole or part of any amount to which she feels she is entitled, a woman can complain to an employment tribunal. Normally, her claim must be presented within three months of the date of the appointment concerned (s 57 ERA). Where a tribunal finds that the complaint is well founded, it must make a declaration to that effect, and if time off has been unreasonably refused, the employer will be ordered to pay a sum equal to that which she would have been entitled to had the time off not been refused. If the complaint is that the employer failed to pay the amount to which she was entitled, the employer must pay the amount that the tribunal finds due to her.

Fathers, husbands, civil partners, and partners are entitled to time off for up to two ante-natal appointments with the pregnant woman with effect from 1 October 2014 as part of the Children and Families Act 2014. This leave is unpaid.

Protection from unfair dismissal

It is automatically unfair to dismiss an employee, irrespective of the length of service, if:

- the reason or principal reason for dismissal is that she is pregnant or which is in any way connected with her pregnancy;
- she is dismissed during her maternity leave period and the reason or principal reason for dismissal is that she has given birth or is connected with her having given birth;
- she is dismissed after the end of her maternity leave period and the reason or principal reason for dismissal is that she took, or availed herself of the benefits of, maternity leave, adoptive leave, or **paternity leave**; or
- she is dismissed during the maternity or adoption leave period and the principal reason for dismissal is that she is redundant and the employer has not offered her any suitable alternative vacancy (see s 99 Employment Rights Act 1996).

Note: these protections do not prevent a woman from claiming sex discrimination (as well) and it may be in her interests to do so because there is no maximum limit to the amount of compensation awarded in a discrimination claim.

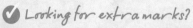 Looking for extra marks?

Pregnant women and those who have recently given birth are given special protection from discrimination. It is important that you consider why this is so. It may be that such women are particularly vulnerable to discrimination and it is important for society to encourage people to have children for the sake of society's future. It is important in exams to know what protection is given and how the courts and tribunals interpret this.

Paternity leave and paternity pay

Paternity leave was introduced by the Employment Act 2002. It is paid (currently about £140 a week) and is of two weeks' duration. However, employers may increase the amount of Statutory Paternity Pay. The qualifications for paternity pay are these:

- the applicant must be an employee who has been continuously employed by the employer for at least 26 weeks at the 15th week before the expected date of childbirth (EWC);

- that employee must be the child's father or the mother's husband, civil partner, or partner (note that this means that paternity leave may be taken by a person who is not the father or by a person who is of the same gender or both); and

- that person must have or expect to have parental responsibility for the child's upbringing.

The employee who is qualified must then inform his or her employer (this notice may be oral unless the employer asks for it to be made in writing) of his or her intention to take paternity leave by the 15th week before the EWC. He or she must inform the employer of:

- the expected week of childbirth (unless this is not reasonably practicable);

- the amount of leave he or she wishes to take; and

- the date on which he or she wishes to start the leave.

When the mother has given birth, or as soon as reasonably practicable thereafter, the person seeking paternity leave must inform the employer of the date of childbirth. An employer may ask the employee to certify that he or she meets the requirements to take paternity leave and that the leave is to look after the mother and/or the baby.

Parental leave

This right must not be confused with shared parental leave (see 'Shared parental leave', above). An employee who has been continuously employed for a period of not less than one year and who has, or expects to have, responsibility for a child is entitled to be absent from work on (unpaid) parental leave for the purposes of caring for that child (reg 13(1) MPL Regulations). He or she must give 21 days' notice and that notice must be in writing if the employer so requires. This right dates back to 1999 in English law and derives from the Parental Leave Directive (96/34/EC). The statutory right is outlined in this section. There may be contractual rights; if so, they will apply if they provide the employee with more rights than does the statutory right to parental leave. Sharing of parental leave (see 'Shared parental leave') and the extension of parental leave to parents whose children are under 18 came into force in 2015.

The entitlement to parental leave originally was in respect of each child under five years old, but from April 2015 the Children and Families Act 2014 extended this right to children

Parental leave

****

under 18 (its having been previously extended to those under 13). The extension from 13 to 18 weeks' leave was a result of the Parental Leave Directive: see the Parental Leave (EU Directive) Regulations 2013. Not more than four weeks per child can be taken in any one year and leave must be taken in blocks of not less than a week.

Regulation 14 MPL Regulations as amended in 2013 provides that an employee is entitled to 18 weeks' leave in respect of any individual child. The leave entitlement is for 'any individual child', so that an employee/parent of multiple-birth children will be entitled to 18 weeks' leave in respect of each child.

There are two important limitations contained in the default procedures. First, an employee may not take more than four weeks' leave in respect of a particular child in any one year and, secondly, that leave must be taken in periods of at least one week, unless the child in respect of whom leave is taken is entitled to a disability living allowance. See *Rodway v South Central Trains Ltd* [2005].

An employee who is absent on parental leave is entitled to the benefit of the terms and conditions of employment that would have applied if he or she had not been absent. This includes any matters connected with the employee's employment, whether or not they arise under the contract of employment, except for matters relating to remuneration. See *Abdoulaye v Régie Nationale des Usines Renault SA* [1998].

Notice provisions

Before employees can exercise their rights to parental leave, they must, unless otherwise stipulated by collective or workforce agreements:

* comply with any request from the employer to produce for inspection evidence of the employee's responsibility or expected responsibility for the child as well as evidence of the child's age;
* give the employer notice of the period of leave that is proposed. This notice must specify the dates on which the leave is to begin and end and be given at least 21 days before the date upon which the leave is to start. Where the leave to be taken is in respect of a child to be adopted and the leave is to begin on the date of the placement, then the notice must specify the week in which the placement is expected to occur and the period of leave. The notice is to be given to the employer at least 21 days before the beginning of that week or, if that is not reasonably practicable, as soon as it is so; and
* ensure that the employer has not postponed the leave.

Postponing parental leave

Schedule 2 MPL Regulations provides that an employer may postpone a period of parental leave, subject to any collective or workforce agreements, where:

* the employee has applied and given the necessary notice; and

- the operation of the employer's business would be unduly disrupted if the employee took leave during the period identified in the notice; and

- the employer permits the employee to take a period of leave of the same length that had been requested within six months of the date on which it was due to begin; and

- the employer gives notice in writing of the postponement stating the reasons for it and specifying the dates on which the employee may take parental leave. This notice must be given to the employee no later than seven days after the employee's notice was given to the employer.

An employee may complain to an employment tribunal if the employer has unreasonably postponed a period of parental leave or attempted to prevent the employee from taking it. The tribunal may award such compensation that it considers 'just and equitable'.

 Looking for extra marks?

You should remember that the MPL Regulations have a default agreement that lays down fairly inflexible rules for those wishing to take parental leave. There is an issue about why these rules should be so inflexible. It is because the rules on this and other 'family friendly' regulations seek to balance the personal needs of the employee and the commercial needs of the employer. Do they succeed in this?

Time off for dependants

Section 57A ERA, dating from 1999 and implementing the Parental Leave Directive, states that an employee is entitled to be permitted by the employer to take a reasonable amount of time off during the employee's working hours, in order to take action which is necessary. There is no entitlement to pay.

These actions include:

- providing assistance on an occasion when a dependant falls ill, gives birth, or is injured or assaulted;

- making arrangements for the provision of care for a dependant who is ill or injured;

- in consequence of the death of a dependant;

- because of the unexpected disruption or termination of arrangements for the care of a dependant; or

- dealing with an incident which involves a child of the employee and which occurs unexpectedly in a period during which an educational establishment which the child attends is responsible for him or her.

There is an obligation on the employee to inform the employer of the reason for absence and of its duration as soon as reasonably practicable. The time off is limited to incidents

Time off for dependants

involving a dependant who is defined as: a spouse or civil partner; a child; a parent; a person who lives in the same household as the employee but who is not an employee, tenant, lodger, or boarder; any person who reasonably relies on the employee for assistance if he or she is ill or assaulted; any person who reasonably relies on the employee to make arrangements for the provision of care in the event of illness or injury. The references to illness or injury include mental illness or injury.

Section 57B ERA asserts that an employee may apply to an employment tribunal to complain about a failure to be allowed time off. The limitation period is the usual three-month period. A tribunal must make a declaration and may award compensation that the tribunal considers 'just and equitable in the circumstances'.

Qua v John Ford Morrison Solicitors [2003] IRLR 184

The EAT considered a situation where a single mother with a child who had medical problems was dismissed after taking time off on 17 different days. The EAT held that the right to time off did not enable employees to take time off for themselves to look after a sick child, except for enabling the parent to deal with an immediate crisis. Such longer-term care would be covered by the employee's parental leave entitlement. There is, said the EAT, no duty on the employee to inform the employer daily of her current situation.

The right to time off is the right to a 'reasonable' amount of time in order to take action that is 'necessary'. The decision as to whether it was necessary depends upon a number of factors, including, for example:

- the nature of the incident that has occurred;
- the closeness of the relationship between the employee and the dependant; and
- the extent to which anyone else was available to help out.

All of this depends upon the individual circumstances. An employee is not, however, entitled to unlimited amounts of time off and the employer may take into account the number and length of previous absences, as well as the dates on which they occurred when deciding whether the time off sought for a subsequent occasion is reasonable. The time off is to deal with unforeseen circumstances. Thus, if a child were known to suffer regular relapses needing attention, then time off for dealing with these illnesses would not come within the terms of s 57A ERA.

 Looking for extra marks?

You should remember that, in determining the reasonableness of the amount of time taken off, the disruption to an employer's business by the employee's absence cannot be taken into account. This, unfortunately perhaps for an employer, is not a relevant factor. When commenting on cases like this in your exam, be prepared to be critical and give your own reasoned views.

Right to request flexible working

Section 47 Employment Act 2002 inserted ss 80F–80I into the ERA 1996 which is concerned with **flexible working**. There are also two sets of Regulations spelling out the details of employee rights. These are the Flexible Working (Eligibility, Complaints and Remedies) Regulations 2002 (SI 2002/3236) and the Flexible Working (Procedural Requirements) Regulations 2002 (SI 2002/3207).

A qualifying employee may make an application to the employer to vary his or her contractual terms in relation to hours of work, times when required to work, or place of work (eg changing a shift pattern, working from home, amending start/finish times). The purpose of the application was originally to enable the employee to care for a child; this right was later extended to caring for the elderly or infirm (**Work and Families Act 2006**); it is now a right for all employees and is no longer restricted to caring for the young or the elderly (**s 131 Children and Families Act 2014**).

A qualifying employee is an individual who has been continuously employed for a period of not less than 26 weeks. Previous restrictions were abolished when the right was extended to all employees with at least 26 weeks' continuous employment.

Commotion Ltd v Rutty [2006] IRLR 171

This case concerned an individual who was employed as a warehouse assistant. After she became legally responsible for the care of her grandchild, she made an application to work three days a week instead of five. Her request was turned down on the ground that it would have a detrimental impact on performance in the warehouse. The EAT, however, held that the employer had failed to establish that they had refused the request on one of the grounds permitted by **s 80G(1)(b) ERA**. Tribunals were entitled to investigate to see whether the decision to reject the application was based on facts and whether the employer could have coped with the change without disruption. In this case the EAT found that the evidence did not support the employer's assertion and the employer had not carried out any investigations to see whether they could cope with what the claimant wanted.

The application for the request must be in writing. The employer must deal with the request 'reasonably' (the previous procedures were abolished when the right to request was extended to all employees with 26 weeks' continuous employment in 2014).

The times and dates of the meetings must be convenient for both parties and the employee has the right to be accompanied by a single companion. The employee may complain to an employment tribunal and obtain an award of up to two weeks' pay if the employer fails to allow and make provision for the employee to be accompanied.

The employer may refuse the application only for one of these reasons:

- burden of additional costs;
- detrimental effect on the ability to meet customer demand;

- inability to reorganise work among existing staff;
- inability to recruit additional staff;
- detrimental impact on quality;
- detrimental impact on performance;
- insufficiency of work during the periods the employee proposes to work;
- planned structural changes; or
- such other grounds as the Secretary of State may specify.

 Looking for extra marks?

Point out that the variation agreed to here is permanent in nature, although the employee may only be looking for a temporary change, that the right is purely a right to *request* flexible working, and that the employer has a panoply of reasons for refusing the request, reasons which are very extensive and can be used to refuse just about all possible requests.

An employee may complain to an employment tribunal that his or her employer has failed to comply with the duty under s 80G or that a decision to reject the application was based upon incorrect facts. The maximum amount of compensation that can be awarded is eight weeks' pay.

Protection from detriment

An employee is entitled not to be subjected to any detriment by any act, or failure to act, on the part of the employer for one of the following reasons (see Pt V ERA):

- that she is pregnant or has given birth to a child;
- that he or she took paternity leave, maternity or adoption leave, or availed herself of the benefits of her terms and conditions of employment during such leave;
- that the employee took parental leave, or time off under s 57A ERA;
- that the employee has been suspended from work on maternity grounds;
- that the employee has refused to undertake 'Keep In Touch' ('KIT') days;
- that the employee declined to sign a workforce agreement for the purposes of the MPL Regulations; or
- that the employee was a representative of the workforce, a candidate for election as a representative, or performed any activities or functions related to being a representative or a candidate.

Breaches of these provisions are heard in the employment tribunal and claims must be brought within three months of the employer's act or omission unless it was not reasonably practicable to do so. If a breach is proved, the tribunal must grant a declaration to that effect and may award such compensation as is just and equitable in the circumstances.

In *Abbey National plc v Formoso* [1999], an employee was held to have suffered detriment when her employer proceeded to hold a disciplinary hearing without the attendance of the employee, who was absent with a pregnancy-related illness. The employee had given notice of the date when she wished her maternity leave to begin whilst she was absent through pregnancy-related sickness. The employer wished to resolve the matter prior to the maternity leave and proceeded with the hearing even though the employee's doctor considered that she was unfit to attend the meeting and would be so until the end of her pregnancy. The EAT confirmed the employment tribunal's view that pregnancy was the effective cause of the disciplinary hearing and that her treatment had amounted to sex discrimination. Similarly, in *GUS Home Shopping Ltd v Green and McLaughlin* [2001] two employees who were absent from work because of their pregnancy were held to have been discriminated against when they did not receive a discretionary loyalty bonus payable to all employees who remained in their posts until a business transferred to a new location. The different treatment meant that they had been unlawfully discriminated against because of sex.

 Key cases

Cases	Facts	Principle
Brown v Rentokil Case C-394/96 [1998] IRLR 445	A pregnant employee, absent from work for a variety of pregnancy-related illnesses, fell foul of her employer's rule that any employee who exceeded 26 weeks' continuous sick leave was dismissed.	The dismissal of a woman at any time during her pregnancy for absences caused by illness resulting from pregnancy is direct discrimination because of sex.
Commotion Ltd v Rutty [2006] IRLR 171	A warehouse assistant became legally responsible for the care of her grandchild and she made an application to work three days a week instead of five. Her request was turned down on the ground that it would have a detrimental impact on her performance in the warehouse.	The employer had failed to establish that they had refused the request on one of the grounds permitted by s 80G(1)(b) ERA. Tribunals were entitled to investigate to see whether the decision to reject the application was based on facts and whether the employer could have coped with the change without disruption.
Dekker v Stichting Vormingscentrum voor Jong Volwassenen Plus Case C-177/88 [1991] IRLR 27	A female applicant was refused an appointment to a post because of her pregnancy, despite the fact that she was the best candidate.	Less favourable treatment because of a woman's pregnancy amounts to unlawful discrimination because of sex.

Key cases
****

Cases	Facts	Principle
Qua v John Ford Morrison Solicitors [2003] IRLR 184	A single mother with a child who had medical problems was dismissed after taking time off on 17 days.	The right to time off is the right to a 'reasonable' amount of time in order to take action that is 'necessary'. The right to time off did not enable employees to take time off for themselves to look after a sick child, only to enable the parent to deal with an immediate crisis.
Rodway v South Central Trains Ltd [2005] IRLR 583	A male employee wished to take one day's parental leave to look after his son. His application was refused, but he took it anyway. As a result he was disciplined.	Parental leave can be taken only in blocks of one week.
Ulrich Hofmann v Barmer Ersatzkasse Case C-184/83 [1984] ECR 3047	The claimant was a man who looked after a child whilst the mother returned to work as a teacher shortly after the birth. He was denied a claim for maternity benefit by the German social security service. The argument, in the legal proceedings that followed, was that the introduction of maternity leave was concerned, not with the protection of the mother's health, but exclusively with the care that she gave to the child. If this argument was correct, it was said, then the leave should be available to either parent and become a form of parental leave.	The ECJ rejected this approach and stated that the **Equal Treatment Directive** was not intended to 'settle questions concerned with the organisation of the family'.
Webb v EMO Air Cargo (UK) Ltd [1994] ICR 770	An applicant was employed initially to cover for another employee who was to go on maternity leave. The new employee discovered that she was also pregnant and the employer dismissed her. She complained of sex discrimination contrary to **s 1(1) Sex Discrimination Act 1975**, now part of the **Equality Act 2010**.	One could not compare a pregnant woman who was not capable of performing the task for which she was employed with a male who was absent through sickness and incapable therefore of carrying out his tasks.

(?) Exam questions

Problem question

Manuella has come to you to ask your advice:

Manuella is a single mother with a three-year-old son; she is in receipt of disability living allowance for his benefit. She has just applied for a full-time job as a lecturer at the University of Middle England. She was shortlisted and, prior to the interview, discovered that she was pregnant. At her interview she told the selection panel of her news and was asked a number of questions about how she could balance a teaching job and having two young children, one of whom was disabled. Her response was that this was not a problem as she was part of an extended family, all of whom would help. She was subsequently turned down for the post and suspects it was because of her personal situation.

See the Outline answers section in the end matter for help with this question.

Essay question

In terms of government regulation on family and parental rights, all the benefits go to women and men receive little help in becoming family friendly.

Discuss.

 Online Resources

To see an outline answer to this question log on to http://www.oup.com/lawrevision/

 Concentrate Q&As

For more questions and answers on employment law, see the *Concentrate Q&A: Employment Law* by Roseanne Russell.

Go to the end of this book to view sample pages.

#7

Working time

- The **Working Time Regulations 1998 (WTR)** implement the **Working Time Directive 1993** and parts of the **Young Workers Directive 1994**.

- The **WTR** impose a maximum 48-hour week during a 17-week reference period and provide rules on night work, rest periods, and annual leave. Note that therefore the maximum is not a 48-hour working week but an average of not more than 48 hours in each 17-week period.

- *UK* **workers** can agree (they may have little choice) to opt out of the 48-hour week and there are EU-wide provisions for determining the rules by collective and workforce agreements.

- Entitlement to paid annual leave arises if an individual has been a worker during all or part of a leave year but does not depend on the person actually performing work.

- Employers must permit employees who are officials of independent trade unions recognised by them to take reasonable time off with pay. Members of a recognised independent trade union are entitled to reasonable time off during working hours for trade union activities and to represent the union.

- A person who has been continuously employed for two years or more and is under notice of dismissal for redundancy is entitled to reasonable time off, during working hours, to look for work.

The Working Time Regulations 1998

The WTR implement the Working Time Directive 1993 and parts of the Young Workers Directive 1994. You should note that certain activities and certain sectors are excluded from the scope of the WTR.

Regulation 36 deals with agency workers, who are not otherwise workers, by deeming the agency or principal to be the employer, depending upon who is responsible for paying the worker.

According to reg 2 WTR, for these purposes **working time** is:

- any period during which the worker is working, at the employer's disposal and carrying out the worker's activity or duties;
- any period during which the worker is receiving relevant training;
- any additional period which is to be treated as working time for the purpose of the Regulations under a relevant agreement.

A **relevant agreement** is defined as a **workforce agreement** (see 'Derogations'), a provision of a **collective agreement** which forms part of a contract between the worker and the employer, or any other agreement in writing that is legally enforceable as between employer and worker. In *Federacion de Servicios Privados del Sindicato Comisiones Obreras v Tyco Integrated Security SL* [2015] the Court of Justice held that time spent travelling from home to the first job of the day and from the last job of the day to home was working time within the Working Time Directive 1993. It must be noted that while these journeys count as working time, they may not necessarily form work which requires payment of the National Minimum Wage or the National Living Wage. That is a matter of national, not EU, law. (There is, it should be added, no EU law on minimum **wages**.)

Maximum weekly hours

One obvious issue here is the position of people who are 'on call' but not necessarily working all the time that they are required to be available.

> **Landeshauptstadt Kiel v Jaeger [2003] IRLR 804**
>
> The European Court of Justice (ECJ) considered the case of a hospital doctor who spent three-quarters of his working hours on call. He was provided with a room where he could sleep when his services were not required. The Court decided that all his hours on call should be counted as working time. The crucial point was that he was required to be present at the place decided by the employer.

Regulation 4 provides that working time, including overtime, must not exceed 48 hours per week (seven days) averaged over a standard reference period of 17 weeks. Employers are required to take all reasonable steps 'in keeping with the need to protect the health and safety of workers' to ensure that this limit is adhered to.

Looking for extra marks?

Point out to the examiner that it is unclear what steps employers must take to fulfil this obligation.

Regulations 4 and 5 allow a worker to opt out of the maximum working week provided that the agreement:

- is in writing;
- relates either to a specified period or applies indefinitely; and
- may be terminable by the worker on seven days' notice, unless a different notice period is specified (subject to a maximum of three months).

Pfeiffer v Deutsches Rotes Kreuz [2005] IRLR 137

The ECJ ruled that this agreement must come from the worker individually 'expressly and freely'. It is insufficient that the **contract of employment** refers to a collective agreement that allows an extension.

Regulation 4(6) provides a formula for calculating the average hours over the reference period.

Night work

Regulation 6 states that a night-worker's normal hours of work must not exceed, in a reference period, an average of eight in any 24-hour period.

Regulation 2 defines **'night-time'** as a period which is not less than seven hours in length and includes the hours of 12 midnight to 5 am.

A **'night-worker'** is a worker who, as a normal course, works at least three hours of working time during 'night-time' or is a worker who is likely, during 'night-time', to work a certain proportion of his or her annual working time as defined by a collective or workforce agreement (see 'Derogations', below).

In *R v Attorney General for Northern Ireland, ex parte Burns* [1999], the court held that the requirement to work at least three hours during night-time as a 'normal course' meant no more than that this should be a regular feature of the individual's work.

Regulation 6(7) obliges the employer to ensure that no night-worker whose work involves special hazards or heavy physical or mental strain works for more than eight hours in any 24-hour period during which night work is performed.

Regulation 7 provides that night-workers are also entitled to a free health assessment prior to taking up night work and at regular intervals thereafter. The reg 7 also stipulates that where a medical practitioner informs the employer that a worker is suffering from health problems connected with working night work, the employer should, if possible, transfer the worker to more suitable work or work that is not night work.

Rest breaks and periods

Regulation 8 imposes a duty on employers to provide adequate rest breaks where the pattern of work is likely to cause health problems, such as where there is monotonous work or a predetermined work rate. In addition, reg 10 entitles adult workers to a rest period of at least 11 consecutive hours every 24 hours. Regulation 11 also entitles adult workers to an uninterrupted weekly rest period of at least 24 hours in each seven-day period. The employer may change this to two uninterrupted rest periods of 24 hours in each 14 days or one uninterrupted rest period of 48 hours every 14 days.

Regulation 12 provides that where an adult worker's daily working time is more than six hours, the worker is entitled to a rest break. The details of this rest break can be in accordance with a workforce or collective agreement, provided that it is for at least 20 minutes and the worker is entitled to spend it away from the work station.

Hughes v Corps of Commissionaires [2011] IRLR 100

This concerned a security guard working on his own for 12-hour shifts. When he had a rest break he had to leave a number at reception where he could be contacted, so sometimes he did not receive his promised 20-minute period of uninterrupted rest. Here the Employment Appeal Tribunal (EAT) said that the employer's obligations were met because he was allowed to take another rest period at a time of his choosing if interrupted.

 ✔ Looking for extra marks?

Point out that, under the Regulations, workers are only entitled to one rest break irrespective of how long they work over six hours.

Holiday entitlement

Regulation 13 provides that in any leave year a worker is entitled to 5.6 weeks' paid leave. (EU law is less: 20 days). Unless there is a relevant agreement for another date, the worker's leave year begins on the date employment commenced and every anniversary thereafter. If the worker commences employment on a date that is different from the date agreed for the commencement of a leave year, he or she is entitled to a proportion for that first year. According to reg 15A, this is calculated on the basis of one-twelfth of the annual entitlement for each month of service. In *Federatie Nederlandse Vakbeweging v Staat der Nederlanden* [2006], the ECJ confirmed that the **Working Time Directive** entitles the worker to the actual rest. Thus, leave cannot be replaced by a payment in lieu, unless the employment is terminated.

Regulation 15 requires the worker to give the employer notice of when he or she wishes to take the leave. This must be equivalent to twice the amount of leave the worker is proposing to take. In effect, the employer can stipulate when holidays are to be taken by giving a counter-notice in accordance with the same Regulation.

✓ Looking for extra marks?

You might draw attention to the fact that holidays not taken by the end of the leave year will be lost, unless the **employee** was on sick leave, on which see later in this section.

Regulation 16 provides that workers are entitled to be paid a sum equivalent to a week's pay for each week of leave. The entitlement to paid annual leave arises if an individual has been a worker during all or part of a leave year but does not depend on the person actually performing work. In *Pereda v Madrid Movilidad SA* [2009], the ECJ stated that the Directive precluded national provisions and collective agreements that prevented workers who are sick during annual leave from taking that leave after recovery, if necessary outside the leave year or carry-over period. There has been much controversy over the years as to which payments are to be included when calculating holiday pay. Commission pay is covered: *Lock v British Gas* [2017] (CA). The Supreme Court refused leave to appeal. In the latest case, *Dudley MBC v Willetts* [2017], the EAT held that even voluntary overtime pay was to be included. The tribunal concluded that such overtime was to be included if there was a sufficient pattern of work extending over a period of time so that it was so regular that it was 'normal'. On the facts, voluntary overtime once every four or five weeks was enough to count as 'normal' for this purpose. Both guaranteed and non-guaranteed compulsory overtime are included, as is payment by commission. This ruling applies to the EU minimum of four weeks' holiday but not to the extra 1.6 weeks under UK law, and is subject to the limit that a three-month gap between payments stops the claim for payments before that break. This UK rule, however, is under fire as a result of the important case discussed next.

In the latest case, *King v Sash Windows Workshop Ltd* [2017], the Court of Justice of the European Union (CJEU) held that the applicant was entitled to holiday pay dating back 13 years to the time when he joined the company. During that time he was paid on a commission-only basis as a salesperson, and while he had taken some unpaid holiday leave, he had not taken 24 weeks of holiday over that 13-year period. It also held that there was no limit on the amount of holiday pay which the claimant could recover. This will certainly have major effects in what is now called the gig economy (see chapter 1). There are two difficulties in applying this law to the UK. First, the UK government has imposed a two-year limit on back claims (**Deduction from Wages (Limitation) Regulations 2014**); secondly, the courts in the UK have held (*Bear Scotland Ltd v Fulton* (2017), a much debated authority, in which it was held that overtime compulsory on the workers but not on the employers was to be included in calculating holiday pay) that where there have been several non-payments of holiday pay, employees cannot claim back beyond a three-month gap in the non-payment of holiday pay. The 2014 Regulations would seem to breach EU law on effectiveness and equivalence; *Bear Scotland* is simply inconsistent with *Sash Window*. *King* was referred to the CJEU by the (English and Welsh) Court of Appeal, to which falls the duty of ruling in 2018 whether or not the **Working Time Regulations** can be read in such a manner as to be compatible with EU law or whether words must be added to the Regulations to make them compatible. It is strongly arguable that both the two-year and three-month rules are contrary to EU law as being contrary to the principle of effectiveness. The position may be resolved by *Shannon v Rampersad* [2015], which is due to be heard by the Court of Appeal in March 2018.

A further complication is that EU law provides for a minimum of four weeks' holiday, whereas UK law gives 5.6 weeks. Potentially (and logically) the Court of Appeal could rule that for the first four weeks EU law applies with the effects stated, but for the remaining 1.6 weeks UK law applies and during this time the two-year and three-month limits continue to apply!

NHS Leeds v Larner [2012] IRLR 825

Here the Court of Appeal ruled that, irrespective of what is stated in a worker's contract, there is no legal requirement that a person on sick leave who wishes to carry forward their entitlement to paid annual leave must serve a notice to the employer during that sick leave.

 Looking for extra marks?

Discuss why an employee who is absent through long-term sickness might choose to have part of it turned into the annual leave entitlement—perhaps because the sick pay entitlement has run out or because the level of sick pay is lower.

Enforcement

Regulation 9 obliges employers to keep records in respect of the maximum weekly working time, night work, and health assessment checks for night-workers. These records must be adequate to show that the relevant time limits are being complied with in the case of each worker employed. Such records must be retained for a period of two years.

The provisions of the Regulations that impose limits are generally to be enforced by the Health and Safety Executive. An employer who fails to comply with any of the relevant requirements will be guilty of an offence and subject to a fine. Inspectors have wide powers to enter premises and investigate and **reg 29** makes it an offence to obstruct them in

Enforcement

✴✴✴✴✴✴✴✴✴✴

their investigations. Regulation 30 entitles a worker to present a complaint (normally) within three months to an employment tribunal (ET) relating to an employer's refusal to permit the exercise of rights provided by the Regulations. Where the tribunal finds such a complaint well founded, it will make a declaration and award compensation or order the employer to pay the worker the amount the tribunal finds is due to the individual in relation to annual leave. The amount of compensation will be such as the ET finds just and equitable and will take into account the employer's default in refusing to permit the worker to exercise the right and any loss sustained by the worker in relation to the matters complained of. In addition, s 12A Employment Tribunals Act 1996 (ETA 1996) allows ETs to impose a financial penalty on employers where there has been a breach of employment rights and the ET thinks that 'the breach has one or more aggravating features'. Normally the penalty must not be less than £100 or more than £5,000 but regard must be had to the employer's ability to pay and there is a 50% discount if payment is made within 21 days.

Section 45A Employment Rights Act 1996 (ERA) gives workers the right not to be subjected to any detriment by any act, or failure to act, on the part of the employer on the grounds that the worker:

- refused, or proposed to refuse, to comply with any requirement in contravention of the WTR;
- refused, or proposed to refuse, to give up a right conferred by the WTR, a workforce agreement (see 'Derogations'), or vary any other agreement with the employer that is provided for by the WTR;
- was a workforce representative or a candidate in an election for such representatives;
- alleged that the employer had infringed the worker's rights under the WTR;
- was bringing proceedings to enforce rights under the WTR.

If the detriment amounts to a dismissal for one of these reasons, then an employee may bring a complaint of unfair dismissal (see chapter 9).

Revision tip

Ensure that you are clear which part of the Regulations imposes limits that are enforceable by the Health and Safety Executive (HSE) and which provide rights that can be exercised at an ET.

Derogations

Apart from the individual's ability to opt out of the maximum working week (see 'Maximum weekly hours'), the WTR allow derogations, in some instances, by agreement between the employer and representatives of the employees. The types of agreement are:

1. collective agreements;

Collective agreements are defined in **s 178 Trade Union and Labour Relations (Consolidation) Act 1992 (TULRCA)** as agreements between employers and **independent trade unions** recognised for collective bargaining purposes.

2. workforce agreements.

Regulation 2 WTR defines a *workforce agreement* as an agreement between an employer and workers employed by him or their representatives in respect of which the conditions set out in **Sch 1** are satisfied.

According to **Sch 1 WTR**, workforce agreements are valid if the following conditions are met:

- the agreement is in writing;
- it has effect for a specified period not exceeding five years;
- it applies to all the relevant members of the workforce or to a particular group within the relevant workforce;
- the agreement is signed by representatives of the workforce or group; and
- before the agreement is signed, the employer provides all the workers concerned with a copy plus any necessary guidance.

If the employer has fewer than 20 workers, a workforce agreement can be reached either by representatives of that workforce or by obtaining the support of the majority of the workforce. Representatives of the workforce are those who are elected.

Both collective and workforce agreements can be used to: (1) extend the reference period for averaging the 48-hour week from 17 weeks up to a maximum of 52 weeks; (2) modify or exclude the application of the Regulations concerning the length of night work, health assessments, daily and weekly rest periods, and daily rest breaks. You should be aware that in these circumstances **reg 24** requires compensatory rest breaks and rest periods.

Time off for trade union duties and activities

No minimum period of service is required before trade unionists can claim time off. According to **s 168 TULRCA**, employers must permit employees who are *officials* of independent trade unions **recognised** by them to take reasonable time off with pay during working hours to enable them to:

- carry out their duties that are concerned with negotiations with the employer that are related to or connected with any of the matters specified in **s 178(2) TULRCA** and in relation to which the employer recognises the union;
- carry out any other duties that are concerned with the performance of any functions that are related to or connected with any matters listed in **s 178(2) TULRCA** and that the employer has agreed may be performed by the union;

Time off for trade union duties and activities

✳✳✳✳✳✳✳✳✳✳

- receive information from the employer and be consulted under s 188 TULRCA 1992 or the **Transfer Regulations 2006** (as amended);
- undergo training in aspects of industrial relations that is both relevant to the carrying out of any of the duties previously mentioned and approved by their trade union or the TUC.

Section 119 TULRCA 1992 states that *an official* is someone who is an officer of the union or branch of it, or someone who is elected or appointed in accordance with the rules to be a representative of its members or some of them. (See chapter 12 on the meaning of 'independence and recognition'.)

The amount of time off allowed, together with the purpose for which, the occasions on which, and any conditions subject to which, time off may be taken, depends on what is reasonable in all the circumstances having regard to any relevant provisions in the **ACAS Code of Practice on Time Off for Trade Union Duties and Activities 2010**. It should be noted that this Code uses the term 'representative' rather than **union official** and does not lay down any fixed amount of time that employers should permit officials to take off.

Officials who are permitted time off should receive normal remuneration as if they had worked. According to s 169(3) TULRCA 1992, where remuneration varies with the work done, average hourly earnings should be paid. No claim can be made for overtime unless it was contractually required and there is no entitlement to be paid for time spent on trade union duties outside working hours.

Paragraph 13 of the Code of Practice recommends that representatives of recognised trade unions should be allowed reasonable time off for duties concerned with negotiations related to or connected with:

- terms and conditions of employment, or the conditions in which employees are required to work;
- engagement or non-engagement, or termination or suspension of employment or the duties of employment, of one or more workers;
- allocation of work, or the duties of employment as between workers or groups of workers;
- matters of discipline;
- trade union membership or non-membership;
- facilities for representatives of trade unions;
- machinery for negotiation and consultation and other procedures.

Paragraph 46 of the Code suggests that management should make available the facilities necessary for representatives to perform their duties efficiently and to communicate effectively with members. According to **para 14**, preparatory and explanatory work by representatives may well be in fulfilment of duties concerned with any of the matters listed in s 178(2) TULRCA.

Time off for trade union duties and activities

✻✻✻✻✻✻✻✻✻✻

What has to be demonstrated is that there is a sufficient connection between the collective bargaining and the duty for which leave is sought. ETs will have to decide whether the preparatory work is directly relevant to one of the matters specified in s 178(2), and if the employer does not negotiate on the issue, the employer's agreement to the performance of the duty will have to be demonstrated.

As regards industrial relations training, again no fixed amount of time is specified but para 26 recommends that representatives should be permitted paid time off for initial basic training as soon as possible after their election or appointment. Time off should be allowed for further training where the representative has special responsibilities or where it is necessary to meet changed industrial relations circumstances. An employer must also permit a member of a recognised independent trade union to take reasonable time off during working hours for trade union activities and to represent the union. However, in the absence of any contractual term to the contrary, an employer does not have to pay for such time off. Trade union activities are not statutorily defined, although para 37 of the Code gives the following examples of the activities of a member:

- attending workplace meetings to discuss and vote on the outcome of negotiations with the employer;
- meeting full-time officers to discuss issues relevant to the workplace;
- voting in union elections.

Paragraph 38 of the Code gives examples of activities where the member is acting as a representative of a union:

- branch, area, or regional meetings of the union where the business of the union is under discussion;
- meetings of official policy-making bodies such as the executive committee or annual conference;
- meetings with full-time officers to discuss issues relevant to the workplace.

Wignall v British Gas [1984] IRLR 493

The EAT rejected the argument that the statute requires each proposed activity on the part of the employee in the service of his or her union to be weighed and tested on its own merits without regard to any other activities or duties on the union's behalf for which the employee might be taking time off.

Thus, every application for time off under s 170 should be looked at on its merits in the particular circumstances.

Time off to look for work
****

Section 171 TULRCA provides that employees wishing to complain of failure to permit time off or to pay the amount required by s 169 TULRCA must apply to an ET within three months of the date when the failure occurred. If the tribunal finds that the claim is well founded, it must make a declaration to that effect. Section 172 TULRCA allows a tribunal to make an award of compensation of such amount as it considers 'just and equitable in all the circumstances having regard to the employer's default ... and to any loss sustained by the employee which is attributable to the matters complained of'. According to *Skiggs v South West Trains Ltd [2005]*, this can include reparation to the official for the wrong done to him or her. In addition, s 12A ETA 1996 allows ETs to impose a financial penalty on employers where there has been a breach of employment rights and the ET thinks that 'the breach has one or more aggravating features'. Normally the penalty must not be less than £100 or more than £5,000 but regard must be had to the employer's ability to pay and there is a 50% discount if payment is made within 21 days.

Time off to look for work

Section 52 ERA allows a person who has been continuously employed for two years or more and is under notice of dismissal by reason of redundancy, reasonable time off during working hours to look for new employment or make arrangements for training for future employment. Such an employee must be paid at the appropriate hourly rate for the period of absence. According to s 53 ERA, this is one week's pay divided by the number of normal weekly hours or, where the number of working hours varies, the average of such hours.

 Looking for extra marks?

Point out to the examiner that it is illogical to give employees an entitlement to be paid 'an amount equal to the remuneration to which he would have been entitled if he had been allowed the time off' and then limit the amount that a tribunal can award to two-fifths of a week's pay.

Under s 54 ERA, a complaint that an employer has unreasonably refused time off, or has failed to pay the whole or any part of any amount to which the employee is entitled, must be presented to an ET, if reasonably practicable, within three months of the day on which it is alleged that the time off should have been allowed or paid for. If the complaint is well founded, the tribunal must make a declaration to that effect and order the employer to pay the amount that it finds is due to the employee. In addition, s 12A ETA 1996 allows ETs to impose a financial penalty on employers where there has been a breach of employment rights and the ET thinks that 'the breach has one or more aggravating features'. Normally the penalty must not be less than £100 or more than £5,000 but regard must be had to the employer's ability to pay and there is a 50% discount if payment is made within 21 days.

(✱) Key cases

Cases	Facts	Principle
Landeshauptstadt Kiel v Jaeger [2003] IRLR 804	There was a disagreement about whether hours spent 'on call' should be treated as working time.	All hours spent 'on call' should be counted as working time if the worker was required to be present at the place decided by the employer.
Pfeiffer v Deutsches Rotes Kreuz [2005] IRLR 137	There was a dispute about the circumstances in which an individual could legally opt out of the limit on working hours.	An agreement to opt out of the limit on working hours must come from the worker individually, 'expressly and freely'.
R v Attorney General for Northern Ireland [1999] IRLR 315	There was a dispute about the circumstances in which an individual should be treated as performing night work.	Performing night work as a 'normal course' means no more than that this should be a regular feature of the individual's work.

(?) Exam questions

Problem question

Karen is an assistant solicitor who has been employed since May 2007 by Moon and Co, a medium-sized commercial legal practice. Frank is a senior partner in the firm and Karen's immediate superior.

Karen's contract of employment states that she 'must work such hours as may be required of her and that her duties may vary from time to time as circumstances dictate'. When she was interviewed ,Frank remarked to Karen that Moon and Co look after their staff and that no one would be expected to do anything that would seriously interfere with their private lives. Karen accepted the post and initially worked Monday to Friday, putting in 48 to 50 hours per week. Three months ago, Frank informed Karen that the company was now 'twice as busy as before' and that 'a special effort would be necessary from her for at least six months'. He explained that she was therefore expected to 'forget about recreational matters and concentrate exclusively on her work'. Frank also indicated that if everything went according to plan a partnership for Karen 'might be on the cards'.

For the past three months Karen has managed to put in 80 to 82 hours per week by working all day on Saturdays and Sundays. Her social life has suffered as a result and she feels that if the

Exam questions

situation continues she may suffer a breakdown. She is certain that if she mentions her concerns to Frank he will consider her not up to the job.

Advise Karen.

See the Outline answers section in the end matter for help with this question.

Essay question

The **Working Time Regulations 1998** are more effective in guaranteeing that workers get paid holidays than controlling excessive hours of work.

Discuss.

 Online Resources

To see an outline answer to this question log on to www.oup.com/lawrevision/

 Concentrate Q&As

For more questions and answers on employment law, see the *Concentrate Q&A: Employment Law* by Roseanne Russell.

Go to the end of this book to view **sample pages**.

#8

Variation, breach, and termination of employment

- Theoretically, neither employer nor employee can unilaterally alter the terms and conditions of employment. A unilateral variation that is not accepted will constitute a breach and, if serious, could amount to a repudiation of the contract. A repudiation does not automatically terminate a contract of employment.

- In order to justify summary dismissal, the employee must be in breach of an important express or implied term of the contract.

- Wrongful dismissal is a dismissal without notice or with inadequate notice in circumstances where proper notice should have been given or where a dismissal has been in breach of agreed procedures.

- An employee is to be treated as dismissed for statutory purposes if his or her contract of employment is terminated by the employer with or without notice, a limited-term contract expires without renewal, or the employee terminates it as a result of the employer's conduct. The second type of dismissal does not apply to the common law action of wrongful dismissal.

- Employees are entitled to treat themselves as constructively dismissed if the employer is guilty of conduct that is a significant breach going to the root of the contract of employment, or which shows that the employer no longer intends to be bound by one or more of its essential terms. The latter is known as anticipatory breach. 'Constructive dismissal' is the same as 'repudiation' as used at common law.

- In order to complain of unfair dismissal, two years' continuous service is required unless the dismissal is for an inadmissible reason.

Variation

The terms and conditions of employment can be varied only by mutual agreement. However, consent to change may be obtained through individual or collective negotiation or may be implied from the conduct of the parties.

> ### *Harlow v Artemis Ltd* [2008] IRLR 629
>
> The High Court recognised that where an employer purports to change the terms of a **contract of employment** unilaterally but they do not immediately impact on the **employee**, then the fact that the employee continues to work does not mean that he or she can be taken to have accepted the variation.

A unilateral variation that is not accepted will constitute a breach and could amount to a repudiation of the contract. In *Société General v Geys* [2013], the Supreme Court ruled that an employer's repudiation does not automatically terminate a contract of employment. There is a requirement for acceptance by the employee. Where there is repudiatory conduct by the employer, the employee has the choice of affirming the contract (by continuing in employment) or accepting the repudiation as bringing the contract to an end. If the latter option is exercised and the employee resigns within a short period, there will be a **constructive dismissal** for statutory purposes (see 'Constructive dismissal', below).

Breach of contract

The options open to an innocent party will depend on whether the breach is of a minor or serious nature. An innocent party may choose to continue with the contract as if nothing had happened (waive the breach), may sue for damages, or, in the case of a serious or fundamental breach, may regard the contract as at an end.

 Looking for extra marks?

Demonstrate your awareness that for an injunction, whether interim or permanent, to be granted a court needs to be satisfied not only that it would be just to make such an order but also that it would be workable. Employment tribunals do not have jurisdiction to grant injunctions.

Employees who are not ready and willing to render the services required by their contracts (eg as a result of taking some form of industrial action) are not entitled to be paid. However, if employers are prepared to accept part-performance, they will be required to pay for such work as is agreed. The principal remedies for breach of contract are an injunction (an order restraining a particular type of action), a declaration of the rights of the parties, and in particular damages.

Section 236 Trade Union and Labour Relations (Consolidation) Act 1992 ensures that an employee cannot be compelled to return to work. Those who seek damages can be compensated for the direct and likely consequences of the breach. In *Gogay v Hertfordshire County Council* [2000], the Court of Appeal confirmed that damages could be awarded for a psychological disorder occasioned by the employer's breach of contract.

The jurisdiction of employment tribunals was extended in 1994 (Employment Tribunals (Extension of Jurisdiction) Order 1994 (SI 1994/1623)) to breach of contract claims that have arisen or are outstanding at the end of employment, provided that the claim is for under £25,000, but does not extend to breaches during employment. In respect of such claims, the tribunals have concurrent jurisdiction with the civil courts. Over £25,000 and the claim must be heard in the civil courts. The £25,000 limit has, despite inflation, not changed since 1994. Under s 3(2) Employment Tribunals Act 1996 (ETA 1996) the claim must be for:

- damages for breach of a contract of employment or any other contract connected with the employment;
- a sum due under such a contract;
- the recovery of a sum in pursuance of any enactment relating to the terms or performance of such a contract.

Certain claims are excluded, for example personal injury, breach of confidence, and **restrictive covenant** cases. An employee's claim must normally be brought within three months of the effective date of termination (see 'The effective and relevant date of termination', below).

Frustration

A contract is said to have been frustrated where events make it physically impossible or unlawful for the contract to be performed, or where there has been a change such as to radically alter the purpose of the contract. As long as the frustrating event is not self-induced, there is an automatic termination of the contract, ie there is no dismissal. This being so, it is not uncommon for an employer to resist a claim for unfair dismissal by alleging that the contract had been frustrated, for example on grounds of sickness. However, if the tribunal wishes to hear the merits of the unfair dismissal claim, it must hold that the contract of employment has not been terminated.

Revision tip

Ensure that you also know the legal principles that have been developed in relation to absences caused by illness (see chapter 9, 'Potentially fair reasons for dismissal'). Ill-health can fall under both frustration and within the law of unfair dismissal incapability, which includes ill-health; however, if the contract is frustrated by illness, there can be no unfair dismissal claim because there is no dismissal, and therefore absences by illness cannot be discussed in the context of an unfair dismissal claim.

Summary dismissal

A **summary dismissal** occurs where the employer terminates the contract of employment without notice. In *McCormack v Hamilton Academical FC* [2012], it was noted by the (Scottish) Court of Session that this is an exceptional remedy requiring substantial justification. Thus it will not be readily sustained where the misconduct only peripherally affects the performance of core duties.

An **instant dismissal** has no legal definition but refers to a dismissal without investigation or enquiry. Whereas an instant dismissal is likely to be procedurally defective in unfair dismissal terms (see chapter 9, 'The Code of Practice and procedural fairness'), a summary dismissal may be lawful both at common law and under statute.

In order to justify summary dismissal, the employee must be in breach of an important express or implied term of the contract, eg be guilty of gross misconduct. Although certain terms are always regarded as important—for example, the duty not to steal or damage the employer's property, the duty to obey lawful orders, and not to engage in industrial action, and the implied term of mutual trust and confidence—the significance of other terms will depend on the nature of the employer's business and the employee's position in it. Gross negligence may constitute gross misconduct: *Adesoken v Sainsbury's Supermarkets Ltd* [2017] (CA). However, Elias LJ cautioned against assuming that gross negligence always amounts to gross misconduct: 'It ought not readily to be found that a failure to act where there was no intentional decision to act contrary to or undermine the employer's policies constitutes such a grave act of misconduct as to justify summary dismissal.'

✅ Looking for extra marks?

You should point out that one consequence of the contractual approach to dismissal is that everything hinges upon the facts of the particular case and previous decisions often have little bearing.

If employees do not invoke the right to end the contract within a reasonable period, they will be taken to have waived their rights and can only seek damages. What is a reasonable period will depend on the facts of the particular case.

Termination with notice

Usually, either party is entitled to terminate a contract of employment by giving notice and once notice has been given it cannot be unilaterally withdrawn. The courts have consistently ruled that for notice to be effective it must be possible to ascertain the date of termination. The length of the notice will be determined by the express or implied terms of the contract and, if no term can be identified, both parties are required to give a reasonable period of notice. What is reasonable will depend on the circumstances of the relationship, for example the employee's position and length of service. Apart from the situation where individuals are disentitled to notice by reason of their conduct, s 86(1) Employment Rights Act 1996 (ERA) provides that certain minimum periods of notice must be given. After a month's service an employee is entitled to a week's notice and this applies until the employment has lasted for two years. At this point, two weeks' notice is owed and from then on the employee must receive an extra week's notice for each year of service up to a maximum of 12 weeks. Therefore, someone who has worked for seven years is entitled to seven weeks; someone who has worked for 20 years receives the maximum, 12 weeks. According to s 86(2) ERA, an employee with a month's service or more need give only one week's notice to terminate. However, there is nothing to prevent the parties from agreeing that both should receive more than the statutory minimum. If there is no **express term**, a minimum period of notice is contractually implied. How long an implied term of notice is depends on all the facts. For example, one newspaper editor may be entitled to six months' notice, whereas another one may be entitled to more than that or less. The statutory length is a minimum and can be extended by contract, whether express or implied. It is part of the 'floor of rights', minimum rights which can be built on by contract but which cannot be reduced by contract.

Although the ERA does not prevent an employee from accepting a payment in lieu of notice ('PILON' in the jargon), in theory an employer must have contractual authority for insisting on such a payment. Without such authority, a payment in lieu of notice will be construed as damages for the failure to provide proper notice. Thus, a payment in lieu can properly terminate a contract of employment if the contract provides for such a payment or the parties agree that the employee will accept a payment in lieu. In *Locke v Candy Ltd* [2011], the Court of Appeal suggested that a PILON clause should be interpreted without the preconception that it necessarily seeks to provide the employee with what he or she would have earned during the notice period. The date of termination at common law is the day notice expires or the day **wages** in lieu are accepted. Except where the notice to be given by the employer is at least one week more than the statutory minimum, s 88(1) provides that an employee is entitled to be paid during the period of notice even if:

- no work is provided by the employer;
- the employee is incapable of work because of sickness or injury;
- the employee is absent from work wholly or partly because of pregnancy or childbirth;
- the employee is absent in accordance with the terms of his or her employment relating to holidays.

It should be noted that any payments by the employer by way of sick pay, maternity pay, paternity pay, adoption pay, holiday pay, or otherwise go towards meeting this liability.

Remedies for wrongful dismissal

A wrongful dismissal is a dismissal without notice or with inadequate notice in circumstances where proper notice should have been given. The expression also covers dismissals that are in breach of agreed procedures. Thus, where there is a contractual disciplinary procedure, an employee may be able to obtain an injunction or declaration from the courts so as to prevent a dismissal or declare a dismissal void if the procedure has not been followed. Judicial review is available where an issue of public law is involved but it will only be exercised in exceptional circumstances. Thus, in the vast majority of cases the employee's remedy will lie in damages for breach of contract.

A person who suffers a wrongful dismissal is entitled to be compensated for such loss as arises naturally from the breach and for any loss that was reasonably foreseeable by the parties as being likely to arise from it. Hence, an employee will normally recover only the amount of wages lost between the date of the wrongful dismissal and the date when the contract could lawfully have been terminated. In *Edwards v Chesterfield Royal NHS Trust* [2012], the Supreme Court ruled that damages were unavailable at common law where an employer had dismissed following disciplinary proceedings which breached express contractual terms: otherwise the statutory scheme of unfair dismissal with its financial cap on the compensatory award (see chapter 9) would be undermined.

✅ Looking for extra marks?

You might draw attention to the fact that one consequence of the *Edwards* case is that, in these circumstances, an injunction or declaration is available for a breach of contract but not damages.

Damages are not available for hurt feelings or the manner in which the dismissal took place (*Addis v Gramophone Co Ltd* [1909] (HL)), even though the manner might have made it more difficult to obtain other employment. There is an exception that where the employers were dishonest and corrupt, employees are entitled to damages for their increased difficulty in obtaining another job if that arises because the company was dishonest and corrupt: *Malik v BCCI* [1997] (HL). Except where employees have a contractual right to a payment in lieu of notice, or are entitled to their full payments during a contractual notice period, they have a duty to mitigate their loss, eg they are obliged to look for another job. Where there is a failure to mitigate, the court will deduct a sum it feels the employee might reasonably have been expected to earn.

The meaning of dismissal for statutory purposes

According to **ss 95** and **136 ERA**, an employee is to be treated as dismissed if:

- the contract under which he or she is employed is terminated by the employer with or without notice; or

- a **limited-term contract** terminates by virtue of the **limiting event** without being renewed under the same contract; or

- the employee terminates the contract with or without notice in circumstances such that he or she is entitled to terminate it without notice by reason of the employer's conduct (this is known as 'constructive dismissal', see 'Constructive dismissal').

Termination by the employer with or without notice

For the giving of notice to constitute a dismissal at law the actual date of termination must be ascertainable.

Practical example: A general warning of impending redundancies will not be treated as an individual notice to terminate.

Section 95(2) ERA states that where an employer has given notice to terminate, an employee who gives counter-notice indicating that he or she wishes to leave before the employer's notice has expired is still to be regarded as dismissed. However, in the case of redundancy this counter-notice must be given within the **'obligatory period'** of the employer's notice.

According to s 136(4) ERA, the 'obligatory period' is the minimum period which the employer is required to give by virtue of s 86(1) ERA (see 'Termination with notice', above) or the contract of employment.

A mutually agreed termination does not amount to a dismissal at law.

✅ Looking for extra marks?

You might suggest to the examiner that, as a matter of policy, tribunals should not find an agreement to terminate unless it is proved that the employee agreed with full knowledge of the implications.

Thus in *Hellyer Bros v Atkinson* [1994] it was held that the employee was merely accepting the fact of his dismissal rather than agreeing to terminate his employment. Whether a mutual agreement is void because of duress is a matter for the employment tribunal. It is possible to have a mutual termination of a contract in a redundancy situation. However, *Lassman v De Vere Hotel* [2003] is authority for the proposition that, where an employer seeks volunteers for redundancy, those who are dismissed will be eligible for a payment despite their willingness to leave.

If employees resign of their own volition, there is no dismissal at law. However, if pressure has been applied the situation will be different, for example where the employee is given the choice of resigning or being dismissed. Problems can arise in determining whether the words used by an employee can properly be regarded as amounting to a resignation. Normally, where the words are unequivocal and are understood by the employer as a resignation, it cannot be said that there was no resignation because a reasonable employer would not have so understood the words. However, exceptions may be made in the case of immature employees or of decisions taken in the heat of the moment or under pressure exerted by an employer. An objective test of whether the employee intended to resign applies only where the language used is ambiguous or where it is not plain how the employer understood the words.

Where a limited term contract expires without renewal

According to s 235(2A) ERA, a limited-term contract is one that terminates by virtue of a limiting event. There are three types of limiting event: the expiry of a fixed term (eg a contract of five years' duration); the performance of a specific task (eg marking 100 Employment Law exams); or the occurrence of an event or failure of an event to occur (eg the end of war in Syria).

Constructive dismissal

In these circumstances, the employer's behaviour constitutes a repudiation of the contract and the employee accepts that repudiation by resigning. Employees are entitled to treat themselves as constructively dismissed only if the employer is guilty of conduct that is a significant breach going to the root of the contract, or that shows that the employer no longer intends to be bound by one or more of its essential terms. If employees continue for any length of time without leaving, they will be regarded as having elected to affirm the contract and will lose the right to treat themselves as discharged. However, provided that employees make clear their objection to what is being done, they are not to be taken to have affirmed the contract by continuing to work and draw pay for a limited period of time. Similarly, where the employer has allowed the employee time to make up his or her mind, there is no need expressly to reserve the right to accept repudiation. It should be noted that even though a repudiatory breach of an express term has been waived, it could still form part of a series of acts that cumulatively amount to a breach of the employer's implied duty to show trust and confidence. It is not necessary to show that the employer intended to repudiate the contract. The tribunal's function is to look at the employer's conduct as a whole and determine whether its cumulative effect, judged reasonably and sensibly, is such that the employee cannot reasonably be expected to tolerate it.

> **Buckland v Bournemouth University [2010] IRLR 445**
>
> The Court of Appeal confirmed that the test for fundamental breach is objective and ruled that a repudiatory breach is not capable of being remedied so as to preclude acceptance. Thus all a defaulting party can do is to invite affirmation of the contract by making amends.

The following have been held to constitute constructive dismissals: a physical assault, demotion, swearing, and significant change in job duties or place of work. A failure to pay an employee's salary or wage is also likely to constitute a fundamental breach if it is a deliberate act on the part of an employer rather than a mere breakdown in technology.

Gardner Ltd v Beresford [1978] IRLR 63

The employee resigned because she had not received a pay increase for two years while others did. The Employment Appeal Tribunal (EAT) accepted that in most circumstances it would be reasonable to infer ('imply') a term that the employer will not treat employees arbitrarily, capriciously, or inequitably in the matter of remuneration.

Many cases have been decided on the basis that the employer failed to display sufficient trust and confidence in the employee (see chapter 2). Thus, unjustified accusations of theft, foul language, or a refusal to act reasonably in dealing with grievances, matters of safety, or incidents of harassment could all give rise to a claim of constructive dismissal.

Revision tip

You should note that, whatever the respective actions of employer and employee at the time of termination, the relevant question is: who really terminated the contract?

The effective and relevant date of termination

Whether a person is qualified to complain of unfair dismissal or has presented a claim within the prescribed time period must be answered by reference to the 'effective date of termination'. Similarly, entitlement to a redundancy payment and the computation of it, together with the time limit for submitting a claim, all depend on ascertaining the 'relevant date' of dismissal. The effective date and the relevant date mean the same thing. **Sections 97 and 145 ERA** provide that:

- where the contract is terminated by notice, the effective or relevant date is the date on which the notice expires even though the employee does not work out that notice. Where the employee gives counter-notice, the effective date is when the employee ceased working in accordance with that notice and the 'relevant date' is the date the counter-notice expires. Unless the contract states otherwise, both written and oral notices start to run the day after they are given (*Wang v University of Keele* [2011]);

- where the contract is determined without notice, the effective or relevant date is the date on which the termination takes effect. The date of termination of people dismissed with payments in lieu of notice is the date on which they are told they are dismissed. Where employees are given notice of dismissal and told to work it, but the employer

Termination by the employer with or without notice

subsequently requires them to leave immediately, the effective or relevant date is the date when they stop working;

- where a limited-term contract terminates by virtue of the limiting event without being renewed under the same contract, the effective or relevant date is the date on which the termination takes effect; and

- where, under the redundancy provisions, a statutory trial period has been served (see chapter 10, 'Offers of alternative employment'), for the purpose of submitting a claim in time the relevant date is the day that the new or renewed contract terminated. This is to be assessed in accordance with the previous three points.

Case law affirms that the effective date of termination is a statutory contract: the parties cannot agree on a different date. The latest authority is *Cosmeceuticals Ltd v Parkin* (2017) (EAT). The employers summarily dismissed their managing director on 1 September. Three days later they put her on garden leave; then on 29 September the chairman wrote to her, notifying her that the contract would be terminated on 23 October. The parties agreed that the last date, 23 October, would be the effective date of termination. The EAT ruled that this was incorrect. Since the dismissal was summary, the effective date was 1 September.

Fitzgerald v University of Kent [2004] IRLR 300

The Court of Appeal confirmed that the effective date of termination, being a statutory concept, is to be objectively determined and cannot be fixed by agreement between the employer and employee.

Whether in a particular case the words of dismissal evince an intention to terminate the contract at once or an intention to terminate it only at a future date depends on the construction of those words. Such construction should not be technical but reflect what an ordinary, reasonable employee would understand by the language used. Moreover, words should be construed in the light of the facts known to the employee at the time of notification. If the language used is ambiguous, it is likely that tribunals will apply the principle that words should be interpreted most strongly against the person who uses them. This is sometimes known as the contra proferentem principle. Where a dismissal has been communicated by letter, the contract of employment does not terminate until the employee has actually read the letter or had a reasonable opportunity of reading it. In *West Midlands Co-operative Society Ltd v Tipton* [1986], the House of Lords indicated that, unless there is a contractual provision to the contrary, the date of termination is to be ascertained in accordance with the formula set out in this section and is not the date on which the employee was informed that his or her appeal had failed.

Key cases

Case	Facts	Principle
Buckland v Bournemouth University [2010] IRLR 445	The claimant resigned after his examination papers he had marked were re-marked against his wishes.	The test for fundamental breach is objective. A repudiatory breach is not capable of being remedied so as to preclude acceptance.
Fitzgerald v University of Kent [2004] IRLR 300	There was a dispute as to whether the effective date of termination could be agreed by the parties.	The effective date of termination is to be objectively determined and cannot be fixed by agreement between the employer and employee.
Gardner Ltd v Beresford [1978] IRLR 63	The employee resigned because she had not received a pay increase for two years while others did.	It was reasonable to infer a term that employers will not treat employees arbitrarily, capriciously, or inequitably in the matter of remuneration.
Gogay v Hertfordshire County Council [2000] IRLR 703	The claimant sought damages for a psychological disorder that resulted from her unlawful suspension.	Damages can be awarded for non-economic losses, here psychiatric harm, in breach of contract claims.
Harlow v Artemis Ltd [2008] IRLR 629	The employee asserted that the employer's enhanced redundancy policy still formed part of his contract of employment.	Where an employer purports to change the terms of a contract of employment unilaterally but they do not immediately impact on the employee, then the fact that the employee continues to work does not mean that he or she can be taken to have accepted the variation.
Lassman v De Vere Hotel [2003] ICR 44	Volunteers for dismissal sought redundancy payments.	Where an employer seeks volunteers for redundancy, those who are dismissed will be eligible for a payment despite their willingness to leave.

 Exam questions

Problem question

There are ten employees in the postroom at Flexico plc. Their contracts of employment provide that their working hours are from 8 am to 4.30 pm with an hour's lunch break. It has recently been

Exam questions

decided by management that, in the interests of efficiency, the postroom staff should work from 9.30 am to 6 pm. After consultation and negotiation, nine of the employees have accepted the change and their contracts have been amended accordingly.

However, Ms Jones has stated that she cannot work the revised hours because she has to be home by 5 pm to take care of her elderly mother when the home-help leaves. She has therefore refused to work the new hours and is currently continuing to work from 8 am to 4.30 pm. Her manager, Mr Smith, is sympathetic and has given an oral undertaking that she may continue to finish at 4.30 pm. He has also indicated that she cannot start before 9.30 am and so she will have to bear the resulting loss of pay.

Discuss the legal issues that arise in this scenario.

See the Outline answers section in the end matter for help with this question.

Essay question

The inherent imbalance of power that exists between employer and employee means, in effect, that breaches of contract can be legally classified as variations of terms and conditions.

Discuss.

 Online Resources

To see an outline answer to this question log on to www.oup.com/lawrevision/

 Concentrate Q&As

For more questions and answers on employment law, see the *Concentrate Q&A: Employment Law* by Roseanne Russell.

Go to the end of this book to view **sample pages**.

#9

Unfair dismissal

Key facts

- Once employees have proved that they were qualified to bring a claim for unfair dismissal (see the next section of this chapter) and were dismissed (see the previous chapter), the employer must show the reason for the dismissal.

- The employer must demonstrate that the reason for the dismissal relates to capability or qualifications, conduct, redundancy, a statutory ban, or some other substantial reason of a kind to justify the dismissal. There are certain reasons such as pregnancy that are automatically unfair.

- Capability is assessed by reference to 'skill, aptitude, health or any other physical or mental quality'.

- Misconduct is a potentially fair reason for dismissal, but the employment tribunal will decide whether dismissal was a reasonable course of action, taking into account all the circumstances. It should be noted that *gross* misconduct is not required (compare wrongful dismissal in the previous chapter).

- 'Some other substantial reason' is a category that gives tribunals the discretion to accept as fair, reasons that have not been defined by statute, such as reasons arising out of the reorganisation of a business or pressure from customers on the employers to sack an employee.

- An employer must act reasonably in treating a reason as sufficient for dismissal. It should be guided by the **ACAS Code of Practice 2015** and must follow contractual procedures.

- The remedies for unfair dismissal are re-employment (reinstatement in the same job or re-engagement in a similar one) or compensation. Compensation will normally consist of a basic award and a compensatory award. Both awards are calculated in a certain way and various sums must be deducted; at that point, if relevant, a statutory maximum is imposed on the compensatory award. The basic award is calculated using a formula; once the sum is ascertained, it is also subject to deductions and a maximum.

Exclusions and qualifications

Employees have the right not to be unfairly dismissed but this generally applies only to those working in Great Britain at the time of dismissal. There are other general exclusions and qualifications, for example the need to have two years' service—s **108 Employment Rights Act 1996 (ERA)**—(see Figure 9.1), and the employee must not be a share fisherman, ie one paid by a share of the catch, or a member of the secret services. The service qualification does not apply if the reason or principal reason for dismissal was 'inadmissible' (see 'Automatically unfair dismissal', below). Continuity is to be calculated in accordance with **ss 210–219 ERA** (see chapter 11) and **s 97(2) ERA** enables employees who are wrongfully deprived of their statutory minimum entitlement to notice, or receive a payment in lieu, to add on that period of notice in ascertaining their length of service.

Revision tip

Remember that employees who are guilty of gross misconduct forfeit their entitlement to notice (see chapter 8).

Potentially fair reasons for dismissal

Once employees have proved that they were dismissed (see chapter 8, 'The meaning of dismissal for statutory purposes'), s **98 ERA** requires the employer to show the reason, or, if there was more than one, the principal reason, for the dismissal and that it falls within one of the following categories:

- it relates to the capacity (a term which includes health) or qualifications of the employee for performing work of the kind that he or she was employed to do;
- it relates to the conduct of the employee;
- the employee was redundant (see chapter 10);

- the employee could not continue to work in the position held without contravention, either on the employer's or employee's part, of a duty or restriction imposed by or under a statute;
- there was some other substantial reason to justify the dismissal of an employee holding the position that the employee held.

It follows that where no reason is given by the employee, a dismissal will be unfair simply because the statutory burden has not been discharged. There is no need to consider whether the dismissal was fair or unfair. Similarly the reason for dismissal must have existed and been known to the employee at the time of dismissal.

Written statement of dismissal

According to s 92 ERA, a person who has been dismissed or is under notice of dismissal has the right to be supplied with a written statement giving particulars of the reasons for dismissal if they have been continuously employed for two years. The employer must provide the statement within 14 days of a specific request being made. A claim that the employer unreasonably failed to provide such a statement or that the particulars given were inadequate or untrue must normally be presented to a tribunal within three months. If the complaint is well founded, a tribunal may make a declaration as to what it finds the employer's reasons were for dismissing (and of course it will take the fact of non-provision, untruth, or inadequacy into account when considering the employer's true reason for dismissal) and must order that the employee receive two weeks' pay. Unlike unfair dismissal's basic award (and redundancy payments), this sum is not subject to the statutory maximum, which changes year by year.

Automatically unfair dismissal

In certain circumstances a dismissal will be unfair because the reason for it was 'inadmissible'. A dismissal is automatically unfair if the reason for it related to any of the following:

- the assertion of a statutory right (see 'Asserting statutory rights');
- trade union membership or activities, or non-union membership;
- pregnancy or maternity (see chapter 6);
- certain health and safety grounds;
- refusing to comply with a requirement which is in contravention of the Working Time Regulations 1998 (WTR);
- the reason, or the principal reason, for the dismissal is that the employee made a protected disclosure;

- the employee is dismissed for trying to enforce the National Minimum Wage or the National Living Wage;
- the proposed or actual performance of any functions or activities as an employee representative or candidate;
- exercising rights in relation to the statutory recognition of a trade union;
- the dismissal of a **worker** within 12 weeks of taking part in protected industrial action;
- the exercise of a statutory right to request a contract variation;
- the exercise of rights under the **Part-time Workers (Prevention of Less Favourable Treatment) Regulations 2000** and **Fixed-term Employees (Prevention of Less Favourable Treatment) Regulations 2002**;
- the exercise of a right in relation to pension enrolment;
- the exercise of a right in relation to study leave or training;
- the existence of a prohibited list under the **Employment Relations Act 1999 (Blacklists) Regulations 2010**;
- political opinions or affiliations (see s 13 **Enterprise and Regulatory Reform Act 2013**).

Additionally, if any of these 'inadmissible' reasons was used to select a person for redundancy, dismissal will also be unfair. Other unfair reasons for dismissal are those connected to: transfers of undertakings (see chapter 11), **protected characteristics** (see chapter 4), and the **Rehabilitation of Offenders Act 1974**.

Asserting statutory rights

Employees are protected if they have brought proceedings against the employer to enforce a 'relevant' statutory right and have alleged that the employer has infringed such a right. The following are examples of 'relevant' statutory rights:

- any right conferred by the ERA which may be the subject of a complaint to an employment tribunal (such as unfair dismissal);
- minimum notice rights under s 86 ERA;
- certain rights relating to the unlawful deduction of union contributions from pay, action short of dismissal on union membership grounds, time off for union duties and activities, and union learning representatives;
- rights afforded by the WTR (see chapter 7);
- rights afforded by the **Trade Union and Labour Relations (Consolidation)**
- **Act 1992 (TULRCA)** in relation to statutory **recognition** of trade unions (see chapter 12);
- rights afforded by the **Transfer of Undertakings (Protection**
- **of Employment) Regulations 2006 (TUPE Regulations 2006)** (see chapter 11).

Discussion of 'potentially fair reasons for dismissal'

Capability or qualifications

According to s 98(3) ERA, 'capability' is to be assessed by reference to 'skill, aptitude, health or any other physical or mental quality'. 'Qualifications' means 'any degree, diploma, or other academic, technical or professional qualification relevant to the position which the employee held'.

In *Abernethy v Mott, Hay and Anderson* [1974], it was held that an employee's inflexibility or lack of adaptability came within his or her aptitude and mental qualities.

It should be noted that in cases of intermittent absences due to ill-health, there is no obligation on an employer to call medical evidence. In deciding whether an employer acted fairly in dismissing, tribunals must determine as a matter of fact what consultation, if any, was necessary or desirable in the known circumstances; what consultation took place; and whether that consultation process was adequate in the circumstances.

Revision tip

Remember that an employee who has become incapable of work through ill-health may have a disability within the meaning of the **Equality Act 2010** (see chapter 4, 'Meaning of disability'). In respect of dismissal the contract may have been frustrated by the employee's ill-health (see chapter 8); in that case there is no dismissal and therefore no unfair dismissal.

Conduct

In this context, conduct may mean actions of such a nature, whether done in the course of employment or outside, that reflect in some way on the employer/employee relationship. It should be noted that tribunals do not have to decide whether misconduct is gross or criminal but whether the employer has, in the circumstances of the case, acted reasonably in dismissing. As a general rule, if an order is lawful, a refusal to obey it will be a breach of contract and amount to misconduct. Theft of an employer's property will amount to a fair reason for dismissal but cases of suspected dishonesty are likely to be more difficult to handle.

> **British Home Stores v Burchell [1978] IRLR 379**
>
> In this case it was stated that tribunals had to decide whether the employer entertained a belief, based on reasonable grounds, in the guilt of the employee at that time. There are three elements to this:
>
> - the employer must establish the fact of that belief;
> - the e mployer must show that there were reasonable grounds upon which to sustain that belief; and
> - at the stage at which the belief was formed the employer must have carried out as much investigation into the matter as was reasonable in the circumstances.

Redundancy

For 'unfair redundancy' see the next chapter.

Statutory ban

Section 98(2)(d) ERA states that if it would be unlawful to continue to work in the position that the employee held, there is a valid reason for dismissing.

Practical example: This reason would apply if a person employed to drive had his or her driving licence withdrawn.

Some other substantial reason

Section 98(1)(b) ERA was included in the legislative scheme so as to give tribunals the discretion to accept as a fair reason for dismissal something that would not conveniently fit into any of the other categories. For example, a genuine but mistaken belief that continued employment would contravene statutory restrictions (*Hounslow LBC v Klusova* [2008]). In *Hollister v National Farmers' Union* [1979], the Court of Appeal ruled that it is sufficient if there is a sound business reason, which means only that there is a reason which management thinks on reasonable grounds is sound. In practice, 'some other substantial reason' is regularly used to justify dismissals as a result of a reorganisation of the business or pressure from a third party, for example a client. If the latter, employers should do everything they reasonably can to avoid or mitigate any injustice brought about by the client's stance (*Henderson v Connect Ltd* [2010]).

Practical example: Where it is necessary to alter hours of work to meet business requirements but employees have a contractual right to resist the change, any resulting dismissals would be for 'some other substantial reason' rather than misconduct.

 Looking for extra marks?

You might comment that employment tribunals will be on the lookout to check whether the employer is using some other substantial reason as a pretext to conceal the real reason for dismissal.

Industrial action and lack of jurisdiction

By virtue of **s 237 TULRCA**, employees cannot complain of unfair dismissal if at the time of dismissal they were taking part in an unofficial strike or other unofficial industrial action. However, **s 238A TULRCA** states that a dismissal will be unfair in certain situations if the reason is that the employee took part in protected industrial action; an example is where the employee is dismissed within 12 weeks of the start of that industrial action.

Reasonableness in the circumstances

According to s 98(4) ERA, where the employer has given a valid reason for dismissal, the determination of the question whether the dismissal was fair or unfair depends on whether in the circumstances (including the size and administrative resources of the employer's undertaking) the employer acted reasonably or unreasonably in treating it as a sufficient reason for dismissing the employee and had regard to equity and the substantial merits of the case. One question that arises here is: whose knowledge or state of mind counts for this purpose? This was answered in *Orr v Milton Keynes Council* [2011], where the Court of Appeal ruled that the relevant person was the one 'deputed to carry out the employer's functions under Section 98'. Thus the knowledge held by other staff cannot be imputed to the designated person if he or she could not reasonably have acquired that knowledge through the appropriate disciplinary procedure.

Anglian Homes Ltd v Kelly [2004] IRLR 793

In this case the Court of Appeal stated that tribunals should not ask themselves whether they would have done what the employer did in the circumstances. Their function is merely to assess the employer's decision to dismiss and decide if it falls within a range of responses that a reasonable employer could have taken.

Tribunals must take account of the wider circumstances. In addition to the employer's business needs, attention must be paid to the personal attributes of the employee, for example seniority and previous work record. Additionally, employers will be expected to treat employees in similar circumstances in a similar way. The words 'equity and the substantial merits' also allow tribunals to apply their knowledge of good industrial relations practice and to ensure that there has been procedural fairness, which is discussed next. The overriding principle is: each case must be considered on its own facts.

The Code of Practice and procedural fairness

According to para 4 of the ACAS Code of Practice on Disciplinary and Grievance Procedures 2015, there are a number of elements to fairness:

- employers and employees should raise and deal with issues promptly and should not unreasonably delay meetings, decisions, or confirmation of those decisions;
- employers and employees should act consistently;
- employers should carry out any necessary investigations to establish the facts of the case;

- employers should inform employees of the basis of the problem and give them an opportunity to put their case in response before any decisions are made (see *Spence v Department of Agriculture and Rural Development* [2011]);

- employers should allow employees to be accompanied at any formal disciplinary or grievance meeting; and

- employers should allow an employee to appeal against any formal decision made. A good appeal can cure defects in the original hearing.

There is much law on procedural fairness, but the student should have the words of s 98(4) ERA in the forefront of his or her mind. Cases are examples of the application of that sub-section. For example, warnings are often (depending on the facts) part of procedural fairness. Unexpired warnings constitute no problem. They can be taken into account when judging whether a dismissal is fair or unfair. What about expired warnings? For example, in *Stratford v Auto Trail VR* [2016] the employers originally thought that a final written warning was the appropriate sanction. However, they relied on 17 expired warnings and the prospect of more warnings in the future to dismiss the employee. The Employment Appeal Tribunal (EAT) held the dismissal to be fair: such expired warnings and belief in future warnings about conduct could be added to the sanction already in mind, a final written warning, to lead to a fair dismissal.

In addition, the foreword to the Code of Practice emphasises the desirability of keeping written records. It should be noted that this Code does not have the force of law but s 207A TULRCA 1992 allows tribunals to adjust any awards by up to 25% for unreasonable failure by the ex-employee or ex-employer to comply with any provision of the Code.

 ✓ Looking for extra marks?

Point out that natural justice is clearly an element in procedural fairness.

Section 10 Employment Relations Act 1999 (ERel Act) gives workers the right to make a reasonable request to be accompanied during a disciplinary or grievance hearing. According to s 13 ERel Act, a disciplinary hearing is one that could result in the administration of a formal warning, the taking of some other action, or the confirmation of previous actions. A grievance hearing is one that concerns the performance of an employer's duty in relation to a worker.

A worker may be accompanied by a single companion who:

- is chosen by the worker;

- is to be permitted to address the hearing;

- is not, however, to answer questions on behalf of the worker;

- is to be allowed to confer with the worker during the hearing.

Looking for extra marks?

Point out that s 10 does not require the worker's choice of companion to be reasonable.

An employer must permit a worker to take time off during working hours in order to accompany another of the employer's workers. **Section 11 ERel Act** provides that an employer who infringes these rights is liable to pay up to two weeks' **wages**. In addition, s 12 protects workers who are subjected to a detriment on the ground that they have exercised a right under s 10 or sought to accompany another worker pursuant to a request under that section.

West Midlands Co-op Society Ltd v Tipton [1986] IRLR 112

The House of Lords confirmed that a dismissal is unfair if the employer unreasonably treats the reason for dismissal as a sufficient one, either when the original decision to dismiss is made or when that decision is maintained at the conclusion of an internal appeal. Whether procedural defects can be rectified ('cured') on appeal will depend on the degree of unfairness at the original hearing. The general rule used to be that the appeal must be a rehearing of the complaint and not merely a review of the original decision, but the modern method is to look at procedure in the round, not at whether there is a rehearing or review.

The remedies
Re-employment

When applicants are found to have been unfairly dismissed, tribunals must explain their power to order reinstatement or re-engagement and ask employees if they wish such an order to be made. Only if such a wish is expressed can an order be made, and if no order is made, the tribunal must turn to the question of compensation. Where re-employment is sought, a tribunal must first consider whether reinstatement is appropriate. Reinstatement occurs when the employee is treated as if he or she had not been dismissed and re-engagement is where there is some other form of re-hiring. If reinstatement is not ordered, the tribunal must then decide whether to make an order for re-engagement and, if so, on what terms. Except in a case where the tribunal takes into account contributory fault, if it orders re-engagement it will do so on terms that are, so far as is reasonably practicable, as favourable as an order for reinstatement.

Practicability is a question of fact for each tribunal. For these purposes reinstatement is defined as treating the complainant 'in all respects as if he had not been dismissed'. An order for re-engagement may be on such terms as the tribunal decides, and the complainant may be re-engaged by the employer, a successor, or an associated employer in comparable or suitable employment. Where a person is reinstated or re-engaged as the result of a tribunal order but the terms are not fully complied with, s 117(2) **ERA** requires a tribunal to make an additional award of compensation of such amount as it thinks fit, having regard to the loss sustained by the complainant in consequence of the failure to comply fully with the terms of the order.

Looking for extra marks?

You might observe that it is a matter for speculation how long re-employment must last for it to be said that an order has been complied with. Employers may well not welcome back their former employees who have won a legal claim against them.

If a complainant is not re-employed in accordance with a tribunal order, he or she is entitled to enforce the monetary element at the employment tribunal. Compensation will be awarded together with an additional award unless the employer satisfies the tribunal that it was not practicable to comply with the order. The additional award will be of between 26 and 52 weeks' pay. In this context, the calculation of the weeks' pay is subject to the same limit as in the basic award (see under 'Compensation') and the amount of the redundancy payment (see chapter 10).

Compensation

Compensation for unfair dismissal will usually consist of a basic award and a compensatory award. Normally, the basic award will be calculated in the same way as a redundancy payment (see the next chapter) and will be reduced by the amount of any redundancy payment received. The current maximum basic award (from April 2017) is £14,670, based on a maximum week's pay of £489. Where the reason or principal reason for dismissal is related to union membership or the employee's health and safety responsibilities there was a *minimum* award of £5,970 from 6 April 2017, subject to any deduction on the grounds stated in the following bullet points.

The basic award can be reduced by such proportion as the tribunal considers just and equitable on two grounds:

- the complainant unreasonably refused an offer of reinstatement. Such an offer could have been made before any finding of unfairness; and
- any conduct of the complainant before the dismissal, or before notice was given.

Section 123 ERA states that the amount of the compensatory award must reflect what a tribunal 'considers just and equitable in all the circumstances having regard to the loss sustained by the complainant in consequence of the dismissal insofar as that loss is attributable to action taken by the employer'. This may include losses resulting from subsequent employment or unemployment if those losses can be attributed to the dismissal. It is specifically mentioned that an individual whose redundancy entitlement would have exceeded the basic award can be compensated for the difference, while a redundancy payment received in excess of the basic award payable goes to reduce the compensatory award. The compensatory award can be reduced in three other circumstances: where the employee's action caused or contributed to the dismissal, where the employee would have been dismissed any-way, and where the employee failed to mitigate his or her loss after it. Before reducing an award on the ground that the complainant caused or contributed to the dismissal, a tribunal must be satisfied that the employee's conduct was culpable or blameworthy, eg foolish, perverse, or unreasonable in the circumstances.

Having found that an employee was to blame, a tribunal must reduce the award to some extent, although the proportion of culpability is a matter for the tribunal. Complainants are obliged to look for work but the onus is on the employer to prove that there was such a failure.

From 6 April 2017, the maximum compensatory award is £80,541 (sic!) or 52 weeks' pay, whichever is the lower amount. The limit applies only after credit has been given for any payments made by the employer and any deductions have been made but any 'excess' payments made by the employer over that which is required are deducted after the amount of the compensatory award has been fixed. As regards deductions, normally an employer is to be given credit for all payments made to an employee in respect of claims for wages and other benefits.

Revision Tip

Remember that where an employee has suffered discrimination as well as unfair dismissal, s 126 ERA prevents double compensation for the same loss.

 Looking for extra marks?

Point out to the examiner that the legislation aims to reimburse the employee rather than to punish the employer. However, s 12A Employment Tribunals Act 1996 (ETA 1996) allows employment tribunals (ETs) to impose a financial penalty on employers where there has been a breach of employment rights and the ET thinks that 'the breach has one or more aggravating features'. Normally the penalty must not be less than £100 or more than £5,000 but regard must be had to the employer's ability to pay and there is a 50% discount if payment is made within 21 days.

It is the duty of tribunals to enquire into the various grounds for compensation, although it is the responsibility of the aggrieved person to prove the loss and for the ex-employer to prove that the ex-employee has not mitigated loss.

The possible heads of loss in the compensatory award have been divided into the following categories:

Loss incurred up to the date of the hearing

Here attention focuses on the employee's actual loss of income, which makes it necessary to ascertain the employee's take-home pay. Thus, tax and National Insurance contributions are to be deducted but overtime earnings and tips can be taken into account. Similarly, any sickness or incapacity benefits received may be taken into account. As well as lost wages, s 123(2) ERA enables an individual to claim compensation for the loss of other benefits. Although, 'expenses reasonably incurred' are mentioned in the statute, complainants cannot be reimbursed for the cost of pursuing their unfair dismissal claims.

> **Dunnachie v Kingston upon Hull City Council [2004] IRLR 727**
>
> The House of Lords held that there can be no award for non-economic loss, for example hurt feelings.

Loss flowing from the manner of dismissal

Compensation can be awarded only if the manner of dismissal has made the individual less acceptable to potential employers. However, economic loss may arise where the person is not fit to take up alternative employment as early as he or she would otherwise have done.

Loss of accrued rights

Tribunals should include a sum to reflect the fact that dismissed employees lose the statutory minimum notice protection that they have built up. Nowadays the figure is around £350.

Loss of pension rights

Basically, there are two types of loss: the loss of the present pension position and the loss of the opportunity to improve one's pension position with the dismissing employer.

Future loss

Where no further employment has been secured, tribunals will have to speculate how long the employee will remain unemployed. However, only rarely will loss be assessed over a career lifetime (*Wardle v Credit Agricole* [2011]). If another job has been obtained, tribunals must compare the employee's salary prospects for the future in each employment and estimate how long it will take the employee in the new position to reach the salary equivalent to that which would have been attained had he or she remained with the original employer.

Making a claim

Claims must normally arrive at an ET within three months of the effective date of termination, unless it was not reasonably practicable to bring the claim within that period. A complaint can also be presented before the effective date of termination provided it is lodged after notice of dismissal has been given. What is or is not reasonably practicable is a question of fact and the onus is on the employee to prove that it was not reasonably practicable to claim in time. You should be aware that the courts and tribunals have dealt with this jurisdictional point on many occasions and have taken the view that, because the unfair dismissal provisions have been in force since 1972, tribunals are strict in enforcing the three-month time limit.

> **Palmer v Southend Borough Council [1984] IRLR 119**
>
> The Court of Appeal interpreted the words 'reasonably practicable' as meaning something between reasonable and reasonably capable of physically being done. The tribunal will look at this issue of reasonableness against all the surrounding circumstances.

The fact that an internal appeal or criminal proceedings are pending does not by itself provide a sufficient excuse for delaying an application. The correct procedure is for employees to submit their applications, known as originating applications, and request that they be held in abeyance.

Although ignorance of the law does not generally afford an excuse, in *Wall's Meat Co Ltd v Khan* [1978] it was decided that ignorance or mistaken belief can be grounds for holding that it was not reasonably practicable if it could be shown that the ignorance or mistaken belief was itself reasonable. Thus, in *Churchill v Yeates Ltd* [1983] the EAT held that it was not reasonably practicable for an employee to bring a complaint until he or she had knowledge of a fundamental fact that rendered the dismissal unfair. In this case, after the three-month period had elapsed, an employee who had been dismissed on the grounds of redundancy discovered that he had been replaced. However, ignorance or mistaken belief will not be reasonable if it arises from the fault of complainants not making such enquiries as they reasonably should have in the circumstances. According to the EAT, where a claimant has consulted skilled advisers, the question of reasonable practicability is to be judged by what the claimant could have done had he or she been given such advice as was reasonable in all the circumstances (*Northamptonshire County Council v Entwhistle* [2010]).

Pre-termination negotiations, conciliation, and settlement agreements

According to s 111A ERA, evidence of pre-termination negotiations normally cannot be heard by an ET. The exceptional circumstances are: where claimants assert that they have been dismissed for an automatically unfair reason; if the ET thinks that there have been improper words or behaviour and it would be just to allow information to be disclosed; and if an offer in relation to costs or expenses was made on the basis that the right to refer to it was reserved.

Most potential applicants must submit details of their case to ACAS before they can lodge an ET claim. This is called 'early conciliation', which came into effect in April 2014. The conciliation officer must endeavour to promote a settlement between the prospective parties within a prescribed period. If during this period the conciliation officer concludes that a settlement is impossible or the period elapses without a settlement being achieved, he or she will give the prospective claimant a certificate to that effect. A claim cannot be lodged without such a certificate but a conciliation officer may continue to endeavour to promote a settlement. Even if it has not received information from a prospective claimant, s 18B(1) ETA 1996 obliges ACAS to promote a settlement where a person requests the services of a conciliation officer in relation to a dispute that is likely to result in ET proceedings against them.

Section 203(2) ERA makes it possible to contract out of the unfair dismissal and redundancy payment provisions if there is an agreement to refrain from presenting a complaint that has been reached after the involvement of a conciliation officer, or satisfies the

Pre-termination negotiations, conciliation, and settlement agreements

✳✳✳✳✳✳✳✳✳✳✳

Figure 9.1 Is the person qualified to claim unfair dismissal?

conditions regulating 'settlement agreements'. According to s 18(4) ETA 1996, where the complainant has ceased to be employed, the conciliation officer must seek to promote that person's re-employment (ie reinstatement or re-engagement) on terms that appear to be equitable. If the complainant does not wish to be re-employed, or this is not practicable, the conciliation officer must seek to promote agreement on compensation. Under s 18(6) and (7) ETA, a conciliation officer is to 'have regard to the desirability of encouraging the use of other procedures available for the settlement of grievances'. Anything communicated to a conciliation officer in connection with the performance of these functions is not admissible in evidence in any proceedings before a tribunal except with the consent of the person who communicated it. It should be noted that a conciliated settlement will be binding even though it is not in writing.

In addition, s 203(2), (3) (3A), (3B), and (4) ERA provide that an agreement to refrain from bringing certain tribunal proceedings can be enforced if it satisfies the following conditions governing 'settlement agreements':

- the agreement must be in writing and relate to a particular complaint or proceedings;
- the employee or worker must have received advice from a relevant independent adviser on the terms and effect of the proposed agreement and its effect on the employee's ability to pursue a complaint or proceedings before an ET;
- there must be an insurance policy in force to cover any claims from the employee in respect of any losses in consequence of the advice;
- the agreement must identify the adviser; and
- the agreement must state that these conditions regulating settlement agreements have been satisfied.

✅ *Looking for extra marks?*

Point out that a settlement agreement might be unenforceable on the grounds of misrepresentation.

Revision tip

Demonstrate your awareness that an ET has jurisdiction to enforce a settlement agreement relating to the terms on which employment is to terminate.

(✱) Key cases

Cases	Facts	Principle
Anglian Homes Ltd v Kelly [2004] IRLR 793	There was a dispute about how tribunals should approach the issue of reasonableness in all the circumstances under s 98(4) ERA.	The function of ETs is to assess the employer's decision to dismiss and decide if it falls within a range of responses that a reasonable employer could have taken.

Cases	Facts	Principle
British Home Stores v Burchell [1978] IRLR 379	It was argued that employers had to prove that the misconduct that led to the dismissal had actually occurred and was not merely suspected.	Tribunals have to decide whether the employer entertained a reasonable suspicion amounting to a belief in the guilt of the employee at that time. There are three elements to this: the employer must establish the fact of that belief; the employer must show that there were reasonable grounds upon which to sustain that belief; at the stage at which the belief was formed the employer must have carried out as much investigation into the matter as was reasonable in the circumstances.
Dunnachie v Kingston upon Hull City Council [2004] IRLR 727	It was argued that employees who are unfairly dismissed can be compensated for non-economic losses.	Compensation for non-economic losses, for example injury to feelings, is not available in these proceedings.
West Midlands Co-op Society Ltd v Tipton [1986] IRLR 112	There was a dispute about the effect of the appeal process on the fairness of a dismissal.	A dismissal is unfair if the employer unreasonably treats the reason for dismissal as a sufficient one, either when the original decision to dismiss is made or when that decision is maintained at the conclusion of an internal appeal.

(?) Exam questions

Problem question

Doris has been employed by Archer Ltd for 18 months. On her appointment it was agreed that she would only be required to work in the despatch area of the factory. A month later Doris received a statement of particulars that informed her that she was to work 20 hours per week and could be required to clean any part of the factory.

Last Monday Doris was asked by her supervisor, Dan, if she would move from the despatch area to the assembly bay and work 25 hours a week 'for a temporary period'. The following day Doris informed Dan that, owing to domestic commitments, she was unable to comply with this request. Dan was upset by this response and told Doris that if she had not changed her mind by Friday she would be regarded as having dismissed herself.

On Saturday Doris received a letter which stated that 'the company has decided to accept your conduct as bringing the contract to an end'.

Advise Doris as to any legal rights she may have.

See the Outline answers section in the end matter for help with this question.

Essay question

The law of unfair dismissal was introduced to provide protection for workers. However, in the twenty-first century it has become a valuable tool for employers in the management of discipline at the workplace.

Discuss.

 Online Resources

To see an outline answer to this question log on to www.oup.com/lawrevision/

 Concentrate Q&As

For more questions and answers on employment law, see the *Concentrate Q&A: Employment Law* by Roseanne Russell.

Go to the end of this book to view **sample pages**.

#10
Redundancy

- Employees are to be regarded as redundant if the employer has ceased or intends to cease carrying on the business for the purposes for which the employees were employed, or in the place where they are employed there has been, or will be, a diminution in the need for 'work of a particular kind'.

- The burden of proof is on the employer to show that any offer of alternative employment was suitable and that any refusal by the employee was unreasonable.

- A trial period may be invoked to consider offers of alternative employment if there is likely to be a difference in terms and conditions of employment.

- The employer should give as much warning as possible of impending redundancies to enable the union and the affected employees to take early steps to consider alternative solutions or possibly find alternative work in the undertaking or elsewhere.

- The size of a redundancy payment depends upon the employee's age, length of service, and the amount of a week's pay. Both of the last two variables are subject to a statutory cap.

The ERA definition of redundancy

According to s 139(1) Employment Rights Act 1996 (ERA), **employees** are to be regarded as being redundant if their dismissals are attributable wholly or mainly to:

- the fact that the employer has ceased, or intends to cease, to carry on the business for the purposes for which the employees were employed; or
- the fact that the employer has ceased, or intends to cease, to carry on that business in the place where the employees were so employed; or
- the fact that the requirement of that business for employees to carry out work of a particular kind, or for employees to carry out work of a particular kind in the place where they were so employed, has ceased or diminished or is expected to cease or diminish.

In this context, 'cease' or 'diminish' means either permanently or temporarily and from whatever cause.

Murray v Foyle Meats Ltd [1999] IRLR 562

The House of Lords, on appeal from Northern Ireland, held that the definition of redundancy requires two factual questions to be answered. These are: have the requirements of the employer's business for employees to carry out work of a particular kind ceased or diminished, or were they expected to cease or diminish? Was the dismissal of the employee attributable, wholly or mainly, to this state of affairs? This means looking at the employer's overall requirements to decide whether there has been a reduced need for employees irrespective of the terms of the individual's contract or of the function that each performed. The House of Lords approved the approach of the Employment Appeal Tribunal (EAT) in deciding that **bumping**' could give rise to a redundancy payment. Bumping is where an individual's (A) job continues but there is a reduction somewhere else in the organisation for the same number of people to carry out the work. If an employee from elsewhere is given A's job, A is to be treated as redundant.

For these purposes, the place where an employee was employed does not extend to any place where he or she could contractually be required to work. The question of what is the place of employment concerns the extent or area of a single place, not the possibility of transfer from one place to another. However, even though an employee may be contractually justified in declining to move because there is no contractual mobility clause, a request to do so may have to be considered as an offer of suitable alternative employment (see 'Offers of alternative employment').

One of the most difficult tasks for tribunals is to determine what constitutes 'work of a particular kind'. It is clear that a change in the time when the work is to be performed (including a change in shift patterns) and a change to the terms and conditions of work will not give rise to a redundancy payment, nor will a reduction of overtime if the work to be done remains the same. Three further points should be noted. First, employees will be entitled to a payment notwithstanding that it could be seen from the commencement of the contract that they would be dismissed for redundancy. Secondly, s 163(2) Employment Rights Act 1996 (ERA) states that an employee who is dismissed is presumed to have been dismissed by reason of redundancy unless the contrary is proved by the employer, ie there is a presumption of redundancy. Thirdly, the statutory definition of redundancy focuses on the employer's requirements rather than needs. Thus—even where there is still a need for the work to be done—if, owing to lack of funds, the requirement for the employee's service has ceased, the employee is redundant.

Offers of alternative employment

If, before the ending of a person's employment, the employer or an associated employer makes an offer, in writing or not, to renew the contract or to re-engage under a new contract which is to take effect either on the ending of the old one or within four weeks thereafter, s 141 ERA has the following effect:

- if the provisions of the new or renewed contract as to the capacity and place in which the person would be employed, together with the other terms and conditions, do not differ from the corresponding terms of the previous contract; or
- the terms and conditions differ, wholly or in part, but the offer constitutes an offer of suitable employment; and
- in either case, the employee unreasonably refuses that offer,

then he or she will not be entitled to a redundancy payment.

The burden is on an employer to prove both the suitability of the offer and the unreasonableness of the employee's refusal. Offers do not have to be formal, nor do they have to contain all the conditions that are ultimately agreed. It should be noted that supplying details of vacancies is not the same as an offer of employment.

 Looking for extra marks?

You should indicate that, although in theory the questions of suitability and the reasonableness of refusal are distinct, they are often run together in practice.

The suitability of the alternative work must be assessed objectively by comparing the terms on offer with those previously enjoyed. A convenient test has been whether the proposed employment will be 'substantially equivalent' to that which has ceased. Merely offering the same salary will not be sufficient, although the fact that the employment will be at a different location does not necessarily mean that it will be regarded as unsuitable. In determining the reasonableness of an employee's refusal, subjective considerations can be taken into account. Thus it might be reasonable for an employee to refuse an offer of employment which, although suitable, involved loss of status. To allow an employee to make a rational decision about any alternative employment offered, s 138(3) ERA states that if the terms and conditions differ, wholly or in part, from those of the previous contract, a trial period may be invoked. Such a period commences when the employee starts work under the new or renewed contract and ends four calendar weeks later unless a longer period has been agreed for the purpose of retraining. Any such agreement must be made before the employee starts work under the new or renewed contract; it must be in writing, and specify the date the trial period ends, and the terms and conditions that will apply afterwards. However, it is not necessary for the employer to provide all the information required by s 1 ERA; the agreement need only embody important matters such as remuneration, status, and job description. If, during the trial period, the employee for any reason terminates or gives notice to terminate the contract, or the employer terminates or gives notice to terminate it for any reason connected with or arising out of the change, the employee is to be treated, for redundancy payment purposes, as having been dismissed on the date the previous contract ended.

Revision tip

Remember that the employee's contract may be renewed again, or he or she may be re-engaged under a new contract in circumstances that give rise to another trial period.

Unfair redundancy

It is possible for a dismissed employee to claim both a redundancy payment and a remedy for unfair dismissal, although s 122(4) ERA prevents double compensation for the same loss being obtained. It should be noted that for unfair dismissal purposes the statutory presumption of redundancy does not apply, so the employer must establish this as the reason, or principal reason, for dismissal. However, tribunals will not investigate the background that led to the redundancy or require the employer to justify redundancies in economic terms.

In *Johnson v Peabody Trust* [1996], the EAT held that employers do not have to show that their requirements for employees to carry out work of a particular kind have diminished in relation to any work that the employees could have been asked to do under their contracts. Thus, where an employee is hired to perform a particular trade, it is that basic obligation that has to be looked at when deciding whether the employer's requirements have ceased or diminished, rather than any work that the employee could be required to carry out in accordance with a contractual flexibility clause.

Section 105 ERA provides that a dismissal on grounds of redundancy will be unfair if it is shown that 'the circumstances constituting the redundancy applied equally to one or more other employees in the same undertaking who held positions similar to the claimant' and either the reason, or principal reason, for which the employee was selected was inadmissible. However, a failure to comply with a procedural requirement to consult trade unions and to consider volunteers will not be automatically unfair. Nevertheless, s 98(4) ERA can still have a considerable impact on dismissals for redundancy (see chapter 9).

Unfair redundancy

✳✳✳✳✳✳✳✳✳✳

Williams v Compair Maxam [1982] IRLR 83

In this case, a leading authority, it was held that it is not enough to show that it was reasonable to dismiss an employee; a tribunal must be satisfied that the employer acted reasonably in treating redundancy as 'sufficient reason for dismissing the employee'. According to the EAT, where employees are represented by a recognised **independent trade union**, reasonable employers will seek to act in accordance with the following principles.

1. The employer will seek to give as much warning as possible of impending redundancies so as to enable the union and employees who may be affected to take early steps to inform themselves of the relevant facts, consider possible alternative solutions, and, if necessary, find alternative employment in the undertaking or elsewhere.

2. The employer will consult the union as to the best means by which the desired management result can be achieved fairly and with as little hardship to the employees as possible. In particular, the employer will seek to agree with the union the criteria to be applied in selecting the employees to be made redundant. When a selection has been made the employer will consider with the union whether the selection has been made in accordance with those criteria.

3. Whether or not an agreement as to the criteria to be adopted has been agreed with the union, the employer will seek to establish criteria for selection that so far as possible do not depend solely upon the opinion of the person making the selection but can be checked objectively against such things as attendance record, efficiency at the job, or length of service.

4. The employer will seek to ensure that the selection is made fairly in accordance with these criteria and will consider any representations the union may make as to such selection.

5. The employer will seek to see whether, instead of dismissing, an employee could be offered alternative employment.

There is no legal requirement that a redundancy 'pool' should be limited to employees doing the same or similar work and it will be difficult to challenge an employer's decision as to who should be in the pool. In selecting employees for redundancy, a senior manager is entitled to rely on the assessments of employees made by those who have direct knowledge of their work. However, employers may need to show that their method of selection was fair and applied reasonably. An absence of adequate consultation with the employees concerned or their representatives might affect their ability to do this (see 'Consultation for unfair dismissal purposes', below). It will not always be possible to call evidence subsequently to show that adequate consultation would not have made a difference to the decision about selection for redundancy. If the flaws in the process were procedural, it might be possible to reconstruct what might have happened if the correct procedures had been followed. However, if the tribunal decides that the defects were more substantive, such a reconstruction may not be possible. The duty to act reasonably in all the circumstances obliges employers to consider the alternatives to compulsory redundancy. Measures for minimising or avoiding compulsory redundancies may include:

- natural wastage;
- restrictions on recruitment;
- reduction or elimination of overtime;
- the introduction of short-time working or temporary lay-off (where this is provided for in the **contract of employment** or by an agreed variation of its terms);

- retraining and redeployment to other parts of the organisation;
- termination of the employment of temporary or contract staff; and
- seeking applicants for early retirement or voluntary redundancy.

'Last in, first out' (LIFO) is at times still used as a criterion for selection and it is assumed to be based on periods of continuous rather than cumulative service. Note, however, that LIFO may be sexually discriminatory.

Selecting employees on part-time and/or fixed-term contracts may also be potentially discriminatory. In *Whiffen v Milham Ford Girls School* [2001], those employees not employed under a permanent contract of employment were the first to be selected in a redundancy exercise. This was held to be a case of indirect sex discrimination because a smaller proportion of women than comparable men was able to satisfy this condition.

As regards alternative employment, 'the size and administrative resources' (s 98(4)) of the employer will be a relevant consideration here. However, only in very rare cases will a tribunal accept that a reasonable employer would have created a job by dismissing someone else.

Consultation for unfair dismissal purposes

An important requirement in redundancy situations is the need for consultation (see 'Consultation about collective redundancies', below, for specific requirements in relation to collective redundancies). Consultation may be directly with the employees concerned or with their representatives. It should be observed that while the size of an undertaking might affect the nature or formality of the consultation, it cannot excuse lack of any consultation at all.

Mugford v Midland Bank plc [1997] IRLR 208

The EAT held that a dismissal on the grounds of redundancy was not unfair because no consultation had taken place with the employee individually, only with the recognised trade union. The EAT described the position with regard to consultation as follows: where no consultation about redundancy has taken place with either the trade union or the employee, the dismissal will normally be unfair, unless the reasonable employer would have concluded that the consultation would be an utterly futile exercise; consultation with the trade union over the selection criteria does not of itself release the employer from considering with the employee individually his or her being identified for redundancy; it will be a question of fact and degree for the tribunal to consider whether the consultation with the individual and/or the trade union was so inadequate as to render the dismissal unfair.

According to *King v Eaton Ltd* [1996], consultation must be fair and proper, which means that there must be:

- consultation when the proposals are still at a formative stage;
- adequate information and adequate time to respond;
- a conscientious consideration by the employer of the response to consultation.

Consultation about collective redundancies
✱✱✱✱✱✱✱✱✱✱✱

Although proper consultation may be regarded as a procedural matter, it might have a direct bearing on the substantive decision to select a particular employee, since a different employee might have been selected if, following proper consultation, different criteria had been adopted. It is not normally permissible for an employer to argue that a failure to consult or warn would have made no difference to the outcome in the particular case. It is what the employer did that is to be judged, not what might have been done. Nevertheless, if the employer could reasonably have concluded in the light of the circumstances known at the time of dismissal that consultation or warning would be 'utterly useless', he or she might well have acted reasonably.

It is also important to note that in *Elkouil v Coney Island Ltd* [2002] the EAT expressed the view that warning and consultation are part of the same single process of consultation, which should commence with a warning that the employee is at risk.

Consultation about collective redundancies

The provisions of Council Directive 98/59/EC on the approximation of the laws of the Member States relating to collective redundancies (the Collective Redundancies Directive) are now contained in Pt IV Ch II Trade Union and Labour Relations (Consolidation) Act 1992 (TULRCA), which outlines the procedure for handling collective redundancies. For these purposes, s 195(1) TULRCA defines a redundancy dismissal as 'for a reason not related to the individual concerned or for a number of reasons all of which are not so related'. This is different from that in redundancy payments litigation considered under 'The ERA definition of redundancy', above. In *University of Stirling v UCU* [2012], the EAT ruled that employees on fixed-term contracts were not dismissed as redundant but for reasons relating to them as individuals. In April 2013, legislation came into force making it clear that fixed-term contracts that terminate at their agreed end point will not count as redundancies for the purposes of collective consultation.

Practical example: It is clear that this definition would cover dismissals that result from a business reorganisation and not just those that fit within the ERA definition (see 'The ERA definition of redundancy').

The duty to consult rests upon an employer who is proposing to dismiss 20 or more employees at one establishment within a period of 90 days or less for reasons of redundancy (s 188). This consultation shall begin 'in good time' and in any event at least 30 days before the first dismissal takes effect, or at least 45 days before the first dismissal takes effect if the employer is proposing to dismiss 100 or more employees at one establishment within a period of 90 days. According to the EAT in *Optare Group Ltd v TGWU* [2007], the numbers include those who volunteer for redundancy; they are in effect volunteering for dismissal. A debatable issue here is at what point in time is the employer 'proposing to dismiss'. It is likely that, except perhaps in a dire situation, there is a period of time during which the decision to dismiss employees by reason of redundancy is reached. There is first the decision in principle to dismiss employees. There may be a second stage where the parts of the organisation in which the redundancies are to take place are identified, followed by a further stage when particular employees are identified.

Hough v Leyland DAF Ltd [1991] IRLR 194

A security manager was asked to prepare a report on the possibility of contracting out the security function. The issue was at what stage the employers could be said to have been proposing to dismiss. The EAT held that this occurred at the time the security manager made his report recommending the contracting out.

Article 2(1) Collective Redundancies Directive states that consultation should begin when the employer is 'contemplating' collective redundancies. In relation to a group of undertakings, the European Court of Justice (ECJ) ruled in *Akavan v Fujitsu Siemens Oy* [2009] that the obligation to consult arises when strategic decisions or changes have been adopted which compel the employer to contemplate collective redundancies. *UK Coal Mining Ltd v NUM* [2008] concerned the closing of a pit in Northumberland. The EAT held that the limitation imposed by using the word 'proposed' did not prevent consultation over the proposal to close when it would lead to redundancies. If there were not going to be redundancies, there would be no need to consult over the closure but in this case the potential job losses necessitated consultation over the reasons for the closure.

 Looking for extra marks?

You should point out that 'contemplating' is clearly not the same as 'proposing' to dismiss and explain the possible consequences of the UK taking a narrower approach than the Directive.

As a result of the ECJ decision in *Junk v Kühnel* [2005], the practice of giving notice at the same time as the consultation process started is not permissible. Indeed, the substantive part of the consultation should be completed before notice is given.

Revision tip

It is unlikely that you would have a question on collective redundancies that did not include a need to discuss when consultation should begin.

Meaning of 'establishment'

The obligation to consult rests upon 20 or more people being made redundant at one establishment.

Consultation about collective redundancies

✱✱✱✱✱✱✱✱✱✱✱

> **Rockfon A/S v Specialarbejderforbundet i Danmark Case C-449/93 [1996] IRLR 168**
>
> The ECJ considered the meaning of the word 'establishment' in this case. The Danish legal interpretation of the word was that an establishment needed a management 'which can independently effect large-scale dismissals'. The Court held that the existence of such separate management was not necessary. The term applied to the unit to which the **workers** who have been made redundant are assigned to carry out their duties.

The Court of Justice of the European Union has held that 'establishment' when dealing with a firm which closes down shops means each individual shop and not the whole business: *USDAW v WW Realisation 1* [2015], the 'Woolworths' case.

Appropriate representatives

The employer must consult with the appropriate representatives of any of the employees who may be affected by the proposed dismissals or by any measures taken in connection with those dismissals.

If an independent trade union is recognised by the employer, the appropriate representatives are the trade union representatives. If there is no such trade union, then they may be either employee representatives appointed or elected by the affected employees for some other purpose but who have authority to receive information and be consulted about the proposed dismissals, or they may be employee representatives elected by the employees for the specific purpose of redundancy consultation. The employer has the choice between these two alternatives but must ensure that consultation takes the form required by the legislation.

The consultation

The consultation should be about ways of avoiding the dismissals, reducing the number of employees to be dismissed, and mitigating the consequences of the dismissals. It is necessary for the employer to consult on each of these three aspects and not on just one or two of them. Thus, if an employer genuinely consults with employee representatives about ways of reducing the numbers involved and mitigating the consequences of the dismissals, they will still have failed in their duty if they have not also consulted about ways of avoiding the dismissals (*Middlesbrough Council v TGWU* [2002]).

There is an obligation for the employer to undertake such consultations with a view to reaching agreement with the appropriate representatives. The employer must disclose the following information in writing to the appropriate representatives (s 188(4) **TULRCA 1992**):

1. the reasons for the proposals;
2. the numbers and descriptions of employees whom it is proposed to dismiss;
3. the total number of employees of any description employed by the employer at the establishment;

4. the proposed method of selecting those to be dismissed and the proposed method of carrying out the dismissals;

5. the proposed method of calculating payments if different from those required by statute; and

6. the number of agency workers working temporarily for and under the supervision and direction of the employer; the parts of the employer's undertaking in which they are engaged; and the types of work they are carrying out.

Whether sufficient information has been given is a question of fact for the employment tribunal (ET) to decide. There is no rule to the effect that full and specific information under each of these heads should be given before consultation can begin (*MSF v GEC Ferranti (Defence Systems) Ltd* [1994]). However, in *Lancaster University v UCU* [2011], the EAT held that sending out a proposed list of redundancies to a union without the information required under s 188(4) TULRCA was a significant breach of the statute.

Special circumstances

There are two 'escape' clauses for employers unable to comply with their obligations under s 188 TULRCA:

1. where there are special circumstances which make it not reasonably practicable for an employer to comply with the consultation and information requirements, they are to take all steps towards compliance that are reasonably practicable in the circumstances;

2. where they have invited affected employees to elect representatives and the employees have failed to do so within a reasonable time, then the employer must give all the affected employees the information set out in points 1 to 6 (see 'The consultation', above).

These are not found in the **Collective Redundancies Directive**.

> **The Bakers Union v Clarks of Hove Ltd [1978] IRLR 366**
>
> The Court of Appeal held that there were three stages involved in deciding whether there was a defence in any particular case. First, were there special circumstances? Secondly, did they render compliance with the statute not reasonably practicable? Thirdly, did the employer take all the reasonable steps towards compliance as were reasonably practicable in the circumstances? In this case, insolvency was not special enough in itself to provide a defence.

'Special circumstances' means something out of the ordinary or something that is not common. In any complaint to an ET, the onus is upon the employer to show that there were special circumstances or that they took all reasonably practicable steps towards compliance (s 189(6) TULRCA).

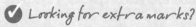

> ✅ Looking for extra marks?
>
> There is a very fine line to be drawn between consultation and negotiation. The obligation here is to consult, but when you think about the obligations placed upon employers, maybe they are really having to negotiate.

Failure to comply

Where an employer has failed to comply with the requirement to consult, a complaint may be made to an ET. If the tribunal finds the complaint well founded it will make a declaration to that effect and may make a protective award covering the protected period. This period is up to a maximum of 90 days and begins with the date on which the first dismissals take effect or the date of the award, whichever is earlier. The award will be of an amount that the tribunal decides is just and equitable (s **189 TULRCA**).

During the protective period the employees covered will receive a week's pay, subject to the statutory maximum, for each week that they would have been paid by the employer. Protective awards resulting from a claim by a trade union can only be awarded in respect of employees for whom the trade union has been recognised. Where a claim is made by an individual, an ET cannot make an award that benefits other employees (see *Independent Insurance Ltd v Aspinall* [2011]). The purpose of the award is to ensure that consultation takes place by providing a sanction against employers who fail to do so properly; in other words, the protective award is penal, not compensatory, in nature. The focus of the award is not on compensating the employees but on the seriousness of the employer's failure to comply with its statutory obligations. The employer's ability to pay is irrelevant. In addition, s **12A Employment Tribunals Act 1996 (ETA 1996)** allows ETs to impose a financial penalty on employers where there has been a breach of employment rights and the ET thinks that 'the breach has one or more aggravating features'. Normally the penalty must not be less than £100 or more than £5,000 but regard must be had to the employer's ability to pay and there is a 50% discount if payment is made within 21 days.

Calculating a redundancy payment

The size of a redundancy payment depends on the employee's length of continuous service (the minimum being two years), his or her age, and the amount of a week's pay. A week's pay is calculated in accordance with ss **220–229 ERA** and in this context means gross pay. The maximum amount of a week's pay is reviewed annually and from 6 April 2017 was £879.

> *Revision tip*
>
> Remember that, unless the contrary is shown, employment is presumed to have been continuous, but this normally only applies in relation to the dismissing employer.

According to s 162 ERA, redundancy payments are calculated according to the following formula, with a maximum of 20 years' service being taken into account. Starting at the end of the employee's period of service and calculating backwards:

- one and a half weeks' pay is allowed for each year of employment in which the individual was 41 and over;
- a week's pay for each year of employment in which the individual was between the ages of 22 and 40;
- half a week's pay for each year of employment between the ages of 18 and 21.

 Looking for extra marks?

You might point out that this method of computation discriminates directly on the grounds of age but it is still permitted.

Thus the maximum statutory redundancy payment was £14,670 in 2017 (ie 30 × £489). Additionally, where a tribunal decides that an employee is entitled to it, compensation can be provided for financial losses that are attributable to the employer's non-payment. In addition, s 12A ETA 1996 allows ETs to impose a financial penalty on employers where there has been a breach of employment rights and the ET thinks that 'the breach has one or more aggravating features'. Normally the penalty must not be less than £100 or more than £5,000 but regard must be had to the employer's ability to pay and there is a 50% discount if payment is made within 21 days.

On making a payment, the employer must give the employee a written statement indicating how the amount has been calculated. Section 165 ERA provides that an employer who, without reasonable excuse, fails to do so can receive a fine not exceeding level 3 on the standard scale, currently £1,000.

Claiming a redundancy payment

Section 164(1) ERA states that employees who have not received a redundancy payment will normally be entitled to make a claim only if within six months of the 'relevant' date (see chapter 8) they have:

- given written notice to the employer that they want a payment; or
- referred a question as to their right to a payment, or its amount, to a tribunal; or
- presented a complaint of unfair dismissal to a tribunal.

Note the six-month limitation period. Normally in employment law that period is three months. Nevertheless, if any of these steps are taken outside this period but within 12 months

Claiming a redundancy payment

****

of the relevant date, a tribunal has the discretion to award a payment if it thinks that it would be just and equitable to do so. In such a case, a tribunal must have regard to the employee's reasons for failing to take any of the steps within the normal time limit.

Figure 10.1 illustrates how a claim for redundancy payment can be progressed.

Figure 10.1 Is the person qualified to claim a redundancy payment?

Key cases

Cases	Facts	Principle
Elkouil v Coney Island Ltd [2002] IRLR 174	There was a discussion about the relationship between consulting and warning in the context of redundancy.	Warning and consultation are part of the same single process of consultation, which should commence with a warning that the employee is at risk.
Hough v Leyland DAF Ltd [1991] IRLR 194	A security manager was asked to prepare a report on the possibility of contracting out the security function.	The issue was: at what stage the employers could be said to have been proposing to dismiss? The EAT held that this occurred at the time the security manager made his report recommending the contracting out.
King v Eaton Ltd [1996] IRLR 199	The parties needed to establish what fair and proper consultation consisted of.	What is required is consultation when the proposals are still at a formative stage; adequate information and adequate time to respond; a conscientious consideration by the employer of the response to consultation.
Mugford v Midland Bank plc [1997] IRLR 208	There was a dispute about the relationship between collective and individual consultation in the context of redundancy.	Where no consultation about redundancy has taken place with either the trade union or the employee, the dismissal will normally be unfair, unless the reasonable employer would have concluded that the consultation would be an utterly futile exercise. Consultation with the trade union over the selection criteria does not of itself release the employer from considering with the employee individually his being identified for redundancy.
Murray v Foyle Meats Ltd [1999] IRLR 562	There was a dispute about the appropriate pool for selecting people for dismissal and the circumstances in which the definition of redundancy would be satisfied.	The following two questions of fact must be answered: (1) Have the requirements of the employer's business for employees to carry out work of a particular kind ceased or diminished, or were they expected to cease or diminish? (2) Was the dismissal of the employee attributable, wholly or mainly, to this state of affairs?

Key cases

****

Cases	Facts	Principle
Rockfon A/S v Specialarbejderforbundet i Danmark Case C-449/93 [1996] IRLR 168	This case considered the Danish legal interpretation of the term 'establishment', which provided that an establishment needed an independent management 'which can independently effect large-scale dismissals'.	The ECJ held that the existence of such separate management was not necessary. The term applied to the unit to which the workers who have been made redundant are assigned to carry out their duties.
The Bakers Union v Clarks of Hove Ltd [1978] IRLR 366	An insolvent employer claimed that the insolvency was a special circumstance obviating the need for consultation in connection with redundancies.	There were three stages to deciding whether there was a defence in any particular case. First, were there special circumstances; secondly, did they render compliance with the statute not reasonably practicable; and, thirdly, did the employer take all steps towards compliance as were reasonably practicable in the circumstances.
Williams v Compair Maxam [1982] IRLR 83	There was a debate about how employers should approach the issue of redundancy consultation when employees are represented by a recognised independent trade union.	Reasonable employers will seek to act as follows: (1) give as much warning as possible of impending redundancies so as to enable the union and employees who may be affected to take early steps to inform themselves of the relevant facts, consider possible alternative solutions, and, if necessary, find alternative employment in the undertaking or elsewhere; (2) consult the union as to the best means by which the desired management result can be achieved fairly and with as little hardship to the employees as possible. In particular, the employer will seek to agree with the union the criteria to be applied in selecting the employees to be made redundant. When a selection has been made, the employer will consider with the union whether the selection has been made in accordance with those criteria; (3) whether or not an agreement as to the criteria to be adopted has been agreed with the union, seek to establish criteria for selection that so far as possible do not depend solely upon the opinion of the person making the selection but can be checked objectively against such things as attendance record, efficiency at the job, or length of service.

Problem question

Florence is a lone parent who started her employment with Nightingale Ltd as a machine-minder at their Enfield factory. Within six months she was promoted to a supervisor's job at the company's Hendon factory, which was ten miles away. A year after her promotion, Florence resigned in order to have a baby. After an absence of two years she returned to work as a supervisor at Hendon, and Nightingale Ltd asked her to sign a document which stated that she must perform 'any tasks reasonably required by the company at any of their factories in North London'. Florence has just been informed that the company is to make 19 employees at the Hendon factory redundant within the next four weeks and that she has been selected for dismissal in accordance with the criterion of 'last in, first out'.

Florence now complains that for the following reasons she has been unfairly treated. First, she complains that her cumulative service with the company was greater than that of many employees who have been retained. Secondly, she argues that the company failed to consider early retirements, short-time working, or calling for volunteers as an alternative to compulsory dismissals. Finally, she claims that since, at the time of dismissal, the company had a vacancy for a supervisor at Enfield she was contractually entitled to be offered employment there.

Advise Florence as to her legal rights.

See the Outline answers section in the end matter for help with this question.

Essay question

To what extent do the statutory provisions on redundancy fairly balance the employer's need for flexibility and an employee's desire for job security?

Discuss.

To see an outline answer to this question log on to www.oup.com/lawrevision/

Concentrate Q&As

For more questions and answers on employment law, see the *Concentrate Q&A: Employment Law* by Roseanne Russell.

Go to the end of this book to view **sample pages**.

#11
Continuity of employment and TUPE

- An employee's period of continuous employment begins on the day on which the employee starts work.

- Any week during the whole or part of which an employee's relations with his employer are governed by a contract of employment counts towards continuity of employment.

- The **Transfer of Undertakings (Protection of Employment) Regulations 2006 (TUPE) (SI 2006/246)** took effect in 2006 and were amended in 2014. They implemented the **Acquired Rights Directive (2001/23/EC)** in the UK. The original Directive dates from 1977 and it was implemented in the UK by Regulations originally dating from 1981.

- A relevant transfer takes place, first, where there is a transfer of an economic entity that retains its identity, and, secondly, where there is a service provision change.

- **Regulation 4(1) TUPE** provides that, except where an objection is made, a relevant transfer shall not operate to terminate any contract of employment of any person employed by the transferor for a reason connected to the transfer.

- The Regulations ensure that an individual's contract of employment will transfer from the transferor employer to the transferee employer when a relevant transfer takes place.

Continuity of employment

Continuity of employment is important as a number of statutory rights, such as the right to be protected from unfair dismissal, redundancy payments, and the right to receive written reasons for a dismissal, depend upon having continuous employment with an employer.

 Looking for extra marks?

It is not likely that you will be presented with a question just on continuity of employment. It is far more probable that it could be included as part of another question. One way of gaining extra marks when dealing with a question on transfers and continuity under TUPE is to also be able to state that there are other situations where continuity of employment can be preserved.

An **employee**'s period of continuous employment begins on the day on which the employee starts work.

General of the Salvation Army v Dewsbury [1984] IRLR 222

A part-time teacher took on a new full-time contract which stated that her employment began on 1 May. As 1 May was a Saturday and the following Monday was a bank holiday, she did not actually commence her duties until the Tuesday, 4 May. She was subsequently dismissed with effect from 1 May in the following year. The issue was whether she had one year's continuous employment required at that time to bring a claim of unfair dismissal. (The qualifying period for this right is now two years.) The Employment Appeal Tribunal (EAT) held that the day on which an employee starts work is intended to refer to the beginning of the employee's employment under the relevant **contract of employment** and that this may be different from the actual date on which work commences.

There is a presumption that an individual's period of employment is continuous, unless otherwise shown (s 210(5) Employment Rights Act 1996 (ERA)). Section 212(1) ERA states that 'any week during the whole or part of which an employee's relations with his employer are governed by a contract of employment counts in computing the employee's period of employment'.

Sweeney v J & S Henderson [1999] IRLR 306

An employee resigned from his employment on a Saturday and left immediately to take up another post. The individual regretted the decision and returned to the original employer the following Friday, to recommence work. The employee was held to have continuity of employment as a result of there not being a week in which the contract of employment did not apply. This was despite the fact that the employee worked for another employer during the intervening period. The employee worked under a contract of employment with the employer during each of the two weeks in question and thus fulfilled the requirements of **s 212(1) ERA**.

A week is defined in **s 235(1) ERA** as a week ending with Saturday or, for a weekly paid employee, a week ends with the day used in calculating the week's remuneration. Thus, if a contract of employment exists in any one week, using these formulae, then that week counts for continuity purposes.

Continuity and absences from work

Absence from work means not performing in substance the contract that previously existed between the parties. There are a number of reasons for which a person can be absent from work without breaking their statutory continuity of employment. These are the following.

1. If the employee is incapable of work as a result of sickness or injury (s 212 ERA).

Absences of no more than 26 weeks under this category will not be held to break continuity. In *Donnelly v Kelvin International Services* [1992], an employee who resigned on the grounds of ill-health, but was then re-employed some five weeks later, was held to have continuity even though they had worked for another employer during the period. There needs, however, to be a causal relationship between the absence and the incapacity for work in consequence of sickness or injury;

2. If there is a temporary **cessation of work**.

According to s 212(3)(b) ERA, absence from work on account of a temporary cessation of work will not break continuity of employment. The word 'temporary' indicates a period of time that is of relatively short duration when compared to the periods of work.

Thus, seasonal **workers** who were out of work each year for longer than they actually worked could not be considered to have continuity of employment, as in *Berwick Salmon Fisheries Co Ltd v Rutherford* [1991]. Other seasonal workers who were regularly out of work for long periods were in the same position, even though, at the beginning of the next season, it was the intention of both parties that they should resume employment. In contrast, an academic who was employed on regular fixed-term contracts to teach was held to have continuity, even though the individual was not employed during August and September each year. During this time the employee prepared for the coming year's teaching and the EAT decided that this amounted to a temporary cessation of work (*University of Aston v Malik* [1984]).

3. Absence from work in circumstances that, by custom or arrangement, the employee 'is regarded as continuing in the employment of his employer for any purposes'.

***Booth v United States of America* [1999] IRLR 16**

The employees were employed on a series of fixed-term contracts with a gap of about two weeks between each contract. On each return to work they were given the same employee number, the same tools and equipment, and the same lockers. Despite the employees arguing that this arrangement was designed to defeat the underlying purpose of the legislation, the EAT could not find an arrangement that would require, in advance of the break, some discussion and agreement that continuity could be preserved. It was clear that the employers did not want such an arrangement. Neither is it likely that an agreement made subsequent to the absence could be used to preserve continuity.

Section 212(3)(c) ERA envisages the arrangement being in place when the employee is absent, so an agreement between an employer and an employee that a break in work would not affect continuity could not be supported because it was made after the employee's return, as in *Morris v Walsh Western UK Ltd* [1997].

Revision tip

It is unlikely that you would be asked a question about continuity of employment without being asked about exceptions; so remember these.

Continuity and industrial disputes

A week does not count for the purposes of computing continuity of service if during that week, or any part of it, the employee takes part in a strike (s 216 ERA). In contrast, periods when the employee is subject to a lock-out do count for continuity purposes. However, in neither case is continuity itself broken.

Continuity and change of employer

Although the continuity provisions normally apply to employment by one employer (s 218 ERA), there are situations where a transfer from one employer to another can preserve continuity of employment. One such situation is when there is a relevant transfer under TUPE (see 'Transfer of undertakings', the next topic).

Where the trade, business, or undertaking is transferred to a new employer, then continuity is also preserved by s 218(2) ERA.

Transfers of undertakings

What happens in law to employees when one company is taken over by another? The effect of TUPE in this situation is discussed next. TUPE requires, however, a change of employer. This means that if on a takeover the employer does not change, as is the case when the first company's shares are acquired by the second one, then the discussion below does not apply. In the UK, shares sales are the usual way of acquiring companies.

The meaning of a transfer of an undertaking

Essentially, TUPE acts to ensure that an individual's contract of employment is transferred in its entirety when the individual employee experiences a change of employer as a result of a transfer. The Regulations also provide that any dismissal for a reason in connection with a transfer will be an automatically unfair dismissal, unless the dismissal is for an 'economic, technological, or organisational reason'.

Transfers of undertakings

✶✶✶✶✶✶✶✶✶✶

Practical example: Favouriterecruits is an employment agency that has a temp division and a permanent placement division. It decides that it does not want to place temps any more and so sells its temp business to another agency, Tempsthebest. This is likely to be a transfer of an undertaking as the temp division has transferred from one agency to another. As a result of TUPE, all the contracts of employment of the employees in the temp division of Favouriterecruits automatically transfer to Tempsthebest.

Regulation 3(1)(a) TUPE states that the Regulations apply, first, to a transfer where there is a transfer of an **economic entity** that retains its identity, and, secondly, to a service provision change. The latter is a UK concept, one not derived from EU law. An economic entity is defined in reg 3(2) as 'an organised grouping of resources which has the objective of pursuing an economic activity, whether or not that activity is central or ancillary'.

 Looking for extra marks?

Does it seem strange that we have a law that ensures that the contracts of employment are preserved for employees who are in a transfer situation? How did such a law come about? For the answer we have to go back to a previous Directive, dealing with the same subject matter, adopted in 1977. One of its purposes was to help with the management of change. Employees, it was reasoned, would be more likely to accept change if their own position was preserved.

There have been many cases in the UK courts and the Court of Justice of the European Union that have resulted in this definition.

Spijkers v Gebroeders Benedik Abattoir CV Case 24/85 [1986] ECR 1119

The European Court of Justice (ECJ) looked at the purpose of the Acquired Rights Directive and concluded that its aim was to ensure the continuity of existing employment relationships. Thus, if the operation that is transferred is an identifiable entity before and after the transfer, then a relevant transfer is likely to have taken place. One needs to look at the situation before the transfer and identify an economic entity and then after the transfer to consider whether the economic entity has retained its identity.

The ECJ in *Spijkers* gave further guidance as to factors that would help in the decision as to whether a transfer had taken place. It was necessary to take all the factual circumstances of the transaction into account, including:

1. the type of undertaking or business in question;
2. the transfer or otherwise of tangible assets such as buildings and stocks;
3. the value of intangible assets at the date of transfer;
4. whether the majority of staff are taken over by the new employer;
5. the transfer or otherwise of customers;

6. the degree of similarity between activities before and after the transfer;

7. the duration of any interruption in those activities.

The Court stated that each of these factors was only part of the assessment. One had to examine what existed before the transfer and then examine the entity after the change in order to decide whether the operation was continued, but these factors might help that consideration.

Revision tip

Spijkers is an important case. It has been cited in many subsequent cases concerning the Directive.

In *Süzen* [1997], the ECJ distinguished between the transfer of an entity and the transfer of an activity. It concerned a school cleaning operation which transferred to a new contractor. On the face of it, there was a relevant transfer because the entity appeared to retain its identity, as evidenced by its continuation and resumption. The ECJ, however, stated that an entity could not be reduced to the activity entrusted to it. Thus the Court distinguished between an entity that transferred and an activity that transferred. An entity, according to the Court, was *an organised grouping of persons or assets facilitating the exercise of an economic activity which pursues a specific objective*. There has, therefore, to be something else, other than the activity taking place, that needs to transfer, such as assets or 'an organised grouping' of people. Without these, there appeared to be only the transfer of an activity.

Another area of controversy for the Regulations has been whether they applied to outsourcing, the contracting-out of services. There are some good examples of this contained in some of the cases.

Kenny v South Manchester College [1993] IRLR 265

This case concerned the provision of education services at a young offenders' institution. After a tendering exercise the contract was won by South Manchester College. The question was whether the undertaking had retained its identity. The High Court stated that 'the prisoners and young offenders who attend, say, a carpentry class next Thursday will, save those released from the institution, be likely in the main to be the same as those who attended the same class in the same classroom the day before and will doubtless be using exactly the same tools and machinery'.

Regulation 3(1)(b) provides that the Regulations apply to a service provision change. These are relevant to outsourcing situations and are meant to ensure a wide coverage of the Regulations. This law is not found in the Directive. Therefore, there may be a **service provision change** (SPC) for the purposes of English law but no transfer within the Directive.

An SPC takes place when a person (client) first contracts out some part of its activities to a contractor; when such a contract is taken over by another contractor (so-called second generation transfers); and when the client takes back the activity in-house from a contractor. Under a 2014 amendment, for the SPC provisions to apply the new activities must be 'fundamentally the same as the activities carried out previously'. According to *Metropolitan Resources Ltd v Churchill Dulwich Ltd* [2009], SPCs are different from transfers under TUPE and merely require a decision on whether one of these three categories of change have happened. There is no need to go through the same process as deciding whether or not a TUPE transfer has occurred. Where a transfer between contractors does take place, however, the work still needs to be done for the same client. Transferring from one contractor to another and working for a different client does not constitute an SPC as in *Hunter v McCarrick* [2012].

Who is to be transferred?

Regulation 4(1) TUPE provides that, except where an objection is made, a relevant transfer shall not operate to terminate any contract of employment of any person employed by the **transferor employer** and assigned to the 'organised grouping of resources or employees that is subject to the relevant transfer'. An 'organised grouping' may consist of one person: *Rynda (UK) Ltd v Rhijnsburger* [2015] (CA).

One problem that has occurred is in deciding who works for the part transferred, when only part of an organisation is transferred to a new employer.

Practical example: If a business decides to contract out its non-core activities and only retain those parts of the business that are concerned with its primary activities, or if only a part of the business is sold off, there are likely to be a number of employees, such as those in Human Resources, who work in the parts remaining, but whose jobs consisted of servicing those parts transferred. This may be the entire content of their jobs or only a part. If such staff remain with the transferor organisation, they may be faced with the loss of their jobs or, at the very least, a significant change in their job activities. The question then is whether these support staff have the right to also transfer.

It was in the case of *Arie Botzen v Rotterdamsche Droogdok Maatschappij BV* [1986] that the ECJ first devised the assignment test to deal with such situations. The Advocate General in the case proposed a test for deciding who should be transferred if only a part of a business was sold off. He said that 'a basic working test, it seems to me, is to ask whether, if that part of the business had been separately owned before the transfer, the worker would have been employed by the owners of that part or the owners of the remaining part'. Some people, of course, would not have been employed in either part if they were separately owned. It may have been because the whole was a certain size that they were employed. This may be especially true of HR departments, as bigger organisations can perhaps have the capacity to employ more specialists, whereas a smaller organisation might demand more generalist abilities. The ECJ held that 'An employment relationship is essentially characterised by the link existing between the employee and the part of the undertaking or business to which he is assigned to carry out his duties'. All that is needed therefore is to establish to which part of the business or undertaking the individual is assigned.

Revision tip

There have been a number of cases in the UK courts where the question of the assignment test has arisen, in particular *Duncan Web Offset (Maidstone) Ltd v Cooper* [1995] and *Michael Peters Ltd v Farnfield* [1995]. In *BT Managed Services v Edwards* [2015], it was held that where an employee is permanently unable to return to work but is still on the books, she is not 'assigned' to an organised grouping. It is otherwise where she is on long-term sick leave but will come back in time.

Regulation 4(3) TUPE also provides that it is only persons employed immediately before the transfer, or who would have been had they not been unfairly dismissed, who are protected, as well as being assigned to such an organised grouping.

> **Litster v Forth Dry Dock & Engineering Co Ltd** [1989] IRLR 161
>
> The receiver of an insolvent company dismissed the entire workforce just one hour before the transfer of the business to a new undertaking. The new undertaking (the **transferee employer**) denied any liability under **TUPE** as there were no employees at the actual time of the transfer. The House of Lords held that not only did the Regulations apply to someone employed immediately before the transfer, but also applied to those who would have been so employed if they had not been unfairly dismissed for a reason connected to the transfer.

Employee choice

Regulation 4(7) TUPE ensures that an employee is not transferred if he or she objects to being so transferred. The result, however, according to **reg 4(8)** is that the employee is then in a 'no man's land'; they have not been transferred, but the transferor cannot be treated as having dismissed the employee. This, and the question of how an employee is to object, was considered in *Hay v George Hanson* [1996]. The EAT held that it was a matter for the employment tribunal in each individual case. If the employee did not know about the transfer until after the event, because there had been no consultation with them, then he or she would still be able to object, as in *New ISG Ltd v Vernon* [2008].

Insolvency

One of the issues, before **TUPE** were amended in 2006, was the obligation for the transferee enterprise to take over all the debts in relation to an insolvent organisation's employees during **relevant insolvency proceedings** and, indeed, to transfer all those employees on their current terms and conditions. It was believed that this would act as a disincentive to the rescue of such enterprises.

Transfers of undertakings

✲✲✲✲✲✲✲✲✲✲✲✲

> **Abels v Administrative Board Case 135/83 [1987] 2 CMLR 406**
>
> The ECJ tried to distinguish between different types of insolvency proceedings in deciding the applicability of the Directive. Mr Abels worked for a company that became insolvent and he and other staff were laid off. The liquidator eventually sold the business to another company who re-employed Mr Abels and others, but did not pay them for the time that they had been laid off. Mr Abels claimed that it was a transfer of an undertaking and that their contracts should have automatically passed to the buyer of the business. If this had happened, then they would have been entitled to continuing pay. The outcome of the case was that the Court distinguished between those situations when the insolvency proceedings were aimed at liquidation of the assets and those situations when the aim, at an earlier stage, was to rescue the business.

TUPE deals with this issue in regs 8 and 9. The outcome is that those elements that the government would normally be responsible for under its statutory obligations towards the employees of insolvent employers do not transfer. The debts owed to employees by the transferor, to the limits of its statutory obligations, will be guaranteed by the Secretary of State. This includes some arrears of pay, notice periods, holiday pay, and any basic award for unfair dismissal compensation under Pt XII ERA. Other debts owed to employees will transfer: see *Secretary of State v Slater* [2008].

In addition to this, there is provision in reg 9 for the employer and employee representatives to agree 'permitted variations' to their contracts of employment. Permitted variations are those that are not due to economic, technical, or organisational reasons entailing a change in the workforce and are designed to safeguard employment opportunities by ensuring the survival of the undertaking (reg 9(7)).

Revision tip

It is very easy to become overwhelmed by the complexity of TUPE. One way of managing this is to deal with each issue in turn—What is meant by a transfer? How is outsourcing affected by them? Who is protected? Do employees have to transfer? What happens if the transferor company is insolvent? And so on.

It is also difficult to dismiss employees in anticipation of achieving a sale. In *Spaceright Europe Ltd v Baillavoine* [2011], the managing director had been dismissed to reduce costs and help achieve a sale, but his dismissal was held to be connected to the transfer thus making it automatically unfair.

Information and consultation

Regulations 13–15 TUPE provide the obligation to inform and consult employees. This includes the possibility of joint liability between the transferor and the transferee for any compensation awarded as a result of a failure to inform and consult (reg 15(8) and (9)).

According to **reg 13(2)**, information should be provided 'long enough before a relevant transfer to enable the employer of any affected employees to consult all the persons who are appropriate representatives of any of those affected employees'.

Institution of Professional and Civil Servants v Secretary of State for Defence [1987] IRLR 373

The High Court decided that the words 'long enough before' a transfer to enable consultation to take place meant as soon as measures are envisaged and *if possible* long enough before the transfer.

The information to be provided should consist of:

1. the fact that a relevant transfer is to take place, approximately when it is to take place, and the reasons for it;
2. the legal, economic, and social implications for the affected employees;
3. the measures that are envisaged to take place in connection with the transfer, in relation to the affected employees or the fact that there are no such measures envisaged.

In *Cable Realisations Ltd v GMB Northern* [2010], the employer appeared to provide the information long enough before a transfer, but two days afterwards there was a factory shutdown during which much of the workforce was away on holiday. As a result, there was not an opportunity to consult on the information provided. This was held to be a breach of **reg 13(2)**. The rules on who are appropriate representatives and the requirements are identical to those rules concerning the appointment of appropriate representatives for the purposes of consultation in collective redundancies. The representatives are the **independent trade union** that is recognised by the employer. If there is no such trade union, then they are employee representatives to be elected or appointed by the affected employees, whether for the purpose of these consultations or for some other purpose. If no employee representatives are elected, something that might happen in small organisations, as in *Todd v Strain* [2011], then there is an obligation to inform the employees individually. From May 2014, where the employers have fewer than ten employees and there is no recognised independent trade union, **TUPE**, as expressly amended, states that consultation may be with the individual employees. As with situations of collective redundancies, there is a special circumstances defence for the employer if it is not reasonably practicable to perform the duty to consult and inform. In such a case, the employer must take all such steps as are reasonable in the circumstances.

Key cases

Cases	Facts	Principle
Abels v Administrative Board Case 135/83 [1987] 2 CMLR 406	Mr Abels worked for a company that became insolvent and he and other staff were laid off. The liquidator eventually sold the business to another company who re-employed Mr Abels and others, but did not pay them for the time that they had been laid off.	The ECJ distinguished between those situations when the insolvency proceedings were aimed at liquidation of the assets and those situations when the aim, at an earlier stage, was to rescue the business.
Litster v Forth Dry Dock and Engineering Co Ltd [1989] IRLR 161	The receiver of an insolvent company dismissed the entire workforce just one hour before the transfer of the business to a new undertaking. The new undertaking (the transferee) denied any liability under **TUPE** as there were no employees at the actual time of the transfer.	Not only did the Regulations apply to someone employed immediately before the transfer, but also applied to those who would have been so employed if they had not been unfairly dismissed for a reason connected to the transfer.
Spijkers v Gebroeders Benedik Abattoir Case 24/85 [1986] ECR 1119	The question was whether a change in the management of an abattoir constituted a transfer of an undertaking. One needs to look at the situation before the transfer and identify an economic entity, then after the transfer to consider whether the economic entity has retained its identity.	Not only did the Regulations apply to someone employed immediately before the transfer, but they also applied to those who would have been so employed if they had not been unfairly dismissed for a reason connected to the transfer.
Süzen v Zehnacker Gebäudereinigung Case 13/95 [1997] IRLR 255	The question was whether the transfer of a school cleaning operation amounted to a transfer of an undertaking.	The ECJ distinguished between the transfer of an entity and the transfer of an activity.
Sweeney v J & S Henderson [1999] IRLR 306	An employee resigned from his employment on a Saturday and left immediately to take up another post. The individual returned to the original employer the following Friday, to recommence work.	The employee had continuity of employment as a result of there not being a week in which the contract of employment did not apply.

Problem question

Terri, Teresa, and Tom are three employees of Highbury Farms Ltd. They all started work for the company on the same day, just over one year ago. Each of them has been dismissed and wants to know if they have a claim for unfair dismissal against the employer, Highbury Farms Ltd. Remember that two years' continuous employment is required before an employee may make a complaint of unfair dismissal.

Terri has suffered a period of illness and was absent for two periods: once for six weeks and once for 13 weeks. Highbury Farms dismissed her at the end of the second period. The illnesses were not as a result of a disability.

Teresa was employed during harvest time. This was for a period of some months during the summer and a short time during the autumn. The company stated that she was just a casual worker and was under no obligation to re-employ her the following year.

Tom was farm manager of one of the company's farms, which has been sold on, and he was made redundant at the time of the sale.

See the Outline answers section in the end matter for help with this question.

Essay question

How does **TUPE** protect employees in the event of a transfer of an undertaking?

To see an outline answer to this question log on to www.oup.com/lawrevision/

Concentrate Q&As

For more questions and answers on employment law, see the *Concentrate Q&A: Employment Law* by Roseanne Russell.

Go to the end of this book to view **sample pages**.

#12

Trade unions: recognition, collective bargaining, and industrial action

Key facts

- The Certification Officer among other mattes decides whether a trade union is entitled to be treated as independent.

- An independent trade union needs to be recognised by the employer in order to enjoy a number of important statutory rights.

- Employers have a duty to disclose to trade unions recognised for collective bargaining purposes information without which they would be impeded in carrying out collective bargaining.

- It is unlawful to dismiss or subject to detriment someone for the purpose of preventing them from joining, or taking part in the activities of, a trade union.

- Statutory immunity is given only to industrial action taken in contemplation or furtherance of a trade dispute.

Independence and recognition

An official called the **Certification Officer** maintains a list of trade unions. (The Certification has a number of functions and the officer's powers have been expanded by the **Trade Union Act 2016**, a statute which changes the Officer's role and led to the resignation of the then Certification Officer.) A trade union whose name is on the list can apply to the Certification Officer for a certificate that it is independent. The Certification Officer is responsible for keeping a record of all applications and must decide whether the applicant union is independent or not.

Section 5 Trade Union and Labour Relations (Consolidation) Act 1992 (TULRCA) deems a trade union to be independent if it is not under the domination or control of an employer or a group of employers or of one or more employers' associations; and it is not liable to interference by an employer or any such group or association, arising out of the provision of financial or material support or by any other means whatsoever, tending towards such control.

Over the years, certain criteria have evolved for assessing whether a union is under the domination or control of an employer.

A Monk Staff Association v Certification Officer and ASTMS [1980] IRLR 431

The Employment Appeal Tribunal (EAT) confirmed that matters such as the union's history, its organisation and structure, its finances, and the extent of employer-provided facilities were relevant. The Court of Appeal has also ruled that the Certification Officer is not required to assess the likelihood of interference by the employer. The degree of risk is irrelevant so long as it is recognisable and not insignificant.

There are some important advantages for trade unions that are 'independent'. If recognised by the employer they have the right to appoint safety representatives, their representatives are entitled to receive information for collective bargaining purposes (see 'Disclosure of information for collective bargaining') and may be consulted in respect of redundancies and transfers of undertakings (see chapter 11, 'Information and consultation'). Their officials can take time off for union activities.

These rights accrue only if the employer recognises the trade union. There is a statutory definition of **recognition** contained in s 178(3) TULRCA. (This definition does not apply to statutory recognition.) Collective bargaining means negotiations relating to or connected with one or more of the matters specified in s 178(2) TULRCA. Although the question of recognition is one of fact for a court or employment tribunal to decide, it is likely that there must be an express or implied agreement between the union and the employer to negotiate on one or more of the matters listed. For agreement to be implied there must be clear and unequivocal conduct over a period of time. Thus, a discussion on **wages** that took place on a particular occasion was held to be insufficient to establish recognition, particularly when the employer's attitude was one of refusing to bargain (see *NUGSAT v Albury Bros* [1978]).

****

It is also possible for a trade union to claim a statutory right to recognition by the employer. The rules are contained in Sch A1 TULRCA. Statutory recognition covers only 'pay, hours, and holidays', a phrase which includes rostering (*BALPA v Jet2.com* [2017]) but excludes pensions. This definition is much narrower than that for voluntary recognition, and indeed the statutory scheme is aimed at encouraging voluntary recognition.

 Looking for extra marks?

Although this procedure enables a trade union to compel an employer to recognise a trade union for specific purposes, it has only been used sparingly. This is because some employers agreed to recognition in anticipation of the union being successful in its claim and also because a voluntary agreement is more likely to be of benefit to both sides than an imposed one.

The Trade Union Act 2016 affects the functions of the Certification Officer but not in relation to the above.

The legal enforceability of collective agreements

A **collective agreement** is defined in s 185 TULRCA as any agreement or arrangement made by, or on behalf of, one or more trade unions and one or more employers, or employers' associations, which relates to one or more of the matters mentioned in s 178(2) TULRCA.

A collective agreement is conclusively presumed not to have been intended by the parties to be a legally enforceable contract unless the agreement is in writing and contains a provision that states that the parties intend the agreement to be a legally enforceable contract (s 179 TULRCA), or the agreement has been specified by the Central Arbitration Committee (CAC), as a result of the statutory recognition procedures. Equally, the parties may declare that one or more parts only of an agreement are intended to be legally enforceable.

Disclosure of information for collective bargaining

For the purposes of all the stages of collective bargaining between employers and representatives of recognised **independent trade unions**, employers have a duty to disclose to those representatives, on request, all such information relating to their undertakings as is in their possession or that of any associated employer, which is both (s 181 TULRCA) information without which the union representatives would be to a material extent impeded in carrying on such collective bargaining and information that it would be in accordance with good industrial relations practice that they should disclose.

An employer can insist that a request for information must be made in writing, and likewise the information itself must be in written form, if that is the wish of the union representatives.

The information can be sought in order to prepare a claim, although it must relate to matters in respect of which the union is recognised.

✳✳✳✳✳✳✳✳✳✳✳

> **R v CAC, ex parte BTP Tioxide [1982] IRLR 61**
>
> The High Court held that the union was entitled to information relating to a job evaluation scheme in respect of which it had no bargaining rights but only the right to represent its members in re-evaluation appeals. Essentially, for information to be disclosed under these provisions it must be both relevant and important. Although each case must be judged on its merits, unions may be entitled to information about groups not covered for collective bargaining purposes.

Attention needs to be given to the **ACAS Code of Practice on Disclosure of Information to Trade Unions for Collective Bargaining Purposes 2003**. To decide what information is relevant, negotiators are advised to take account of the subject matter of the negotiations and the issues raised during them, the level at which negotiations take place, the size of the company, and its type of business.

The duty to disclose is subject to the exceptions detailed in s 182 TULRCA. Employers are not required to disclose information:

- the disclosure of which would be against the interests of national security;

- that could not be disclosed without contravening other legislation;

- that has been communicated to the employer in confidence;

- relating specifically to an individual unless he or she has consented to its disclosure;

- the disclosure of which would cause substantial injury to the employer's undertaking for reasons other than its effect on collective bargaining;

- obtained by the employer for the purpose of bringing or defending any legal proceedings.

Section 182(2) TULRCA provides that employers are not obliged to produce, allow inspection of, or copy, any document other than a document conveying or confirming the information disclosed, and are not required to compile any information where to do so would involve an amount of work or expenditure out of reasonable proportion to the value of the information in the conduct of collective bargaining.

A union that feels that its representatives have not received the information to which they are entitled can complain to the CAC. If the complaint is upheld, the declaration will specify the information in respect of which the CAC believed the complaint to be well founded, the date on which the employer refused or failed to disclose information, and the period within which the employer ought to disclose the information specified (s 183 TULRCA). If the employer still does not cooperate then the CAC, after hearing the parties, awards the terms and conditions detailed in the claim or others that it considers appropriate. Such an award will relate only to matters in respect of which the trade union is recognised. The terms and conditions awarded take effect as part of the **contracts of employment** of the **employees** covered.

****

 Looking for extra marks?

The provisions concerning the obligation of the employer to provide information are very weak. It is interesting that all through the period when legislation weakening trade unions was being adopted in the 1980s and 1990s, these provisions were left untouched.

Protection for trade unionists

Section 137(1) TULRCA makes it unlawful to refuse employment to people because they are or are not members of a trade union, or because they refuse to accept a requirement that they become a member or cease to be a member, or to impose a requirement that they suffer deductions if they fail to join.

With regard to job advertisements, if one indicates, or might reasonably be understood as indicating, that employment is open only to people who are or are not union members, then if people who do not meet the relevant condition are refused employment, it will be conclusively presumed that this was because they failed to satisfy the condition.

Section 138 makes it unlawful for an agency that finds employment for **workers**, or supplies employers with workers, to refuse its services to people because they are or are not union members or are unwilling to accept a condition or requirement of the type mentioned in s 137(1)(b). The provisions relating to advertisements also apply to such agencies. A complaint about the infringement of these provisions must normally be presented to an employment tribunal within three months of the date of the conduct complained about.

Provision is made for conciliation, but if a complaint is upheld, the tribunal must make a declaration to that effect and may make an order obliging the respondent to pay compensation, which is to be assessed on the same basis as damages for the tort of breach of statutory duty and may include damages for injury to feelings.

Section 146 TULRCA gives employees the right not to be subjected to any detriment as an individual by any act, or any deliberate failure to act, by an employer if the act or failure takes place for the purpose of preventing or deterring them from being or seeking to become members, or taking part in the activities, of an independent trade union or penalising them for doing so. Section 152 also makes a dismissal unfair if the reason was that the employee was or proposed to become a member of an independent trade union or take part in its activities.

Industrial action

The statutory immunity in tort for various types of industrial action depends on that action taking place *in contemplation or furtherance of a trade dispute*. This is the so-called 'golden formula'. So long as the action taken is in contemplation or furtherance of a trade dispute, the TULRCA immunities apply irrespective of whether or not the action is in breach of a disputes procedure.

However, if the 'golden formula' does not apply, it will be relatively easy for an employer to show that at least one of the economic torts is being committed, and to obtain an interim injunction on that basis.

Revision tip

Industrial action taken in contemplation or furtherance of a trade dispute is provided with immunity from action in tort. You should point out that the most common torts are likely to be inducing a breach of contract, interference with a contract or business, intimidation, and conspiracy. Torts other than the economic torts do not fall within this law and therefore unions are liable for these torts used when the golden formula applies.

Section 244 TULRCA defines a **trade dispute** as a dispute between workers and their employer that relates wholly or mainly to one or more of the following:

- terms and conditions of employment, or the physical conditions in which any workers are required to work;
- engagement or non-engagement, or termination or suspension of employment, or the duties of employment of one or more workers;
- allocation of work or the duties of employment as between workers or groups of workers;
- matters of discipline;
- the membership or non-membership of a trade union on the part of a worker;
- facilities for officials of trade unions; and
- the machinery for negotiation or consultation and other procedures relating to any of the foregoing matters, including the recognition by employers or employers' associations of the right of a trade union to represent workers in any such negotiation, or consultation, or in the carrying out of such procedures.

University College London Hospital NHS Trust v UNISON [1999] IRLR 31

The union gained an overwhelming majority in favour of strike action in support of a demand for employment guarantees associated with the building of a new hospital under the Private Finance Initiative (PFI). This would have involved the transfer of some workers to a new employer. The Court of Appeal held that the dispute was about terms and conditions that would apply to workers not currently employed by the NHS Trust and that such a dispute about future employment with a new employer was outside the provisions of **s 244**.

A 'worker' is defined to cover only those employed by the employer in dispute. The word 'contemplation' refers to something imminent or likely to occur, so the 'golden formula' cannot be invoked if the action was taken too far in advance of any dispute. 'Furtherance' assumes the existence of a dispute and an act will not be protected if it is not for the purpose of promoting the interests of a party to the dispute (eg if it is in pursuit of a personal vendetta) or occurs after its conclusion.

McShane v Express Newspapers [1980] IRLR 35

The House of Lords held that while the existence of a trade dispute had to be determined objectively, the test for deciding whether an act is in furtherance of such a dispute is a subjective one: 'If the person doing the act honestly thinks at the time he does it that it may help one of the parties to the dispute to achieve their objective and does it for that reason, he is protected' (per Lord Scarman).

Apparently there is no requirement that a union should act exclusively in furtherance of a trade dispute; it is sufficient if the furtherance of a trade dispute is one of its purposes.

Ballots and notice of industrial action

Trade unions and their officials can benefit from immunity provided by s 219 TULRCA only if the union has authorised or endorsed the industrial action, having gained majority support in a ballot of the members concerned not more than four weeks before the start of the action. Industrial action in favour of other workers, often called 'sympathy strikes' or 'secondary action', such as non-NHS unions calling out members in support of striking nurses, is illegal. That illegality has been upheld by the European Court of Human Rights: *National Union of Rail, Maritime and Transport Workers v UK* [2014]. The Court held that while freedom of association is the subject of and protected by Art 11 European Convention on Human Rights, the government had a defence, a legitimate aim, within Art 11(2), protection of the rights and freedoms of others. Sympathy strikes can impinge on the rights of those not involved in the dispute and can cause disruption to the economy and disrupt services to the public. The Court also held that the ban was necessary in a democratic society within the words in Art 11(2). These strikes were not core union activities; because they were only ancillary, the state had a wide margin of appreciation to regulate unions' conduct in this regard. National parliaments were in a better position than the Court in respect of determining whether such action should be lawful. The ban on secondary action had lasted for 20 or more years, and it had endured through several governments of various hues. Therefore, the consensus in the UK was that such action should remain unlawful.

For s 219 TULRCA immunity to be available, a number of detailed requirements must be met. These include the trade union sending out a notice of a ballot to its members; providing the employer with certain information about its membership and a sample of the ballot paper; sending out a ballot paper that will contain a statement specified in s 229 TULRCA, which warns the voter that taking part in a strike or other industrial action may be in breach of the contract of employment. It also, however, tells the voter that if he or she is dismissed for taking part in a strike or other industrial action that is called officially and is otherwise lawful, the dismissal will be unfair if it takes place less than eight weeks after he or she started taking part in the action, and depending on the circumstances may be unfair if it takes place later. The Trade Union Act 2016 added requirements that the union gives 14 days' notice of industrial action (unless the parties agree on seven days' notice), the union tells the employer which type of action will take place, the union notifies the employer whether the action will be continuous or discontinuous, and the union informs the employers which groups of workers and their location are being called on to take the action.

Members are also invited to vote for industrial action or action short of a strike. Industrial action will not be regarded as having the support of a ballot if a member who was likely to be induced into taking part in the action was not accorded the right to vote. As soon as is reasonably practicable after the ballot, the union must take such steps as are reasonably necessary to ensure that all those entitled to vote and every relevant employer are informed of the number of votes cast, the numbers voting 'yes' and those voting 'no', and the number of spoiled ballot papers. If there is a failure to inform one or more relevant employers, the ballot and subsequent action will still be valid in relation to the other employers who were informed correctly (ss 231–231A TULRCA). After this, the union must provide written notice to the employer of the industrial action to be taken and when. In the first High Court case on this point after the Trade Union Act 2016 came into force on 1 March 2017, *Thomas Cook Airlines Ltd v. British Airline Pilots Association* [2017], Lavender J held that the ballot paper need only relate to the periods during which industrial action may take place and need not specify the dates when such action will take place. The Act reduces the period at the end of which the ballot loses its effect to six months but the union can put that six-month period on the ballot. This decision provides the parties to the dispute with the flexibility they need to come to a settlement.

Unions have for a long time complained that the law restricts ballots to ones conducted via the post, arguing that electronic ballots are faster and cheaper to run than postal ones as well as producing higher turnouts. During debates on the Trade Union Act 2016, the government agreed under pressure to institute a review of such balloting. It could hardly do otherwise when, for example, ballots within the Conservative Party, including votes for the leader, are conducted electronically. The review under Sir Ken Knight was published in December 2017. It proposed pilots on non-statutory votes (eg testing the water for support for a strike, which unions already perform electronically). This outcome unsurprisingly has disappointed unions.

The Trade Union Act 2016 affects the law stated in the previous section of this book. In particular, pre-industrial action ballots are valid only if 50% of eligible voters turn out to vote; and 40% of those eligible to vote must vote in favour of the action where the action is to involve an essential public service; unions have to give 14 days' notice of industrial action rather than seven (this works as a cooling-off period); and there is a time limit of four months placed on how long a ballot will remain valid for. New union members have to opt in to the political fund.

Revision tip

You need to be aware of why the procedural rules for calling industrial action are so complex. They are designed to discourage unions from taking such action.

Remedies

Section 22(2) TULRCA limits the amount of damages that can be awarded 'in any proceedings in tort' against a trade union that is deemed liable for industrial action. The words 'in any proceedings' are crucial, since separate proceedings may be brought by all those who have suffered from the industrial action. The limits set are between £10,000 and £250,000, depending upon the size of the union. These amounts were set in the 1980s and have not been amended since.

Injunctions

If an employer is suffering economic harm as a result of unlawful industrial action, the employer may resort to seeking an injunction to stop the action. In situations of extreme urgency an *interim* injunction can be sought. This is a temporary measure that endures until a named day and can be obtained on the basis of sworn statements submitted by the applicant alone. If the respondent is absent, this used to be known as an *ex parte* (one-sided) injunction and is now known as a 'without notice' injunction. According to **s 221 TULRCA**, a court shall not grant an application if the party against whom the injunction is sought claims (or in the court's opinion might claim) that the act was done in contemplation or furtherance of a trade dispute unless all reasonable steps have been taken to give that party notice of the application and an opportunity of being heard.

Before granting an interim injunction, a judge will have to consider the following questions.

- Is there a serious question to be tried?
- Does the balance of convenience lie with the claimant?
- Where the party against whom the injunction is sought claims that the action was in contemplation of furtherance of a trade dispute, is there a likelihood of the defendant establishing a defence to the action under **s 219** or **220 TULRCA**?

In exercising its discretion, a court will need to take into account the possibility of a defendant succeeding in establishing a trade dispute defence.

NURMTW v Serco Ltd [2011] IRLR 399

This concerned a union's failure to include a small number of people in the ballot for strike action. The Court of Appeal allowed an appeal against an interim injunction saying that accidental errors should not invalidate the ballot.

Failure by **union officials** to comply with an injunction may amount to contempt of court, for which the union is vicariously liable.

Acts done in the course of picketing are illegal unless the picketing falls within the immunity conferred within **s 220 TULRCA**. This immunity does not extend to the non-economic torts such as nuisance and trespass and it does not extend to crimes. By **s 219(3)**, picketing is also unlawful if it is not at or near the picket's place of work. This provision is aimed at prohibiting secondary picketing; that is, picketing in support of those taking industrial action elsewhere.

The law on picketing has been further narrowed by the **Trade Union Act 2016**. There has to be a 'picket supervisor' appointed by the union, and the union has to give advance notice of the picket line to the police.

Intriguingly, and for the first time, the Welsh Assembly has voted to repeal several sections of the **Trade Union Act 2016**, in particular the provision on the 40% threshold on industrial action ballots involving important public services: see 'Ballots and notice of industrial action', above. This is a devolved matter. Who would have believed that Wales and England would have different employment laws! The gig economy discussed in chapter 1 may sound new and trendy with its apps and bookings via the internet but it isn't; but Wales and England have not have separate employment law since the **Laws in Wales Acts 1535** and **1542**.

The delights of Brexit await us and after Brexit the Prime Minister promises to repeal the **European Convention on Human Rights**. For employment law, we live in interesting times: the ground is shifting beneath our feet.

 (✳) Key cases

Case	Facts	Principle
McShane v Express Newspapers [1980] IRLR 35	The National Union of Journalists staged a strike against provincial newspapers and called for action by members not directly working for these newspapers.	While the existence of a trade dispute has to be determined objectively, the test for deciding whether an act is in furtherance of such a dispute is a subjective one. Lord Scarman said: 'If the person doing the act honestly thinks at the time he does it that it may help one of the parties to the dispute to achieve their objective and does it for that reason, he is protected.'
A Monk Staff Association v Certification Officer and ASTMS [1980] 1 IRLR 431	A staff association applied for a certificate of independence.	The Certification Officer is not required to assess the likelihood of interference by the employer. The degree of risk is irrelevant so long as it is recognisable and not insignificant.

Exam questions

Cases	Facts	Principle
R v CAC, ex parte BTP Tioxide [1982] IRLR 61	A union sought disclosure of information about a job evaluation scheme, but the employers refused, arguing that the union was not recognised for collective bargaining purposes with regard to the information sought.	The union was entitled to information relating to a job evaluation scheme in respect of which it had no bargaining rights but only the right to represent its members in re-evaluation appeals. Essentially, for information to be disclosed under these provisions it must be both relevant and important. Although each case must be judged on its merits, unions may be entitled to information about groups not covered for collective bargaining purposes.
University College London Hospital NHS Trust v UNISON [1999] IRLR 31	The union gained an overwhelming majority in favour of strike action in support of a demand for employment guarantees associated with the building of a new hospital.	The dispute was about terms and conditions that would apply to workers not currently employed by the NHS Trust and that such a dispute about future employment with a new employer was outside the provisions of s 244 TULRCA.

 (?) Exam questions

Problem question

Meena and Sonya are members of the National Workers Union, which is an independent union recognised by the employer for whom they both work.

The employer has withdrawn from a collective agreement reached with the union and is proposing not to give their employees the previously agreed pay rise.

Meena is outraged and wants the union to take legal action against the employer for breaking an agreement.

Sonya is also very angry and wants to call all the affected employees together and have a vote on strike action to start immediately.

Consider the legal principles at issue on these facts.

See the Outline answers section in the end matter for help with this question.

Essay question

The statutory controls on trade unions are necessary to make sure that they do not take industrial action too easily and damage the economy.

Discuss.

 Online Resources

To see an outline answer to this question log on to www.oup.com/lawrevision/

 Concentrate Q&As

For more questions and answers on employment law, see the *Concentrate Q&A: Employment Law* by Roseanne Russell.

Go to the end of this book to view **sample pages**.

Exam essentials

The integration of individual and collective employment law

Depending on the title of your exam, you are likely to need a thorough knowledge of both individual and collective employment law if you want to achieve the best results. Although individual and collective aspects are often taught separately, the issues overlap considerably. Remember that individual contracts of employment are the normal starting point for the exercise of rights at work and these may contain terms incorporated from collective agreements. Certain collective rights can be regarded as free-standing, for example the statutory recognition provisions, but others are closely associated with individual employment law, for example the requirement to consult over dismissals for redundancy.

Building topics from first base

You need to be able to distinguish an employee from other types of worker because different rights are given to these categories. For example, only employees can claim unfair dismissal or a redundancy payment whereas workers are entitled to the National Minimum Wage and holiday pay as well as being protected from discrimination under the Equality Act 2010. By understanding the sources of express and implied terms in a contract of employment you will be able to identify whether or not there has been a breach of contract in a particular factual situation. It is important to know when there is a fundamental breach because this may lead to a complaint of unfair constructive dismissal. Whether or not an employee is qualified to claim will normally depend on the statutory provisions on continuity of service being satisfied. Similarly, statutory provisions have been introduced in the light of the common law background. Thus, contractual terms will demonstrate whether or not statutory rights are being adhered to, for example in relation to pay, hours, and holidays. Finally, discrimination in employment may be evidenced by unequal contractual terms.

Common examination topics

Your lecturers will have placed emphasis on the key issues as they deliver the syllabus but you may also wish to study past exam papers to confirm the themes that are frequently explored. However, we set out here some topics that have proved popular with examiners.

- How and why is an employee distinguished from other types of worker?
- What is the relationship between express and implied terms in contracts of employment?
- How do collective agreements impact on individual contracts of employment?

Exam essentials
✳✳✳✳✳✳✳✳✳✳

- Have the statutory provisions on pay been successful in providing minimum rights to workers?

- How important is the common law today in protecting employees on termination of their employment?

- Does the law of unfair dismissal provide effective job security for workers?

- Do the unfair dismissal provisions provide a suitable balance between the rights of workers and those of management?

- How have the courts and tribunals interpreted the terms direct and indirect discrimination?

Essays and problem questions

Law exams tend to consist of a mixture of essay and problem questions. The first invite you to display your knowledge and analytical skills on a particular subject. Often essays consist of a requirement to comment on a particular statement or quotation. Remember to stick to the subject and look at relevant statutes as well as the important cases that have interpreted that legislation. The questioner is looking for evidence of your knowledge, prior reading, and analytical skills. Do not waste time and space in quoting from statute books—you will not score marks for this, you waste time, and create a poor impression of your work; and you can assume that the questioner knows their content already! Problem questions require you to apply your legal knowledge to particular situations. There are likely to be a number of actors in the scenario outlined. Remember to deal with each one individually and make sure that you deal with them all! It is important not to let your personal feelings and prejudices influence your advice. You are required to apply the relevant law to each situation, so you should do so in a dispassionate way. Often there is no clear-cut solution so you will need to discuss the options available. The questioner is looking for evidence of your legal knowledge and your ability to apply that knowledge to particular situations.

Reading and research

Whether you are answering an essay question or a problem question, you need to show evidence of your reading and research. Those who receive the best marks in exams are those people who have read around the subject and researched beyond the basic textbook and course handbook/manual or VLE, for example by reading articles in the Industrial Law Journal, probably the leading employment law journal in the world.

Outline answers—problem question answers

Chapter 1

Problem answer

• You should point out that the first issue to consider is whether George was an employee when he worked at the factory. All the circumstances need to be taken into account, including any documentation supplied to him. In terms of control, you should state that it would be relevant to know the following. Was he required to produce a minimum number of shoes? What degree of supervision was he subject to? Draw to the examiner's attention that you do not know whether tax and National Insurance were deducted during this period.

• You should make clear that people who work from home may well be employees.

• In terms of the declared intention of the parties, you might infer that this was designed to alter his status rather than confirm it. In which case it will be of no value if the new relationship is a sham. You should refer to *Autoclenz Ltd v Belcher* [2011] ('The intention of the parties'). However, if there is doubt the declaration can be used to resolve ambiguity. You should refer to *Massey v Crown Life Assurance* [1978] ('The intention of the parties').

• You should suggest that it looks as though George was and is still an employee. There appears to be a continuing mutual obligation on the employer's part to supply materials and on George's part to produce shoes. You should refer to *Carmichael v National Power plc* [2000] ('Mutuality of obligation').

• You should state that the failure to make deductions is not conclusive of his status, although his contract will be tainted with illegality if he participates in a deliberate fraud on HMRC. (On illegality, see chapter 2.)

• For more examination material you should read *Questions and Answers Employment Law 2014 and 2015* by Richard Benny, Michael Jefferson, and Malcolm Sargeant, published by Oxford University Press.

Chapter 2

Problem answer

• You should discuss whether the further secretarial duties and covering the switchboard are both within her capabilities and appropriate to her post as a 'personal secretary'. You could point out that it would be relevant whether she had performed such additional duties in the past.

• You should state that it is important to know whether the increased workload is likely to be permanent or temporary and whether this was communicated to Mildred. If temporary, she may be obliged to cooperate if she will not suffer a detriment by doing so. If permanent, the employer may be expected to engage additional staff or at least share the additional burdens.

• You might point out that covering the switchboard might break an express term in her contract on working hours or the WTR. The employer must also comply with the common law duty of care and the Health and Safety at Work etc Act 1974. You might refer to *Walker v Northumberland County Council* [1995] ('Safe system of work').

• You should suggest that Mr Smith's abusive behaviour might be regarded as a breach of the duty of trust and confidence but Mildred is choosing to affirm the contract. You might refer to *Malik v BCCI [1997]* ('To cooperate with the employee').

• You should state that if Mildred raises a grievance she will need to make clear whether it relates to the extra duties, her treatment by Mr Smith, or both.

Chapter 3

Problem answer

• You should point out that Pt II ERA requires certain qualifications, for example to submit a claim in time.

Outline answers—problem question answers

✷✷✷✷✷✷✷✷✷✷

- You should note that, although Alex has not fully performed his part of the bargain, unless his contract states otherwise he is entitled to be paid for the work he has done.
- You should emphasise that the employer may have a cross-claim for damages but this does not affect Alex's right to wages under Pt II ERA.

Chapter 4

Problem answer

You might begin your answer by stating generally that this question is about discrimination in employment. The relevant legislation is the Equality Act 2010 which, amongst other measures, replaced the Sex Discrimination Act, the Race Relations Act, and the Employment Equality (Religion or Belief) Regulations 2003.

First, consider the case of Mrs Nice. On the face of it there does seem to be an example of direct race discrimination by Mr Dodgy, so you should discuss direct discrimination and that it requires less favourable treatment of an individual on the grounds of their race, colour, etc (*James v Eastleigh BC* [1990]). The question is how does this help Mrs Nice who is white and is not herself apparently being discriminated against? You should point out that the Equality Act 2010 makes it unlawful for a person to instruct another to commit an unlawful act. You will also need to refer to the case of *Weathersfield v Sargent* [1999], whose facts are very similar to this situation, concluding that Mrs Nice would be able to claim constructive dismissal and have a claim under the Equality Act 2010.

Mona's case will lead you to consider indirect discrimination under the Act. Is this a rule that amounts to a provision, criterion, or practice that will be of detriment to a larger number of women than men (*Whiffen v Milham Ford Girls School* [2001])? Is it also of detriment to Mona herself? This seems likely and you will want to raise the issue of whether there is any objective justification for the rule, whether there is a 'proportionate means of achieving a legitimate aim'. You could also raise the situation with regard to the burden of proof. Mr Dodgy will have to show that the rule was for

another reason than one that amounted to discrimination against women.

Mr Singh might also have a claim for discrimination under the Equality Act 2010 as Sikhs have been recognised as an ethnic group (*Mandla v Dowell Lee* [1983]), but it is also possible that he might have a claim under the religion or belief provisions of the Act—whether an unjustifiable rule concerning hair length is likely to discriminate against people of a particular religion. The employer would have to show that the rule was a proportionate means of achieving a legitimate aim.

Chapter 5

Problem answer

You might begin by stating that these candidates have issues related to disability and that the Equality Act 2010 now contains the relevant provisions previously in the Disability Discrimination Act 1995.

For Agnes it is a question of how she is being treated for a disability-related reason. This is similar to the examples given in the DRC Code of Practice (see the Equality and Human Rights Commission website). She cannot type fast because of her disability, not because of a lack of knowledge of how to type. There is an important issue, therefore, about the selection of the correct comparator. There is also a possibility of age discrimination, because the employer may have prejudices about older workers and their speed of work. You will need to consider this, maybe by asking for information about the ages of other candidates interviewed and the ages of the successful ones.

Delilah has had a problem with her interview related to her disability. Questions to be asked include whether the employer had prior knowledge of her ailment and the consequences of this; as well as the employer's duty to make reasonable adjustments.

Chapter 6

Problem answer

This question is inviting you to demonstrate your knowledge of the law relating to discrimination in relation to sex, especially pregnancy. You might need to cross-reference with the information in chapter 4 when considering your answer. It is also inviting you to describe the measures that exist with regard to parental leave and time off for emergencies.

It would be best if you started off by stating what the statutory position is as contained in the Equality Act 2010.

You should also mention the **Pregnancy Directive** and the **Equal Treatment Directive** which, at an EU level, have provided protection for pregnant women and those who have recently given birth. This will give you the opportunity to display your knowledge of some of the key cases, especially *Dekker* [1991] and *Brown v Rentokil* [1998]. In summary, discrimination against a pregnant woman can be direct discrimination, for which there can be no justification defence. The questions that she was asked at the interview might reveal the possibility of discrimination in the decision-making role of the selection panel.

With regard to her present child, Manuella will have the right to parental leave. You have an opportunity here to display your knowledge of the **Maternity and Parental Leave Regulations** and to describe what Manuella is entitled to, eg 13 weeks' leave for each child with a maximum of four weeks' in any one year. You will want to consider relevant cases such as *Rodway v South Central Trains Ltd* [2005] and *Abdoulaye v Régie Nationale des Usines Renault SA* [1998].

Finally, you should include the provisions of s 57A ERA, which is concerned with time off for emergencies. Of particular interest will be *Qua v John Ford Morrison Solicitors* [2003].

Chapter 7

Problem answer

• You should comment on the precise terms of Karen's contract. For example, is Frank's remark about interference with her private life enforceable? If so, it could be argued that her contract has been varied but Karen's continuation in employment has indicated her consent to the change.

• You should observe that it is likely that Karen can be required to work additional hours so long as it is safe for her to do so and the WTR are adhered to.

• You should point out that, where these Regulations apply, regs 4 and 5 impose a 48-hour limit over a reference period unless the individual has opted out. You might refer to *Pfeiffer v Deutsches Rotes Kreuz* [2005] ('Maximum weekly hours').

• You should note that Karen might find it difficult to refuse to work more than 48 hours as she seems to have done so since her employment commenced. Equally, she will not be keen to get the Health and Safety Executive involved in enforcing the limit as this will not be conducive to her achieving a partnership. If Karen is in a union she might ask her representative to raise the matter.

• You might advise Karen to inform Frank that she is concerned about her health and that she needs to reduce her hours temporarily in order to recharge her batteries. You should also mention the employer's common law duty of care (see chapter 2, 'To take reasonable care of the employee') and its obligations under s 2 Health and Safety at Work etc Act 1974.

Chapter 8

Problem answer

• You should note that Ms Jones appears to be abiding by her contractual terms. It seems unlikely that Flexico have the right to vary her hours simply because others have agreed to the change. You might refer to *Harlow v Artemis Ltd* [2008] ('Variation').

• You should mention that an express term, individual or collective, could provide authority for unilateral variations but Mr Smith has not suggested that this is the case here.

• You should comment that Mr Smith's oral undertaking can be relied on but any resulting loss of pay may amount to an unlawful deduction under s 13 ERA (see chapter 3, 'Wages and unauthorised deductions')

• You should state that both parties have a duty to cooperate with each other. Flexico should try to find a job for Ms Jones that will enable her to work her contractual hours.

Outline answers—problem question answers
✱✱✱✱✱✱✱✱✱✱✱

Equally, Ms Jones should try to adjust her domestic arrangements so that she could get home later. On the reciprocal duties of the parties, see chapter 2.

• You might note that if the parties do not resolve their differences, Ms Jones may be dismissed for 'some other substantial reason' (see chapter 9, 'Some other substantial reason') even though Flexico are in breach of contract.

Chapter 9

Problem answer

• You should point out that in order to bring a claim for unfair dismissal, Doris must show that she is qualified and not excluded. For example, she should ensure that her complaint is submitted to the employment tribunal in time.

• You should comment that, on the wording of the question, Doris could regard herself as either expressly or constructively dismissed. You might refer to *Buckland v Bournemouth University* [2010] (chapter 8, 'Constructive dismissal').

• You should note that Doris could use s 92 ERA in order to request a statement of reasons for dismissal. However, it would seem that the real issue is the refusal to work extra hours rather than the place of work.

• You should record that on these facts the failure to cooperate with the employer might be better classified as 'some other substantial reason' for dismissal rather than misconduct. You might refer to *Hollister v National Farmers' Union* [1979] ('Some other substantial reason').

• In discussing whether it was reasonable to dismiss under s 98(4) ERA, you should observe that Doris has given a good reason for not acceding to the employer's request and that you have no information about whether it was feasible for someone else to cover the extra hours. You might refer to *Anglian Homes Ltd v Kelly* [2004] ('Reasonableness in the circumstances').

• You should state that Doris has a right to notice under her contract or s 86 ERA, depending on which is more favourable.

• You should mention the remedies that might be available to Doris for unfair dismissal and breach of contract.

Chapter 10

Problem answer

• You should point out that Florence needs two years' continuous service to claim unfair dismissal and to obtain a redundancy payment.

• You should examine why the criterion of 'last in, first out' was applied. If it was agreed with a trade union or other employee representatives, Nightingale Ltd might argue that it is good practice for employers to agree and then implement redundancy criteria. You might refer to *Williams v Compair Maxam* [1982] ('Unfair redundancy'). On the other hand, you should explain that 'last in, first out' might cause indirect discrimination if it is based on continuous service. If this method of selection has had a disproportionate impact on females at Nightingale Ltd, it will need to be justified. You might refer to *Whiffen v Milham Ford Girls School* [2001] ('Unfair redundancy').

• Various methods of avoiding dismissals are found on the ACAS website. Some of these methods are mentioned in the question. In addition, unfair dismissal case law emphasises the need for warnings and consultation with individuals. This would be relevant to Florence because if she had been consulted she would know whether or not she was considered for the vacancy at Enfield and why she did not get the job. You might refer to *Mugford v Midland Bank plc* [1997] and *King v Eaton Ltd* [1996] ('Consultation for unfair dismissal purposes').

• You should observe that s 98(4) ERA requires suitable vacancies to be offered. However, the wording of the document she signed does not give Florence a contractual right to such employment.

• You should draw attention to the fact that Florence has a right to notice of dismissal under s 86 ERA or her contract if that is more favourable.

Chapter 11

Problem answer

This question, of course, is about continuity of employment and you will probably need to start with an analysis of the provisions contained in the ERA. Remember that there is a presumption of continuity that should be of assistance to all three individuals.

Terri should be able to claim continuous employment as the total period adds up to less than 26 weeks' absence. There were no disability issues, so it is unlikely that she would also be protected by the Equality Act 2010.

Teresa is a casual worker and you will need to review the statute and cases on such employees. If she has been only employed for two periods during one year, then it seems unlikely that she could claim continuity of employment.

Tom's case might well be a dismissal as a result of a TUPE transfer. Such a dismissal would be unfair. You will need to spend some time on ensuring that he was employed at the time of the transfer and whether the sale of the farm could constitute a TUPE transfer that would automatically have transferred his contract of employment to the new farm owner.

Chapter 12

Problem answer

This question is about trade unions and industrial action.

You would probably start off the reply to this question with an analysis of what is meant by a trade union being referred to as independent and the implications of recognition for collective bargaining purposes: so write something about s 5 TULRCA and the role of the Certification Officer citing what cases you could. Then move on to what is meant by recognition and collective bargaining (s 178). You might also speculate on what purpose the recognition is for. To get extra marks you might also mention that recognition can also be achieved through statutory means.

You can then look at the individual issues raised by the workers concerned.

Meena—this is about the fact that collective agreements are not normally regarded as legally binding between the parties to them. However, you should point out that they may be enforceable by individuals if their terms have been expressly or impliedly incorporated into contracts of employment.

Sonya—her action raises the issues related to balloting and the procedure necessary to go through in order to take industrial action, including the consequences of not going through this procedure, ie the removal of protection from immunities in tort. Mention must be made of changes brought about by the Trade Union Act 2016.

Glossary

Bumping This is where an individual's job continues but there is a reduction somewhere else in the organisation for the same number of people to carry out the work.

Certification Officer The official organisation that holds the list of independent trade unions and adjudicates as to their independence or not.

Cessation of work Work that has permanently or temporarily ceased to exist.

Collective agreement Any agreement or arrangement made by or on behalf of one or more trade unions and one or more employers, or employers' associations, which relates to one or more of the matters mentioned in s 178(2) TULRCA.

Compulsory maternity leave This is not to be less than two weeks in length, commencing with the day on which childbirth occurs, and it is included in the maternity leave period.

Constructive dismissal This is where an employee terminates the contract with or without notice in circumstances such that he or she is contractually entitled to terminate it without notice by reason of the employer's conduct.

Contract of employment A contract of service or apprenticeship, whether express or implied, and (if it is express) whether oral or in writing.

Direct discrimination When a person is treated, on a forbidden ground, less favourably than a comparable person is or would be treated by the employer.

Disability-related discrimination When an employer discriminates against a disabled person and when it is for a reason related to his or her disability; the treatment is less favourable than the treatment given, or that would have been given, to others to whom the reason does not or would not apply, and the employer cannot show that the treatment in question can be justified.

Economic entity An organised grouping of resources that has the objective of pursuing an economic activity, whether or not that activity is central or ancillary (**reg 3(2) TUPE**).

Employee An individual who has entered into or works under (or, where the employment has ceased, worked under) a contract of employment: **s 230 ERA**.

Employee shareholder A person who receives a minimum of £2,000 paid up shares in a company but relinquishes certain statutory rights including a remedy for being unfairly dismissed.

Expected week of childbirth The week, beginning with midnight between Saturday and Sunday, in which it is expected that childbirth will occur.

Express terms Those terms that are expressly stated to form part of the contract. They may be oral or in writing.

Flexible working This concerns the right of some employees to request to vary their hours of work for the purposes of caring for certain dependants. If the employer grants the variation, that change is permanent.

Gender reassignment This is a process that is undertaken under medical supervision for the purpose of reassigning a person's sex by changing physiological or other characteristics of sex, and includes any part of such a process.

Harassment This is said to occur when a person engages in unwanted conduct that has the purpose or effect of violating that other person's dignity, or creating an intimidating, hostile, degrading, humiliating, or offensive environment.

Implied term in fact Where there is a gap in the contract of employment it is possible to imply a term if a court or tribunal can be persuaded that it is necessary to do so in the circumstances of the particular case.

Glossary

Implied terms in law These are terms that are regarded by the courts and tribunals as being inherent in all contracts of employment.

Independent trade union A trade union that is judged not to be under the domination or control of an employer or a group of employers and is not liable to interference by an employer, arising out of the provision of financial or material support or by any other means whatsoever, tending towards such control.

Indirect discrimination (sex) A person discriminates against a woman if he applies to her a provision, criterion, or practice which he applies or would apply equally to a man, but which is such that it would be to the detriment of a considerably larger proportion of women than of men, and which he cannot show to be justifiable irrespective of the sex of the person to whom it is applied, and which is to her detriment. Justification involves the employer proving that she used 'proportionate means of achieving a legitimate aim'.

Instant dismissal This has no legal definition but refers to a dismissal without investigation or enquiry.

Limited-term contract A contract that terminates by virtue of a limiting event such as the end of a war.

Limiting event There are three categories: the expiry of a fixed term; the performance of a specific task; or the occurrence of an event or failure of an event to occur.

Maternity leave A statutory period of leave to which women who are pregnant or who have recently given birth are entitled.

Night-time A period that is not less than seven hours in length and includes the hours of midnight to 5 am.

Night-worker A worker who, as a normal course, works at least three hours of working time during 'night-time' or is a worker who is likely, during 'night-time', to work a certain proportion of his or her annual working time as defined by a collective or workforce agreement.

Obligatory period The minimum period that the employer is required to give by virtue of s 86(1) ERA or the contract of employment.

Occupational requirement There are certain situations, when it is an essential part of the nature of the job, where it is permissible to use sex, racial origin, religious or other belief, or sexual orientation as a criterion in the selection of an applicant or in providing access to promotion and training.

Parental leave Time off associated with a child of less than 18 years of age that entitles the employee to a period of 18 weeks' unpaid leave per child. This must not be confused with shared parental leave (see chapter 6).

Paternity leave This is a period of leave given for the purpose of caring for a child or supporting the child's mother. This leave must be taken between the date of the birth and a date 56 days thereafter.

Protected characteristic The Equality Act 2010 lists nine protected characteristics. These are the characteristics, such as sex or race, in relation to which discrimination is unlawful.

Reasonable adjustments Where the disabled person is placed at a substantial disadvantage compared to persons who are not disabled because of a provision, criterion, or practice applied by or on behalf of an employer, or any physical feature of premises occupied by an employer, it is the duty of the employer to take reasonable steps, in all the circumstances of the case, to prevent the provision, criterion, practice, or feature from having that effect.

Recognition Recognition in relation to a trade union means the recognition of the union by an employer, or two or more associated employers, to any extent for the purpose of collective bargaining. It may be achieved voluntarily or through statute.

Relevant agreement A workforce agreement, a provision of a collective agreement that forms part of a contract between the worker and the employer, or any other agreement in writing that is legally enforceable as between employer and worker.

Glossary

✳✳✳✳✳✳✳✳✳✳

Relevant insolvency proceedings Insolvency proceedings that have been opened in relation to the transferor not with a view to the liquidation of the assets of the transferor and that are under the supervision of an insolvency practitioner.

Restrictive covenant An express clause in the contract of employment that restrains competition by employees when they leave.

Service provision change A transfer that takes place when an undertaking first contracts out some part of its activities to a contractor, when such a contract is taken over by another contractor, and when the client takes back the activity in-house from a contractor.

Service-related pay and benefits This may include salary scales, holiday, etc, all or some of which may be related to length of service.

Summary dismissal This occurs where the employer terminates the contract of employment without notice.

Trade dispute A dispute between workers and their employer that relates wholly or mainly to terms and conditions of employment, engagement, or non-engagement or termination or suspension of employment; allocation of work or the duties of employment as between workers or groups of workers; matters of discipline; membership or non-membership of a trade union; facilities for officials of trade unions; and the machinery for negotiation or consultation about these matters.

Transferee employer The employer to whom staff are transferred in a TUPE transfer.

Transferor employer The employer from whom staff are transferred in a TUPE transfer.

Union official Someone who is an officer of the union or branch of it, or someone who is elected or appointed in accordance with the rules to be a representative of its members or some of them.

Vicarious liability Employers are liable to third parties for the torts committed by employees in the course of their employment. For a special application of this doctrine in discrimination law, see chapter 5.

Victimisation When a person is treated less favourably than other persons are treated or would be treated in the particular circumstances, and the reason that the person is victimised is because that person has brought proceedings or exercised rights under any of the relevant Acts.

Wages Any sum payable to the worker in connection with his employment (s 27(1) ERA).

Worker An individual who has entered into, or works under, a contract of employment or 'any other contract, whether express or implied and (if it is express) whether oral or in writing, whereby the individual undertakes to do or perform personally any work or services for another party to the contract whose status is not by virtue of the contract, that of a client or customer of any profession or business undertaking carried on by the individual': see s 230 ERA.

Workforce agreement An agreement is a workforce agreement if it is in writing; it has effect for a specified period not exceeding five years; it applies to all the relevant members of a workforce or all the relevant members who belong to a particular group; it is signed by the representatives of the group; copies of the agreement are readily available for reading prior to the signing.

Working time Any period during which the worker is working, at the employer's disposal and carrying out the worker's activity or duties; any period during which the worker is receiving relevant training; any additional period that is to be treated as working time for the purpose of the WTR under a relevant agreement.

Young worker An individual who is at least 15 years of age, over the compulsory school leaving age, and who has not yet attained the age of 18 years.

Index

Index

Index

****

Index

****

Concentrate QUESTIONS & ANSWERS

Revision & study guides from the **No. 1** legal education publisher

Q&A
EMPLOYMENT LAW

Roseanne Russell

practise technique › boost your confidence › achieve success

→ LOOK INSIDE

OXFORD

Employment status

2

ARE YOU READY?

In order to attempt this chapter you must have covered the following areas in your revision:

● The definitions of 'employee' and 'worker' contained in employment legislation with particular reference to the differences in definitions across various legislation

● Which rights attach to different categories of 'employee' and 'worker'

● The importance of policy considerations behind the different definitions and associated rights

● The common law tests to determine whether a contract is a contract of service or a contract for services (such as control, integration, economic reality, and mutuality of obligation)

● The changing nature of the labour market and the difficulties in determining employment status for certain groups (e.g. agency workers; zero hours contractors)

 ## KEY DEBATES

Shifting patterns of work in today's flexible labour market mean that it can be difficult to determine a person's employment status. This has given rise to renewed debates on whether the current tests remain appropriate.

Debate: Changing labour market

Does the rise of the 'gig economy' mean that we have to reconsider the common law tests of whether a contract is a contract of employment? Do the common law tests remain relevant when applied to today's labour market?

Debate: Unscrupulous behaviour

How does the law allow or inhibit unscrupulous behaviour regarding employment status? Is it too easy for workers to claim self-employment for advantageous tax reasons? Does the law adequately prevent 'sham' self-employment practices by employers?

⊙

Debate: Zero hours contracts

What are the advantages and disadvantages of zero hours contracts? Are they used disproportionately amongst certain groups (such as care workers) and what are the implications of this?

QUESTION | **1**

The courts have resolved questions of employment status over the years by the application of various tests. Critically examine, by reference to case law, the tests used and briefly indicate the advantages and disadvantages of each test.

CAUTION!

- As with any question, take time to read precisely what the examiner is asking of you. Here you are being asked to 'critically examine'. This requires doing more than describing the various common law tests or 'telling all you know' about the topic. Critically examining a concept means that you have to discuss it in detail and give your view (supported by evidence) of the pros and cons of each test.

- There is no right way or wrong way to structure an essay answer but it is always worth spending a few minutes planning how best to present your material. Jot down the key points (including cases) that you want to mention and then think about what structure will allow you to present your argument in the most clear and convincing way.

- This area is dominated by case law, which the question asks you to discuss. Remember that it is usually the ratio that is most important so show the examiner that you understand the ratio, any relevant obiter comments, and the importance of any dissenting judgments. Lengthy descriptive accounts of the facts of a case should be avoided.

- To demonstrate your knowledge of the wider labour market context, a 'critical examination' could also highlight the continued relevance (or otherwise) of these tests.

DIAGRAM ANSWER PLAN

Why is it necessary to consider case law (employee-worker distinction and limited statutory definitions)?

Various tests—control, integration, economic reality, mutuality of obligation, personal service

Development of each test as a response to problems with previous tests

▼

Problem areas in a changing labour market

SUGGESTED ANSWER

[1] Your opening sentence reassures the examiner that you understand the question and introduces the subject area of your answer.

The question of who is an employee is central in employment law but determination of employment status has sometimes proved difficult.[1] **Section 230(1)** of the **Employment Rights Act ('ERA')** defines an employee as 'an individual who has entered into or works under (or, where the employment has ceased, worked under) a contract of employment'. **Section 230(2) ERA** defines a 'contract of employment' as 'a contract of service or apprenticeship, whether express or implied, and (if it is express) whether oral or in writing'. While some protections in the employment field extend to workers (such as the **Working Time Regulations 1998** and the **National Minimum Wage Act 1998**), employees have certain important rights that other categories of workers do not have such as the right in **s94(1) ERA** not to be unfairly dismissed. For that reason being an 'employee' is important.

[2] This opening paragraph shows succinctly that you understand the relevant statutory law and its limitations.

As the statutory definitions are of limited assistance[2] to help distinguish the nature of the relationship, the courts have developed a range of tests to help identify whether a contract is one of employment.

[3] An explanation of a 'classic statement' is given here to show the depth of your knowledge.

The first test was the 'control test'. This asked what was the degree of control the alleged employer ('the master') exercised over the alleged employee ('the servant'). The classic statement[3] concerning this test was given by MacKenna J in *Ready Mixed Concrete (South East) Ltd* v *Minister of Pensions and National Insurance* [1968] 2 QB 497, where he said that a contract of service exists if three conditions are fulfilled: (1) The servant agrees that, in consideration of a wage or other remuneration, he will provide his own work and skill in the performance of some service for his master, (2) he agrees, expressly or impliedly, that in the performance of that service he will be subject to the other's control in a sufficient degree to make that other master, and (3) the other provisions of the contract are consistent with its being a contract of service. Subsequent cases have taken this statement as a guide when determining employment status. Although this test appears simple, as work has become more complex and technology has increased, the test has proven to be inadequate as the sole determinant of employment in today's labour market. Although an essential component in a contract of service, it is a crude measure and, as Kahn-Freund argued, 'based upon the social conditions of an practise technique ❯ boost your confidence ❯ achieve success

[4] Authority to support a particular point can be found in articles. This shows your wider reading and lends weight to your argument.

[5] This paragraph is a good example of the PEA method: the point is identified (control test), it is explained in detail by reference to a key case, and it is analysed with support from academic authority.

[6] This sentence helps structure the answer by showing the development of tests over time.

[7] Here the use of 'advantage' and 'disadvantage' allows you to analyse the test critically rather than just explain what the test involves.

earlier age' **(O. Kahn-Freund, 'Servants and independent contractors' (1951) 14 *Modern Law Review* 504).**[4] Highly skilled or senior employees or those with a significant degree of flexibility in their working conditions cannot be said to be 'controlled' by their employer in any real sense while carrying out their work. Although important, 'control' is no longer seen as conclusive.[5]

The second test that developed was the integration test. It was first identified in *Cassidy* v *Ministry of Health* **[1951] 2 KB 343, CA,** where it was applied to establish that a doctor working within the NHS was an employee of the Health Authority. Denning LJ referred again to this test in *Stevenson, Jordan and Harrison Ltd* v *MacDonald and Evans* **[1952] 1 TLR 101.** It asks whether a person is employed as part of the business, whether his or her work is done as 'an integral part of the business', or whether it is merely accessory to it. The test appears straightforward although it proved to be of limited use since, in asking whether a person was an integral part of the organisation, it was unclear precisely what constituted 'integration' into an 'organisation'.

The courts gradually moved away from seeing one factor as determinative of the issue of employment status.[6] A more flexible approach was taken by adopting what is known as the multiple test, i.e. no single factor will be conclusive—all factors are considered and weighed to decide the question (this is sometimes called 'the multifactorial approach'). The question asked is, looking at all the factors, some of which may point to self-employment status and others to a finding of employment, does the evidence overall point to the person being an employee? This multi-factorial test was applied by Cooke J in *Market Investigations* v *Minister of Social Security* **[1969] 2 QB 173.** Cooke J stated that the fundamental question was: 'Is the person who has engaged himself to perform these services performing them as a person in business on his own account?' In other words, looking at the economic reality of the situation, does the individual bear the economic risk as a self-employed person? Factors to consider include whether the worker hires his own helpers; what degree of financial risk he takes; what degree of financial responsibility he has for investment; and any management responsibility undertaken.

One distinct advantage[7] of the multiple test is that it allows the court or tribunal great flexibility: all relevant factors are considered, with no single factor being decisive. This approach is particularly useful when some factors may go towards self-employment, such as the contractual right given to the worker to substitute another worker for him- or herself, while other factors may point towards employment status, such as the unrestrained power to control the time and manner in which the work is performed. By looking at all the circumstances of the case, and giving appropriate weight to these (possibly